FREELY CHOSEN REALITY

Ralph Austin Powell, O.P., Ph.D. (Louvain)

UNIVERSITY
PRESS OF
AMERICA

Copyright © 1983 by

University Press of America, Inc.

P.O. Box 19101, Washington, D.C. 20036

ISBN (Perfect): 0-8191-2925-9
ISBN   (Cloth): 0-8191-2924-0

DEDICATION

This essay is dedicated to the memory of William Humbert Kane, O.P., 1901-1970. For many years he studied the natural origin of human knowledge in Thomas Aquinas. One of his favorite texts was the following one that frequently appears in this essay (*Summa Theologiae*, I, q. 11, art. 2 ad 4):

"Unde unum ponitur in definitione multitudinis, non autem multitudo in definitione unius. Sed divisio cadit in intellectu ex ipsa negatione entis. Ita quod primo cadit in intellectu ens, secundo quod hoc ens non est illud ens et sic apprehendimus divisionem, tertio unum, quarto multitudinem."

"So unity enters the definition of the many, but the many does not enter the definition of unity. Now division arises in the mind simply by negating existence. So that the first idea to arise in the mind is the existent, then that this existent is not that existent and so we grasp division, thirdly unity, and fourthly the many."

EXPLANATION OF REFERENCE STYLE

Essential to this book is the thesis, as enunciated by Gilson (1937), that historical experience is essential to the progress and sound development of philosophical understanding. The reference style has been adapted according-ly, using the system worked out by John Deely over the course of our thirteen years collaborating on the 'excavation' of John Poinsot's 1632 *Treatise on Signs* (see Deely, 1982, 1983). This system cites all sources used in the course of the work in the list of "References" given at the back of the book, arranged alphabetically by author, as is standard bibliographical technique in existing style sheets, but with the novel twist of dating these sources in a linear column under the names according to the period of composition (in the case of ancient authors) or original publication (in the case of modern authors) of the works cited, with dates of modern editions used or of translations consulted being given inter-nally to the reference.

This system, called by its deviser the *historical layering of sources*, thus, makes it possible for the first time conveniently and directly to reflect the historical period of origin of the contributions to the work, within the text as well as in the list of references proper. The relationship of conceptual thought to experi-ence and the historical continuities underlying the material differences of philosophical projects are brought to the foreground in this style of reference and made unmistakable.

I expect that this new device, simple in its conception but revolutionary in its transformation of the reader's sensitivity to the historicity built into the very condition of human existence, will eventually establish itself as a standard bibliographical technique supplanting the more cumbersome and historically confused systems that have been standard up till now.

The details of applying the system of historical layering will eventually re-quire the writing of a new "manual of style." But the essentials of the method are simple, as outlined above, and the variant details, as exhibited in this manuscript—for example, in addition to following the traditional practice (Tur-abian, 1973: 3.99) of using square brackets to interpolate quotations, I have used square brackets around parts of texts cited in the notes to the chapters that were *not cited* within the chapters themselves, in order to permit the reader to see the context of the original more clearly—should not cause the reader any prob-lems. On the contrary, the system is adopted precisely to enhance the reader's grasp of issues in the way proper to (however neglected within recent) philos-ophy, which is itself, when seen in anything approaching its proper dimen-sions, one of the finest historical achievements of Western consciousness.

v

TABLE OF CONTENTS

FOREWORD

With this essay "intelligent realism" should rightfully regain the center of the contemporary philosophical stage. "Intelligent" is used here, not just in contrast to "naive," but in the sense proposed by Ralph Powell and consecrated by the tradition since Aristotle: the ability to read in things the difference between the *real* and the *unreal*— these terms too being used in Powell's carefully developed sense. Powell situates this intelligent realism in its rapport with all the other presently popular forms of realism: certain forms of empiricism in the "analytic" tradition; behaviorism; Marxism; Heidegger's realism of *Sein*; and, of course, Neo-thomism, which Powell is at pains in some respects to correct, in the process finding himself closer to the mind of St. Thomas than his potential objectors.

Because Powell employs a phenomenological method (one closer to Pfänder than to Husserl), he is able to describe an experience of things which takes account of classical and modern aporia, including problems arising from the figure-background discovery of Gestalt psychology, which, under the author's sure guidance, far from leading to relativism and skepticism, turn our attention towards the prowess of our cognitive faculties exercising their daily "self-discipline" as they correct the impression to accord with the full, true reality gained from total experience. Because Powell so masterfully develops the foundations of his philosophy in the theory of knowledge he sketches for us, showing both its foundations in the natural and its founding the cultural, he is able to suggest in a few deft strokes an ontology which holds promise of being able to support both a philosophy of science and an ethics. Indeed, "ethics" is here too modest a term—Powell suggests nothing less than a concept of human freedom, grounded in the way we relate through knowledge to things, and thus both an anthropology and a foundation for political philosophy.

Powell's is neither a constitutive phenomenology nor a phenomenology of Being-in-the-world. Rather Powell appeals to ordinary experience in its manifest pragmatic success in relating to things both in "real" relations, in which things are seen to affect one another as a matter of fact (and this both publicly and privately); and in "unreal" relations, those which exist only in the minds of the knowers but which, by influencing action, can have a powerful effect on things and therefore ultimately upon real relations. Powell thus distinguishes and describes both our knowledge of things (and real relations between things) and our knowledge of certain conceptions to which nothing independent of thought corresponds. *Unfreedom*, he shows, is failure to recognize such unreal relations for what they are—our own creations—not necessarily arbitrary, meaningless, or worthless (although sometimes pathological), but in any event subject to alteration directly by thought and hence more controllable and malleable than the person who naturalizes them will ever realize. Our notions are, after all, the engines of man's cultural achievement. But in failing to distinguish the unreal from the real, man has become unperceiving prisoner of his own creatures rather than creative master of them. (One hopes that in later works Powell will develop more description of the domineering role of the unconscious). Only through fully intelligent relationship to the real can man become master of his own culture. Intelligent relationship to the real includes, not only the ability to discern the real from the unreal, but to realize that the real always founds the unreal; and that the unreal, by guiding our action and by stretching out beyond the real into the not yet, can influence the real. Freedom is the ability to choose the real. It is freedom from illusion, confounding the fantastic with the real. But it is also the ability of fantasy (Powell should make this clear) to work out from the real towards the yet to be attained—a certain freedom from the real which allows man to bring new reality into existence, provided he can insert the products of his fancy into the fabric of already existing relations. Powell relates the fundamental ontological principle of freedom which he describes for us admirably to the theories on freedom of the entire tradition, making use of M. Adler's excellent work in doing it, demonstrating in the process the primordiality and solidity of his own position.

There is one respect in which Powell's intelligent realism is, I believe, unduly timid. There are good reasons for the author's stressing that we know neither the intrinsic natures nor just mere external accidents but rather it is things themselves which we know, however imperfectly. Yet Powell is so concerned to protect intelligent realism from any accusation of naivete that he hesitates to develop sufficiently a phenomenology of the knowledge of kinds of things as well as knowledge of distinct individuals, although he obviously presupposes both kinds of knowing. We indeed do not know the intrinsic nature of an oak or of a granite boulder yet we unfailingly distinguish them. Moreover, when I recognize in the boulder the result of igneous formation and in the shale, sedimentary, I read in (in-telligo) their structure marks of their respective histories. While there will always be much I do not know about these stones, what I do already know presents itself as a *structure*, that is, a whole set of relationships into the belonging together of whose parts I enjoy some insight. This in-sight permits a reading-in which allows me to abstract from the peculiar local conditions of the structure's manifestation in *this* stone a formal type which can be understood even if every ontic exemplar of it were to cease to exist (Langan, 1972).

There is another side to the basic ontology implied in Powell's seminal work which deserves a much fuller phenomenological exploration than he has chosen to give it here. Powell makes it clear that unreal relations not only are not always mere *Gehirnsgespenste*—phantoms of the imagination—but on the contrary are both anchored in the real and influential, through human action, upon it. But he is so concerned to distinguish real from unreal relations and then to relate both to choice that he does not here take the trouble to describe phenomenologically the kind of real-unreal relationship which distinguishes a genuine project from an unhealthy fantasy. Nor does he explain very well just why a set of unreal relations, like a monetary system, for instance, has weight, consistency, mobilizing power, capable of cementing a vast planetary system of economic relations. These explorations must await subsequent essays which we trust will follow now that Powell's pioneering effort has shown the way.

Thomas Langan
University of Toronto

AUTHOR'S PREFACE

Freely Chosen Reality asks whether any reality can be a free effect of choice. It is a search for some reality that cannot exist except while being freely chosen. It may well be that no such reality exists. Freedom is indeed a public object famed for its presence in such institutions as free speech, free elections, and freedom of religion. But public freedoms may not express any *mind-independent reality*. Such freedoms may be mere illusions disguising the lifeless energy of mechanical necessity, illusions inherited from prescientific ages that believed in spiritual realities.

Today, any philosophical search for "reality" must sooner or later meet the challenge of historical relativism. This challenge cannot be escaped by "benign neglect," as happens in the United States and Britain wherever analytic philosophy predominates. The analytic school does not champion historical relativism, but more or less neglects the historical dimension of human experience. Yet all human experience, especially ethical experience, is always directly concerned with a given historical culture. Significantly, in ethics analytic philosophy finds itself more and more vulnerable to the criticisms of relativists.

Thus recently several noted analytic philosophers in ethics have been converging on the view that ethics can only speak in ethnocentric moral norms. Now ethnocentric moral norms are the norms of one's own culture as distinct from those of other cultures. "Ethnocentric moral norms" is thus only a polite phrase for "tribal mores." In today's world, with highly competitive opposed cultures in daily contact, an ethnocentric ethics can offer nothing to the search for a world community and world peace. Yet flatly ethnocentric positions are taken by such noted analytic philosophers as G.E. Moore (1903: 161); Stephen Toulmin (1950: 153); Alasdair MacIntyre (1966: 266). The most unabashed declaration of ethnocentricity by an analyst comes from Charles Stevenson (1944: 252):

> When the terms are *completely* neutralized one can say with tranquility that all moralists are propagandists or that all propagandists are moralists (Stevenson's emphasis).

These writers have failed to find any way for analytic philosophy to break out of tribal mores. Would it not be better to abandon ethics rather than to indulge in propaganda under the guise of philosophy?

Alasdair MacIntyre pictures current analytic ethics as "the graveyard for fragments of culturally dead large scale philosophical systems" (MacIntyre, 1979: 20). But because analytic philosophers consider history of philosophy an "optional extra," they "do not recognize that they have been retreading the ground of the great eighteenth and nineteenth century debates and now emerge with no greater success than their predecessors" (*ibid.*, p. 18). MacIntyre holds that the epistemological foundations of analytic philosophy lie in an eighteenth century philosophy that subsequent philosophy has repudiated. These forgotten, repudiated foundations are the foundations both of analytic ethics and of our contemporary liberal morality. Our contemporary analytic ethics and our contemporary morality are *foundationless* just because their *true historical foundations* have been *rightly* repudiated by subsequent philosophy (*ibid.*, p. 22):

> That recent moral philosophy should function in this protective way is scarcely surprising if I am right in identifying that philosophy as the heir of the eighteenth century; for the morality that it protects is the heir of the eighteenth century too. But the eighteenth century claimed for its liberalism epistemological foundations of a kind philosophy has since had to repudiate; *we* hold no nontrivial truths to be self-evident, *we* cannot accept Bentham's psychology or Kant's view of the powers of reason. Thus liberalism itself became foundationless; and since the morality of our age is liberal we have one more reason to expect the search for the foundations of ethics to be unrewarded.

According to MacIntyre, the lack of epistemological foundations reduces the characteristic concepts of analytic moral philosophers to the status of arbitrary taboos. Just as the Polynesians cannot agree on what they mean by "taboo," so our philosophers cannot agree on what they mean by "good," "obligatory" and "right" (*ibid.*, pp. 18-19). Thus analytic ethics has lost its status as philosophy because its characteristic concepts are totally subject to historical determinism.

Nor can the efforts of a few analytic philosophers such as Marcus George Singer to establish universal moral principles that "by definition transcend the geographical and temporal boundaries of particular societies" (Singer, 1961: 334) be judged successful. Singer distinguishes moral principles from moral rules. Moral rules do *not* apply to all societies without exception because of socio-cultural differences of persons and circumstances. In concentration camps, among gangsters and on waterfronts, something approaching Hobbes' state of nature exists. In such places even fundamental moral *rules* like truth telling do not generally oblige. But the universality of moral *principles* implies the fallacy of epistemological relativism. Singer in fact asserts as self-evident that epistemological relativism is false. Speaking of the diversity of codes of moral *rules* around the globe, he says (*ibid.*, p. 333):

> It is curious that this has not been thought with any frequency to justify an epistemological . . . relativism. This could not be so much as stated without contradiction.

Now epistemological relativism is the most fundamental aspect of historical relativism. Its infrequent assertion (at least in the U.S. and Britain) does not prove it to be false.

MacIntyre showed above the serious consequences of analytic philosophers considering history of philosophy as an "optional extra." Likewise Singer just above intimates that historical relativism has not been considered a serious option in the U.S. and Britain. Philosophers in these countries may stumble onto the difficulties inherent in historical relativism. But experience of historical relativism has not become part of the ordinary formation of professional philosophers. Consequently, historical relativism remains an unwelcome discovery that is never subjected to concerted open debate among philosophers.

This comparative neglect of historical relativism contrasts with the dominant philosophy in continental Europe, phenomenology. Prominent among phenomenologists is Heidegger. He has made historical relativism the fundamental experience of his philosophy. According to Heidegger, the history of philosophy is "the reign of mystery in error" (Heidegger, 1949: 347). In his view, analytic philosophy would be only one fateful experience of "Being" among many others in the history of philosophy. The analytic philosopher's efforts to refute other philosophies as nonsensical and as posing meaningless questions are interpreted by the Heideggerians as hopeless efforts to escape the historical relativity of his own thought. Heidegger's historical relativism explicitly repudiates that conformity truth of which analytic philosophy is but a variant interpretation. Marxism has gone so far as to deny to philosophy, ethics, law and politics the status of conformity to transcultural reality. But Marxism retains belief in conformity truth for technology and for "Marxist science." Heidegger repudiated *conformity truth of every kind*. This challenge to conformity truth I try to meet in this essay.

Singer's claim that epistemological relativism cannot be asserted without contradiction may indeed be valid, but only if he can point out experiential evidence that such assertion contradicts, which he fails to do. I myself believe, however, that such evidence exists: namely, our experience of real relations. As *real*, such relations transcend socio-cultural differences just because they are independent of the mind, whereas cultures are mind-dependent. In this essay, I will try to show that real relations are directly experienced as self-evident realities which transcend cultures. Epistemological relativism can thus be refuted by evidence found in direct experience.

While Singer appeals to self-evident rational principles that transcend cultures, in this essay I will try to show that *distinct* objects of intelligence are not directly experienced. Hence, rational principles cannot be directly experienced as distinct objects. The necessary principles to which Singer appeals were founded by ancient and medieval philosophy on the claimed knowledge of the necessary nature of things. Such necessary principles are not available as data unless we admit that we directly experience the distinction of *substance and accidents*, which even such great opponents of scepticism as Aquinas, Locke, Kant, and Hegel all deny. For the necessary nature of a thing is its substance as *distinct* from its accidents. The claim to self-evident rational principles as *original data* is generally rejected by traditional philosophy and by contemporary philosophy alike.

Thus, analytic philosophers who remain faithful to merely experiential data are reduced to ethnocentric ethics. Singer, who espouses universal moral principles, is not faithful to mere experiential data. I claim that ethics can be founded on real human relations that are directly experienced. Such real relations transcend cultural limits just because they are physical parts of the universe. Analytic philosophy is a valuable method of analysis of the usage of ethical terms. But I claim that it cannot yield an ethics worthy of the name because its data are not directly experienced as culture-transcending realities.

Epistemological relativism is likewise destructive of claims to the transcultural universality of logic. Like other rational principles, the ancients and medievals grounded the universality of logic on their claim to know the necessary nature of things. Once we restrict ourselves to experiential data, the transcultural claims of logic must be excluded as *original data*. Consequently, W.V.O. Quine has been able to show that logical necessity can be dispensed with in the philosophy of science (Quine, 1962: 110).

The problem of historical relativism is the problem of discontinuity among philosophies. Historical relativism is the irreducible difference of doctrines between philosophies stemming from different cultures. The general laws of historical determinism seem sufficient to account for the *dis*continuity of philosophical systems, since the variation of socio-cultural factors in different historical epochs produces incompatible systems of thought. But the *continuity* or agreement of diverse systems on certain basic facts of experience is not so easily accounted for simply by historical determinism. Rather, it seems a sign of permanent, trans-cultural realities, for which every philosophy has to account, no matter from what it is engendered.

If very different philosophical systems arising from very different cultures have all agreed that we cannot experience the natures of things directly, yet have also agreed that if we can experience reality at all, what we directly experience are real relations, then this agreement is strong evidence for the epistemological validity of this experience of real relations, and counter-evidence to historical relativism and skepticism. The real relations that are directly experienced in this way include the real social relations that constitute the social order: e.g., relations between husband and wife, between workers and managers, relations between political candidates and electors.

Those of my readers who are unfamiliar with medieval and renaissance authors may be impatient with my discussion of Scotus and Suarez and their speculations about the Christian eucharist, and ask what this has to do with modern philosophy. However, historical relativism can be overcome only if we compare current modes of thought with those of different times and cultures. Scotus and Suarez did their philosophy in the context of their own time and culture. If we do acknowledge (as we must) their influence on modern philosophy, we must examine their thought in its theological setting. Otherwise our thought is historically determined in an uncritical way by our own culture. What emerges from a philosophical examination of Scotus and Suarez is something like a medieval version of Positivism. That is a sign that pure historical relativism cannot explain agreement in the understanding of experience between radically diverse cultures.

I claim that ethics can be founded on real human relations *exclusively*. I mean that ethics can be written using human relations as their *unique data*, excluding any claim to knowledge of a supposed human nature. If human relations are *real* relations, they can supply the epistemological foundation for an ethics. Inasmuch as such realities are mind-independent social relations, they are transcultural data that escape the confines of tribal mores. Inasmuch as such real relations are the effects of free choice, they are the proper subject matter of ethics.

Some philosophers hold that ethics can survive as a discipline even though all human behavior is completely subject to psycho-social-biological determinism: these philosophers are called ''soft determinists.'' Other philosophers hold that ethics cannot survive such a deterministic removal of free choice: they are called ''hard determinists.'' But if I can prove the existence of freely chosen realities, I can solve the doubts of both sides of this argument as to whether there is a proper subject matter for ethics.

Although philosophers holding either ''soft'' or ''hard'' determinism agree that belief in complete psycho-social-biological determinism of all human behavior is an arguable opinion, among social scientists deterministic denial of free choice is the common view. Milton Rokeach, the social psychologist, states the situation thus (1973: 338):

> [The] matter of determinism, while still a philosophical issue, is rarely debated nowadays as a scientific issue. Social scientists of all theoretical persuasions, from Skinner at one extreme to Lewin, the symbolic interactionists, and Freud at the other, have long agreed that human behavior is determined by genetic endowment and by environmental circumstances.

Hence my argument for freely chosen realities both answers a question debated in philosophy and challenges a prevailing opinion in social science.

Hence, in this essay, I shall deal with three problems:

1) The problem of historical relativism:
I will show that philosophers of extremely different tendencies, and coming from very different cultures, have agreed at least on one point: namely, that although we do not have direct experience of natures, we do have direct experience of real relations.

Hence, there is trans-cultural agreement on an experiential basis for philosophy. Therefore from the *historical point of view itself*, historical relativism is *unconvincing*.

2) The problem of real relations:
Here I demonstrate that this transculturally accepted doctrine is in fact *philosophically* true. Hence historical relativism is *false*, inasmuch as it claims to exclude *all* transcultural truth.

3) The problem of real relations as effects of free choice:
Here, I will show that *some* real relations are the effects of free choice, and thus constitute a basis for a valid ethics. Hence MacIntyre's position is false.

4) In a concluding Chapter V, I will show the wider implications of my thesis for philosophy as a whole.

This book is intended to be the first in a series. The second book is now being written. It is called *Totally Empirical Ethics*. In it I treat ethical problems in terms of real relations only. That some real relations are empirically given as freely chosen is the outcome of this present book. Such freely chosen real relations are proper subject matter for a transcultural ethics. The third book will attempt to pass from experience of things in their extrinsic relations into knowledge of their intrinsic natures. For it may be that extrinsic relations *sufficiently experienced indirectly manifest* the intrinsic natures. Finally a fourth book will consider the philosophical problem of God.

Some remarks about the genesis of the present essay may facilitate readers' understanding of the entire series. During a three day discussion in 1970, Dr. John Deely convinced me that intuitive concepts are real relations, according to John Poinsot. That discussion began my collaboration with him in translating the *Treatise on Signs* of John Poinsot, forthcoming from the University of California Press. Working on that translation, I found that the eminent seventeenth century Thomist held that real and unreal relations have the same sign value. This reminded me of the famous doctrine at the beginning of Hegel's Logic: Being and Non-Being are the same. That conjunction of Hegelianism and Thomism led me first to reformulate the epistemological question in terms of experience of real relations as the primordial basis of all knowledge. Eventually, it led me to attempt to prove free choice from real relations only. Furthermore, in this essay I make frequent reference to experience of the identity and distinction of real and unreal relations, e.g., between the words and gestures of people conversing. This account of experience is derived from the doctrine of real and unreal relations as having the same sign value.

It only remains for me to thank the many people who contributed substantially to this work. My debt of thanks to my brethren of the Dominican Province of St. Albert the Great and to my colleagues at the Aquinas Institute of Theology cannot be measured, particularly inasmuch as what I was writing in this essay must often have seemed to them beyond the fringe. To them I owe the many years of quiet study without visible product that went into this book, all conducted in an atmosphere of free search for truth in the venerable tradition of the Order.

My special thanks go to Benedict Ashley, O.P., who edited the entire manuscript. He rephrased many expressions throughout the work. He understood my thought fully in every instance. I am truly amazed at the amount of thought and work that he devoted to the manuscript, and I am very grateful.

I must also thank especially Dr. John Deely for the immense labor and skill he devoted to setting up the notes and bibliography according to the style explained on page v above, and I thank Felicia Kruse, Gene Dolfi, and Samuel Torvend for their zealous bibliographical research under Dr. Deely's direction. Mr. Gerald "Bud" MacFarlane of Composition Specialists in Dubuque, Iowa, assisted in the layout and design of this volume, and Ms. Felicia Kruse bore the main burden of proofreading.

Saint Louis University
Aquinas Institute of Theology
10 October 1982

FREELY CHOSEN REALITY

GENERAL INTRODUCTION

Section 1. Some behaviorists deny free choice.

"To man *qua* man we readily say good riddance," writes B.F. Skinner (1971: 200-201). The man to be abolished is the *inner man*, the man defended by the literatures of freedom and dignity (*ibid.*). He is to be replaced by the scientific picture of man determined entirely from the outside by his biological and social environment (Skinner, 1971: 211). Skinner's disciples now occupy key chairs in our major universities and thus Skinnerian psychology has become a common university discipline organizing innumerable endeavors of the academic public. Nor are these endeavors confined to university laboratories. According to Kenneth Goodall, the Skinnerians' laboratory is the real world, "classrooms, kitchens, mental hospitals, rehabilitation wards, prisons, nursing homes, day-care centers, factories, movie theaters, national parks, community mental health centers, stores, recreation centers and right next door" (Goodall, 1972: 54). Moreover, Goodall finds that Skinnerians are not significantly different from their chief rivals, the humanists, who do not however approve their frank espousal of planned social control of the masses (*ibid.*, 60, 62).

Moreover, independently of the Skinnerians, by use of sophisticated sampling techniques behavioral science seems to have reduced another area of apparent free individual choice to the predictable calculation of social environment: the area of voting behavior. According to V.O. Key, Jr. (1966: 5), the conventional wisdom of political science holds: "Given knowledge of certain characteristics of a voter—his occupation, his residence, his religion, his national origin, and perhaps certain of his attitudes—one can predict with high probability the direction of his vote. The actions of persons are made to appear to be only predictable and automatic responses to campaign stimuli." Thus Orthodox Marxism's denunciation of free elections as empty sham concealing popular servitude finds justification in the purest academic circles of Western Democracy.

1

Section 2. Some behaviorists discern free choice in real relations.

However, some behaviorist political scientists do not agree that all voting behavior is a predictable and automatic response to social environment. Indeed, these political scientists admit that the vote of the majority is a predictable and automatic response to social environment. They admit that the majority do not vote responsibly because most voters do not connect their vote with the actual behavior of government. The reason is that most voters are found not to understand the political language in which politicians define political objects. Political objects are defined in terms of the spectrum of liberal versus conservative policies. The majority of voters are found not to understand this language. So the majority of voters do not understand what the politicians are doing. Yet these political scientists have found a minority of voters who do understand political language; who do thereby identify what politicians are actually doing; and who do realistically relate their vote to the actual behavior of candidates. These voters they call "responsible voters": voters who actually participate in democratic government.

Now what these political scientists describe as behavior of a minority of voters seems to be what traditional philosophy called "exercise of free choice." For the minority seems to be making a rational choice between the alternatives of liberal and conservative objects. But these political scientists are behaviorists. Traditional philosophical notions of *human nature*, and its faculties of *intellect, will,* and *sense* are lacking in their discipline. Their description of responsible voting uses two categories exclusively: 1. *Real communication* between voters and government: 2. *Shared political language* empirically found to be required for this real communication. Now real communication is a case of communicability of our knowledge. And for Kant "universal communicability of our knowledge—is presupposed in every logic and every principle of knowledge that is not one of scepticism" (Kant, 1790: 84).[1] Hence, for Kant real communication is the presupposition of all philosophy. Now according to Aristotle, communication is a case of *real relation*. In Aristotle's time, communication between master and slave was an everyday experience. For Aristotle (335-322BCa: 6b29-30), such communication was a case of real relations, illustrating the category of relation:

> All relatives have their correlatives. 'Slave' means slave of a master, and 'master' in turn implies slave.[2]

Now we shall see below that Kant not only held real relations; he held also that real relations were the only realities we directly experience. So perhaps philosophy can turn the data of these political scientists into an *argument for free choice from real relations only*.

Section 3. Can philosophers experience free choice in real relations alone?

But traditional philosophy has never tried to adjudicate the existence or non-existence of free choice except in the categories of *human nature* and its faculties of *intellect, will* and *sense*. Traditional philosophy has never tried to adjudicate the existence of free choice in terms of real relation only. This essay will try to *manifest free choice exclusively by real and unreal relations*, with no suppositions made about any *human nature* or any faculties of *intellect, will* and *sense*. If this can be done then the data of these political scientists will be converted into a philosophical argument for free choice.

These political scientists attempt to distinguish *real* communication between electorates and government from apparent communication between them. In their discipline the difference between real and apparent communication is the difference between democratic elections as a valid form of government and democratic elections as deceptive propaganda. This difference between real and apparent communication is therefore crucial to their methodology. Real communication is understood by them as what is independent of subjective belief as opposed to apparent communication which is dependent on subjective belief. Hence in their methodology the *real* understood as mind-independent has become an object of methodological discrimination.

Now it is a good question whether philosophers have ever made a methodological study of reality at the stripped down minimal level manifest in the methodology of these political scientists: reality in terms of what Aristotelians would call *real relations only*. Indeed, for Whitehead (1929: 499) real relations are minimum "facts of nature" required for the truth of modern science. But he does not seem to have made a methodological study of reality seen merely in terms of real relations. I have asserted without sufficient proof that Kant considered real relations a minimum penetration of reality. This assumes that Kant admitted to knowing mind-independent reality. That seems a dubious interpretation of Kant. On the other hand, can one assume Aristotelians could think of real relations *otherwise than as accidents in substances*. It seems that in fact Aristotelians cannot do it. But if Aristotelians cannot understand real relations otherwise than as inhering in substances, then they cannot think reality as expressed in the methodology of these political scientists. For these political scientists are behaviorists. Like other positivists, they do not acknowledge the existence of substances in the Aristotelian sense of substance.

The question is whether philosophers like Kant and the Aristotelians could think *reality as experienced* in terms of real relations only. It seems that pure empiricists such as these behaviorists have so experienced reality. The question concerns the mind-independent content of experience. This question is a truly philosophic one. It asks what is the reality-content of philosophical experience, a capital question for the origin of philosophy in experience. It would be strange if such philosophers had never faced it. The question is inevitable if the data of these political scientists is to be converted into philosophical argument.

Section 4. Is philosophical experience totally subject to historical determinism?

The question whether philosophers can think reality at the level of these political scientists assumes that *some* philosophers have some common understanding of reality. Since Kant, any philosophic claim to understand mind-independent reality can only be regarded as open to question. At best we can admit *without examination* a claim to understanding reality as commonly *believed* in one philosophical tradition, e.g., among Aristotelians. But we cannot assume a common understanding of reality between traditions as different as Aristotelianism, British Empiricism and Kantian Criticism. Such an assumption can only be justified by manifesting philosophers in these different traditions who did share some common understanding of reality. Until we have done so, we cannot assume that these different traditions any more share a common doctrine of reality than does world literature.

Is philosophy anything but imaginative literature? Perhaps the only valid part of the philosophical traditions is not their claim to know reality but their value as imaginative literature as, for example, Plato's dialogues. Like imaginative literature, the philosophical traditions would bring to expression the typical subjective experiences of given historical epochs. Philosophy would be a very serious form of world literature because it would be a very good analysis of subjective experience in a given age and civilization. But philosophy would have *no valid claim to publicly verified knowledge of reality*. The rightful claim to publicly verified knowledge of reality would devolve exclusively on the sciences. This understanding of philosophy would imply that philosophical experience is completely subject to historical conditioning; for philosophy would be only the expression of the historically conditioned experience of a given society in a given epoch.

This contention that all philosophical experience is completely subject to historical determinism excludes publicly verified truth from every philosophical knowledge claim. For no knowledge claim can dispense with some grounding in experience. For example, any philosophy of ethics or religion would be reduced to expressing the ethnocentric experience of one class or nation as opposed to that of others. This contention that all philosophical experience is completely subject to historical determinism has been well argued by Heidegger. The conclusion of his position is that philosophy is *beyond responsible* human control: it is "the reign of mystery in error" (Heidegger, 1943: 347)[3]. Heidegger concedes that physical science can make correct statements corresponding to reality (see Powell, 1970: 125). But philosophy could not achieve correspondence to reality because it is completely subject to historical conditioning in its experience of human existence and of all things.

According to Heidegger, diverse philosophies differ by the historically determined light in which beings of their world are philosophically experienced. Diverse historically determined lights of philosophical experience manifest the beings of the world in incompatible metaphysical interpretations. Heidegger calls all philosophies "metaphysics" because he defines philosophies by their *incompatible interpretations of the nature of beings*. For one philosophy, the historically determined light of its philosophical experience manifests the nature of beings as *matter*; for another philosophy, the historically determined light of its philosophical experience manifests the nature of beings as *becoming* and *life*; for another philosophy, the historically determined light of its philosophical experience manifests the nature of beings as *idea*; for another philosophy, the historically determined light of its philosophical experience manifests the nature of beings as *will*; and so on; as the historically determined light of philosophical experience is diversified, diverse philosophies experience beings in such further incompatible "metaphysical" interpretations as: substance, subject, energeia, and eternal return of the selfsame (Heidegger, 1949: 207-208).[4]

So there is a historically determined difference in the light of philosophical experience that gives incompatible interpretations to the nature of all beings in the diverse philosophies. This difference in the light of philosophical experience is the Fate of Being (*Geschick des Seins*) for any one philosophy. This difference is just an inexplicable fateful stamp (*geschicklichen Prägung*) of the nature of all beings in that philosophy.[5] But philosophers have never been aware of the inevitable historical fate that determines the light of their philosophical experience. This unawareness of philosophers is the famous Heideggerian "forgottenness of Being" (cf. Richardson, 1963: 742). Moreover, the fate of philosophies has now run its course: No further possibility of raising fundamental metaphysical questions remains open since Nietzsche's philosophy (Heidegger, 1961; Magnus, 1970[6]).

Despite the fatefulness of philosophy's "metaphysical" thinking, "metaphysical" thinking nevertheless provides the "rare and simple decisions of history" (Heidegger, 1943[7]). Thus Heidegger's understanding of fatefulness would enhance rather than diminish our usual estimate of the historic power of metaphysical thought. Despite its historic power, "metaphysical" thinking is fated because it precludes correspondence truth as regards the difference between Being and the beings. All philosophies are "metaphysical" because they experience the nature of all beings in forgetfulness of Being. Any philosophical experience is fated because its fundamental experience concerns a *given fated difference of Being and the beings without experiencing this difference as such*. "The forgetfulness of Being is forgetfulness of the difference of Being and the beings," writes Heidegger (Heidegger, 1950: 336, my translation).[8] The difference of Being and the beings is the difference between the fatefully distinctive light of a philosopher's experience as contrasted with all beings as lit up for him under that light. Not even the most fundamental metaphysical experience can correspond to its most primordial determinate; namely, its own characteristic experience of the difference of Being and the beings. In this sense, the root philosophical experience is a forgotten fate that determines all subsequent thinking in that "metaphysical" system. Correspondence truth in the experience of the difference of Being and the beings would precisely destroy that Heideggerian "freedom" that consists in "wandering" fatefully from one metaphysical system to another. The pre-essence of philosophical truth consists precisely in this fateful wandering—erring from one incompatible system of metaphysics to another (Heidegger, 1943: p. 347 of English trans.). Heidegger allows for some correspondence truth, as I have pointed out above. But correspondence truth in the experience of the difference of Being and the beings he cannot admit. For Heidegger's fatefulness of *Sein* consists in the meta-physical thinker's incapacity to experience the beings except "in this or that fated *Sein* coinage" (*geschicklichen Prägung*) (Heidegger, 1957: 134).

Section 5. Diverse philosophers with a common doctrine of experienced reality would challenge total historical determinism of experience.

Now I believe that I have shown below that diverse systems (metaphysical systems in Heidegger's sense) *do agree by correspondence truth* in original philosophical experience of the difference of Being and the beings. I believe that I have shown that Aristotelians, Locke, and Kant agree in a doctrine of philosophical experience; and that, according to them, philosophical experience revealed reality as ambiguous to the *as yet unknown nature of the beings*. They held that philosophical experience attained reality as independent of subjective experience, but that experience *could not* directly reveal the intrinsic nature of the beings. If I am right in this claim, then their fundamental philosophical experience of reality was not a fatefully determined *geschickliche Prägung des Seins* in the nature of the beings. Their fundamental experience was not an "experience" in one or the other fated *Sein* "coinage." These diverse metaphysical thinkers would not be "wandering" from one another in their fundamental experience of reality. Their fundamental experience would be proved corresponding to reality as different from the as yet unknown true nature of the beings. That experience of the beings as real would reveal that the nature of the beings cannot be directly experienced. Only after having reasoned to the nature of the beings as understood in their particular system would each metaphysical thinker experience that characteristic *Sein*-"coinage" of the Being of beings. But that subsequent experience would depend on their prejacent reasoning. For example, an Aristotelian having reasoned to the existence of *substance* would subsequently experience substance as the nature of beings. But in the original philosophical experience, the reality of the beings would be experienced as different from their as yet unknown true nature. The Being of the beings in a particular *Sein*-"coinage" would not yet be experienced. These thinkers would experience the beings as different from their own system's *Sein*-"coinage" or any other system's. Therefore beings as *directly* experienced would be *philosophically* experienced as *possibly* corresponding to various "differences." And that would constitute correspondence truth of the beings in their "difference." That conclusion is incompatible with Heidegger's doctrine on fated experience in only one or the other fated *Sein*-"coinage." Historical determinism of philosophical experience would not be complete.

What I show below concerning the Aristotelians, Locke and Kant can be briefly outlined as follows. Philosophical experience for the Aristotelians is experience of concrete realities that subsequently become known as accidents, but which are *not experienced* as accidents. Only later are they *understood* as needing inherence in a substance. Philosophical experience is experience of *concrete realities* prior to abstract knowing of *Being* or any other abstract universals. This turns out to be also Locke's doctrine of experiential knowing. This account of experienced realities is not explicitly either Aristotelian or Lockean philosophy. Aristotelians and Locke held that this account of experienced reality was open to the interpretations of Parmenides, Spinoza and Hobbes, albeit falsely.

I believe that Kant can be shown to hold a similar doctrine of experimental knowing as prejacent to his system. His system explains the integration of the individual's experience thanks to a priori principles; namely, thanks to a priori forms of sense and a priori concepts of the understanding. But Kant held that human communication was "presupposed to every principle of knowledge that is not one of scepticism" (Kant, 1790: 239—text cited in note 1 of this chapter). Thus Kant saw communication as a fact prior to his own or any other non-sceptical philosophical explanation. Moreover, Kant admitted experienced real relations to the "transcendental object" which cannot be experienced in its intrinsic nature. This realm as term of real relations is outside of and foreign to Kant's systematic philosophy, but it is presupposed to his philosophy. Kant's "thing-in-itself" is first of all the "transcendental object," which is the *term of experienced real relations*. Now a term of experienced real relations which is not itself experienced in its intrinsic nature makes sense. It makes the same sense as experienced reality of real relations according to the Aristotelians. They also held that we experience real relations but that we cannot experience directly the substantial natures of the thing-terms of real relations. Aristotelians held that we cannot experience the substantial nature of the thing-terms that are really related.

Therefore I claim that Aristotelians, Locke, and Kant can be shown to share a similar doctrine of experiential knowing of reality. According to them philosophically experienced reality is not explicitly Aristotelian, Lockean or Kantian: it could be falsely interpreted as that of Parmenides, Spinoza, Hobbes or any nonsceptical philosophy. I believe these facts challenge Heidegger's claim about complete historical determinism of philosophical experience.

I believe that I show below that Aristotelians, Locke and Kant agree in their understanding of experiential knowing. Now although experience is sometimes deceptive, no other knowledge claims can be valid that are not somehow grounded in experiential knowing. In this sense, experiential knowing is in a general way the origin of philosophy and science. Moreover, I believe I can show that the conjunction of Aristotelians and Kant in experiential knowing happens in the experience of real relations. Hence their conjunction coincides with political scientists who claim to describe human freedom in terms of real relations only. So we would have found philosophers capable of thinking reality at the level of those political scientists.

This essay considers only the doctrine of experiential knowing of real relations in the Aristotelians, Kant and some other philosophers. We will neglect the subsequent systematic philosophy of these philosophers. Our purpose would be frustrated either by the Aristotelian doctrine of substance and the remaining categories or by the Kantian doctrine of a priori forms of sense and a priori concepts of understanding. Our purpose is to think reality at the level of those political scientists who use real relations only. *Our purpose is to match experiential knowing in those political scientists with experiential knowing in these philosophers.*

Section 6. Does experience of real relations constitute the origin of all philosophy and science?

Furthermore, real relations seem a minimum content of mind-independent reality, for the real relation does not directly reveal the intrinsic nature of things, but only the real external order among things. A city dump reveals real relations among things in the dump, but does not tell us anything about the intrinsic nature of what is in the dump. So the claim to experience real relations is merely the claim to experience some real concrete order. But this is a minimum claim to experiencing reality. Now I believe that I have also shown below that real relations between communicators is the minimum experienced reality required for actual communication. Hence the real relation is not only a minimum claim to experiencing reality. It would also be required for public verification, since public verification is actual communication.

Now experiential knowing is a general supposition of all philosophy and science. Experiential knowing of real relations seems to be a minimum claim to experiencing reality; namely, the claim to experience real concrete order. Real relations, moreover, seem to me needed to verify publicly the claim to experiencing real relations. Now let us assume that I can show that real relations exist; that they are a minimum of experienced reality; and that they are the minimum of experienced reality required for actual public verification. Under these assumptions real relations would be: a) experienced realities; b) publicly verified realities; c) *the minimum publicly verified realities* presupposed to all other publicly verified realities. Hence, publicly verified real relations would be the *critically verified origin of all publicly verified philosophy and science.* Thus we would have the critical philosophical answer to the claim that philosophical experience is completely determined by historical conditioning. For experienced real relations publicly verified would be *extrahistorical* realities common to philosophy and science: they would be realities mind-independent of and prior to all publicly verified philosophy, science and historical experience. Real relations would be first publicly verified facts on which philosophy must be built.

Section 7. The outcome of the general introduction. The division of the essay.

These introductory considerations have the following outcome. We have asked whether philosophers can think reality at the level of mere real relations, as do political scientists who claim empirical verification of human free choice thanks to mere real relations. Our preliminary answer is: No!: philosophers cannot do so. For we must assume that philosophical experience is completely subject to historical determinism; and so it cannot distinguish mind-independent reality from its own historical conditioning. However, the assumption that philosophical experience is completely subject to historical determinism is only an assumption based on a warning sign. That warning sign consists in the interpretation of divergent philosophical traditions as having incompatible doctrines of experiential knowing. However, I believe that this interpretation is false in the case of such notably diverse philosophical traditions as those arising from Aristotle, Locke, the British Empiricist and Kant, the continental Rationalist. If I prove this agreement among them, I remove a considerable part of the basis for the assumption that philosophical experience is completely subject to historical determinism. Moreover, in achieving agreement in the doctrine of experiential knowing among these traditions, our further investigations will be understandable in all three traditions. For all three traditions refer their systems to experiential knowing.

But removing that warning sign is but a preparation for our philosophical task. The task will then be to find the critical origin of all publicly verified philosophy and science in mind-independent reality. For mind-independent reality is free from historical determinism. Having found that critical origin in publicly verified real relations, we can finally approach the question: Can freely chosen reality be manifested exclusively by real and unreal relations? Accordingly, this essay will be divided thus:

Part I. A historical part comprising a single chapter, Chapter I. Experience of real relations as common epistemological ground for philosophies of experience.

Part II. Philosophical Analysis. This part comprises the remaining four chapters.

Chapter II. Why the Problem of Realism Involves Direct Experience of Public Objects.

Chapter III. Experience of Real Relations.

Chapter IV. Freely Chosen Reality.

Chapter V. The Republic of the Free.

Chapter I

EXPERIENCE OF REAL RELATIONS
AS COMMON EPISTEMOLOGICAL GROUND
FOR PHILOSOPHIES OF EXPERIENCE

Introduction to Chapter I: the Goal of This Chapter.

Heidegger claims philosophical experience is totally subject to historical determinism. A most persuasive case for this difference in philosophical experience is found in the chasm that separates ancient and medieval philosophy from modern philosophy. This chasm was opened by Descartes, the "father of modern philosophy." But philosophy did not become fully aware of this chasm until Locke and Kant had done their work. Hegel then came to seal the new philosophical experience by reconciling old and new in his own fashion. First, I try to show in this chapter that a chasm separating ancient and medieval Aristotelians from these moderns *does not exist* because, like the moderns, these Aristotelians denied experience of natures. Secondly, I will show that philosophers of extremely different tendencies, and coming from very different cultures, have agreed at least on one point; namely, that although we do not have direct experience of natures, we do have *direct experience of real relations*. Hence, there is transcultural agreement on an experiential basis for philosophy. Therefore from the *historical point of view itself*, historical relativism is *unconvincing*.

Section 1. Aristotle on the ignorance of the distinction of substance and accidents in the Pre-Socratics.

Aristotle's methodology is aimed primarily at distinguishing the real from the unreal. This is the significance of his discussion in the *Categories* (Aristotle, 335-322BCa: pp. 4-6) of the use of singular and universal names. Singular names can be used to name real things which are always singular and concrete. As terms of propositions (e.g., *this man* is an animal, *this whiteness* is a color) they can function as subjects but not as predicates. On the other hand universal names such as *animal* or *color* can function as predicate terms. However, since they do not directly name something real, but are only predicable of the real, universal names cannot simply be said to name something real. As universal, therefore, they name something unreal; i.e., there is no such thing in reality as "animal" or "color," but only animal singulars and colored singulars. While Aristotle is certainly not a Nominalist, he also is not a Platonic realist. Rather, he is insistent that the intelligence affirms the real only in the act of affirming or denying a universal predicate of a singular subject, an act dependent on the power to discriminate between the real and the unreal element in knowledge.

Besides the distinction of the real and unreal, Aristotle's analysis of linguistic usage reveals distinction within the real singulars. Names of real singulars such as *this whiteness* are always names as *present in* an individual subject. But not even universal names such as *manhood* are ever used to mean *present in* a subject: "For manhood is not *in* a man" (Aristotle, 335-322BCa:3a11). Moreover singulars named by such names as *this whiteness* cannot exist apart from the individual subject in which they are present. Such a singular individual subject as *this man* or *this horse* Aristotelians call *individual or primary substances*. All real singular entities that can only exist as present in an individual substance they called *accidents*. Aristotle enumerates nine kinds of accidents (*Categories*, 335-322BCa: 1b25-2a3). So Aristotle (*ibid.*, 2b3-6) can make the following statement about everything namable: "In fine, then, all things whatsoever save what we call primary [individual] substances are [either merely mental unreal] predicates of primary substances or [are real as] present in such as their subjects. And were there no primary substance, nought else could so much as exist."[1]

Thus linguistic analysis revealed the distinction of substance and accidents to Aristotle. But he held that this distinction was *conceptual* and *not given in sensory experience*. Aristotle's criticism of Parmenides in Book I of the *Physics* is significant in this regard. Almost all Aristotle's arguments against him turn on the conceptual difference between substance and accidents (for an outline of the arguments see Ross, 1936: 473[2]). Parmenides' error lay in his failure to make the conceptual distinction of substance from its accidents where experience could find nothing separate to be experienced. But Aristotle also argues against him *from the experiential difference* between a continuum and its parts. Thus the experiential evidence of the distinction of the continuous whole from its parts in that argument sets up a contrast with the mere conceptual distinction between substance and accidents in the other arguments.

Parmenides assumed that "being" has but one meaning and that there is nothing besides "being." And he concluded that all things were one. By substituting the *one* experiential object "white" for the one conceptual object "being," Aristotle argues against him thus. Even if "white" has but one meaning and nothing exists besides "white," still a plurality is manifested in two ways. First, the experiential distinction of the continuous white whole from its parts manifests a plurality. Secondly, the conceptual distinction of the substance from its accident "white" manifests a plurality. The argument from a continuum has already been explained as manifesting a plurality of whole and parts (Aristotle, 335-322BCb: *Physics*, Book I, 185b6-15). And so the following text (*ibid.*) makes only summary reference to the argument from the continuum:

> His assumption is false inasmuch as he treats "being" as having only one meaning, whereas in reality it has several. And his inferences are false, because, even if we accepted such a proposition as "nothing that is not white exists," and if "white" had only one meaning, still the white things would be many and not one. Obviously not one in the sense of a homogeneous continuum. Nor in the sense of a conceptual identity, for there remains a conceptual distinction between the subject in which the whiteness is seated, and the qualification of "being white," and that distinction does not involve the separate existence of anything alongside of "that which is white"; because the plurality is established not by there being something separate, but by there being a conceptual distinction between white and the subject in which it inheres. But Parmenides had not yet arrived at this principle. (*Physics*, Book I, 186a25-32).[3]

In the text *logos* in the dative is translated *conceptual*.

Section 2. Aristotle explained by Aquinas-Commentator: the ignorance of the distinction of substance and accidents in several pre-Aristotelians.

Aristotle's texts are better understood when read in conjunction with such a philosopher-commentator as Aquinas. On the above text he comments as follows (Aquinas, 1269-1270):

> In the time of Parmenides it was not yet considered that something could be one as a subject and many conceptually [ratione]. And therefore he believed if nothing existed separated from a given subject that it followed it was one only. But this is disproved both by the argument from multiplicity of parts and by that from the diverse rationale of the subject and its accidents. (My translation). (*In I Physicorum*, lect. 6, n. 40).[4]

For Aquinas, the contrast of the two arguments lies in the experiential difference of whole and parts as against the merely intelligible difference of rationale between subject and accidents. In the time of Parmenides, this intelligible difference of substance and accidents had not yet been considered. But Aquinas certainly did not think that in Parmenides' time people had not yet considered the experiential difference between a whole and its parts.

Aristotle and Aquinas commenting criticized Parmenides because he did not grasp the distinction of substance and accidents whereby the world as a whole is divided into distinct individual existing substances. But they did not deny that Parmenides had a true experience of the world as a whole: he grasped reality (being) but not its distinctions (substances).

But Parmenides was not the only philosopher known to Aristotle and Aquinas who did not distinguish between substance and accidents. They knew of other philosophers who evaded this distinction, each in his own way.

One way of evading the distinction of substance and accidents was by holding a doctrine incompatible with the existence of substance. Now substance for Aristotle and Aquinas was a composite of intrinsic components, namely substantial form and prime matter. These intrinsic components were nature in the proper sense. "Nature" so understood was the principle of all motion *and rest* that occurred to substances. Hence any doctrine that eliminated substantial form and prime matter *as principles of rest* eliminated the existence of substance. For substance was composed of these intrinsic principles by its intrinsic nature.

Philosophers holding for everything in perpetual motion had just this way of evading the distinction of substance and accidents. By neglecting nature as principle of rest, they consequently rejected the existence of substance as understood by Aristotle and Aquinas.

For nature is the inherent content of substance (Aristotle, 335-322BCb: *Physics*, Book II, Chapter I, 192b32-34):

> This, then, being what we mean by "nature," anything that has in itself such a principle as we have described may be said to possess a "nature" of its own inherently. And all such things have a substantive existence.[5]

Aquinas' commentary emphasizes that substance is not "nature" but a composite derivative from its contents, substantial form and prime matter. Substantial form and prime matter are "nature" in the proper sense:

> Because substantial form, prime matter and their composite, substance, are all called "substance" one might believe that the composite is "nature." But Aristotle excludes this by saying the composite of matter and form, such as a man, is not "nature" but "from nature" [*a natura*] (Aquinas, c. 1269-1270: *In II Phys.*, lect. 1, no 152).[6]

According to Aristotle and Aquinas, "nature" is the principle of motion inherent in a substance. But nature is also *principle of rest from motion*. They indeed granted perpetual motion in the heavenly bodies. But certain types of accidental change resulted in change of substance: as when sickness so changed the accidents of an organism as to result in death. Once substantial change occurred, all accidents of the organism ceased to exist as well, since they depended for existence on the living organism. When the accidents ceased to exist, of course they ceased to change. Hence not all kinds of change could go on without ceasing. The transition from existence to non-existence by corruption and the transition from non-existence to existence by generation put absolute limits on these types of change. These types of change are said to be "between contradictory limits," i.e., between existence and non-existence or vice versa. Change between positive limits also occurs, e.g., change of a surface from red color to green. The positive limits in such change they called "contrasting limits" (Aristotle, 335-322BCb: 225a1-13). But no change could be without limit:

> Nor can any change be without limit; for we have agreed that every change is from this to that, whether the 'this' and 'that' are contrasted or contradictory. Thus the limits of changes between the contradictories are the positive and the negative, e.g., existence as the limit of genesis and non-existence of extinction; and in the case of contrasts the contrasted qualities in question, for such are the extreme points of the change. This applies to every form of modification, for modification must be from one quality to another contrasted with it (Aristotle, 335-322b: *Physics*, Book VI, ch. 10, 241a27-32).[7]

Aquinas comments (1269-1270):

> He intends to show that no change is without limits. This is against Heraclitus . . . First he shows that no change is without the limit of a *determinate* outcome . . . His first argument is this. It is said above that every change is from something to something. Some changes are between contradictories, such as generation and corruption, some changes are between contraries such as qualitative change and growth or decrease of size in living beings.
>
> Evidently these changes all have limits. In changes between contradictories, the limits are positive and negative. Generation is terminated at existence, and corruption is terminated by non-existence. Similarly in changes between contraries, these contraries themselves are the limits or ultimates in which such changes cease. (My translation of *In VI Phys.*, lect. 13, nn. 879-880).[8]

So Aquinas understands all change as limited because any change *results in something determinate*, not in something indeterminate. He understands determinacy of outcome as excluding the "infinity" of motion. Determinate outcome of motions manifests some motions as substantial generation or corruption: it manifests other motions as resulting in accidents. *Determinacy of motions manifests the real distinction of substance and accidents.* By denying determinacy of motions, Heraclitus is evading the real distinction of substance and accidents!

Aristotle and Aquinas commenting compare Parmenides' denial of any motion with this doctrine of everything in perpetual motion. They hold Parmenides is more opposed to Nature as the basic presupposition of natural philosophy. But nevertheless, this doctrine is also opposed to its fundamental principle that Nature is the *principle of both motion and rest* (Aristotle, 335-322BCb):

> The physicist is not concerned to argue with the man who denies the existence of motion, for he starts with the datum that Nature is the principle of movement. As to [everything moving perpetually] it is about right to say that it is palpably false, but not quite so defiant of the whole discipline of Physics as the other; for though in our discourse on Physics it was laid down that Nature is the principle of rest as well as motion, yet it is motion that is primarily germane to the matter (*Physics*, Bk. VIII, ch. 3, 253b4-10).[9]

Aquinas comments (1269-1270), identifying Heraclitus as holding for everything perpetually changing:

> First he compares this opinion to the preceding one claiming that everything is in perpetual rest. He says holding everything perpetually changing as Heraclitus did is indeed false and contrary to the basic principles of natural philosophy. However it is less opposed to the fundamentals of the discipline than the previous opinion [of Parmenides]. Nevertheless it is manifestly opposed to the fundamental supposition of natural philosophy that *Nature is not only principle of motion but also of rest* (emphasis added; my translation of *In VIII Physicorum*, lect. 5, n. 1007).[10]

In general, according to Aristotle and Aquinas commenting, the doctrine of *everything* perpetually changing removes nature as *principle limiting any motion whatsoever*. Because some changes are intrinsically limited by the substance or accidents being produced, *not everything* is changing without limit. Since *limits of some changes* are fixed by the nature of substances, even perpetual local motion of the heavenly bodies is only a limited change within a cosmos where limits of change are fixed by the natures inherent in substances. It is these limits that makes "nature" principle of rest.

In particular, Heraclitus did not acknowledge generation or corruption of substances as the natural limit manifest in substantial change. Nor did he acknowledge any sort of accidental change as limited by the production of a determinate accident, *leaving the substance as such unchanged*. In other words, for Aristotle and Aquinas, Heraclitus' neglect of the "limits" of change *evaded the real distinction between substance and accidents*. By neglecting nature as principle of rest, he evaded the real distinction of substance and accidents. Denying "rest" understood as intrinsic limit to change is a doctrine incompatible with the existence of substance. For, so understood, "rest" means the determinate intrinsic nature of substance. Denying "rest", therefore, removes substance by removing its intrinsic nature.

Aquinas believed Plato held accidents were non-being. This understanding of Plato is not clearly found in Aristotle. It may not be the true understanding of Plato. But it does show that for Aquinas a philosopher could evade the real distinction between substance and accidents. His understanding of Plato is as follows:

> Plato said an accident is non-being. Although he said an accident is non-being, nevertheless he did not say an accident is nothing. He said it is something. (My translation of Aquinas, 1269-1270: lib. 1, lect. 7, n. 49).[11]

Now, for Aquinas, an accident is real and really distinct from its substance. But its reality is to be the "being of a being" (1269-1272a: lib. 12, lect. 1, n. 2419); accidents exist yet "accidents can exist only in a subject" [a substance] (*ibid.*, n. 2422). Indeed, they do not exist but rather the substance exists by them (Aquinas, 1266-1274j):

> These accidents, as long as the bread and wine remained, had not themselves got existence; for it was their substance that existed, which existed in this way or that because of them. Thus we say that snow exists as white (or is white) because of its whiteness (*Summa theologiae*, III, q. 77, art. 1 ad 4).[12]

Hence by holding that accidents were non-being, Plato evaded the real distinction between substance and accidents defended by Aquinas.

According to Aquinas (1269-1272a), Protagoras held that the properties and natures of things existed only while being sensed and thought:

> Now if potency is present in a thing only when it is acting, it follows that nothing is hot or cold, sweet or bitter, and so forth, except when it is being sensed through a change in the senses. But this is clearly false; for if it were true it would follow that Protagoras' opinion would be true, since he said that all the properties and natures of things have existence only in being sensed and in being thought (*In IX Met.*, lect. 3, n. 1800).[13]

Thus Protagoras evaded the distinction between the substance as potency respecting its action as accident. For it is thanks to their substantial natures that sensible things exist when not acting on the senses, according to Aquinas. So Protagoras' view ignored the substantial existence of things whereby they exist independently of their action on our senses (but in potency to such action).

Section 3. Aquinas' position in his independent writings: the distinction of substance and accidents excluded from the realm of the naturally known.

We have no evidence that Parmenides, Heraclitus, Plato or Protagoras ever heard of the real distinction between substance and accidents. Indeed, Aristotle explicitly tells us Parmenides had not yet arrived at this distinction, as seen above. In any case, all of them found different ways of evading the distinction.

Aquinas thought they evaded in their several ways that real distinction. But he does not charge any of them with not believing their own opposed view. But he does assert that Heraclitus *could* not believe his denial of the principle of contradiction (1269-1272a):

> That this principle must meet the conditions given above he shows as follows: it is impossible for anyone to think, or hold as an opinion, that the same thing both is and is not at the same time, although some believe that Heraclitus was of this opinion. But while it is true that Heraclitus spoke in this way, he could not think that this is true; for it is not necessary that everything that a person says he should mentally accept or hold as an opinion. (*In IV Met.*, lect. 6, n. 601).[14]

The text refers to conditions the first principle must meet. "The conditions given above" were:

> that there could be no error regarding it; that it is not hypothetical; and that it comes naturally to the one having it (*ibid.*, n. 599).[15]

So we must now enquire about the content of what is naturally known according to Aquinas. For if the distinction of substance and accidents were included in what is naturally known, these philosophers could not have believed their evasion of that distinction. But Aquinas does not charge them with denying the naturally known truth of that distinction. Why does he exclude the real distinction of substance and accidents from what is naturally known?

In order to see why Aquinas excluded the distinction of substance and accidents from what is naturally known, we must grasp his doctrine on experiential knowing. What was naturally known to intellect included not merely intellectual objects, it included also objects of sensory experience. In general, what was naturally known to intellect was the nature of material things. The nature of material things was the proper object of our intellect. Hence the nature of material things specified our intellectual power just as color specified the power of sight and sound specified the power of hearing. However, since what specified our intellect existed only in individual bodies, our intellectual knowledge naturally included objects of sensory experience (Aquinas, 1266-1274d):

> The reason for all this is that cognitive faculties are proportioned to their objects. For instance, an angel's intellect, which is totally separate from corporeal reality, has as its proper object intelligible substances separate from corporeal reality, and it is by means of these intelligible objects that it knows material realities. The proper object of the human intellect, on the other hand, since it is joined to a body, is a nature or

"whatness" found in corporeal matter—the intellect, in fact, rises to the limited knowledge it has of invisible things by way of the nature of visible things. But by definition a nature of this kind exists in an individual which has corporeal matter, for instance, it is of the nature of stone that it should exist in this or that particular stone, or of the nature of horse that it should exist in this or that particular horse, etc. Thus the nature of stone or any other material reality cannot be known truly and completely except in so far as it exists in a particular thing. Now we apprehend the particular through the senses and imagination. Therefore if it is actually to understand its proper object, then the intellect must needs turn to sense images in order to look at universal natures existing in particular things. (*Summa theologiae*, I, q. 84, art. 7).[16]

The complete natural object of human knowledge was both intellectual and sensory. The intellectual judgment "Socrates is a man" showed that the intellect understood Socrates who was an object of sensory experience. The intellect directly understood only the abstract universal nature "man." But, indirectly, intellect reflected on the origin of its abstract universal in the sense experience of the individual Socrates (Aquinas, 1266-1274d):

Directly and immediately our intellect cannot know the singular in material realities. The reason is that the principle of singularity in material things is individual matter, and our intellect—as said before—understands by abstracting species from this sort of matter. But what is abstracted from individual matter is universal. Therefore our intellect has direct knowledge only of universals. Indirectly and by a quasi-reflection, on the other hand, the intellect can know the singular, because, as mentioned before, even after it has abstracted species it cannot actually understand by means of them except by a return to sense images in which it understands the species, as Aristotle says.

Therefore, in this sense, it is the universal that the intellect understands directly by means of the species, and singulars (represented in sense images) only indirectly. And it is in this way that it formulates the proposition, "Socrates is a man." (*Summa*, I, q. 86, art. 1).[17]

In fact, intellect brought to full actuality of the universal an item common to singulars already experienced by sense. For sense experience already perceived some item common to different individual men (Aquinas, 1269-1272b):

Then he elucidates something asserted in the preceding solution, namely, that the universal is taken from *experience bearing on singulars*. And he says that what was stated above, albeit not clearly—namely, how from the experience of singulars the universal is formed in the mind—must now be discussed again and explained more clearly. For if many singulars are taken which are without differences as to some one item existing in them, that one item according to which they are not different, once it is received in the mind, is the first universal, no matter what it may be, i.e., whether it pertains to the essence of the singulars or not . . .

> But how this one item can be taken he now explains. For it is clear that sensing is properly and per se of the singular, but yet there is somehow even *a sensing of the universal*. For *sense knows* Callias not only so far forth as he is Callias, but also as he is *this man*; and similarly Socrates, as he is *this man*. As a result of such an attainment pre-existing in the sense, the intellective soul can consider *man* in both. But if it were in the very nature of things that sense could apprehend only that which pertains to particularity, and along with this could in no wise apprehend the nature in the particular, it would not be possible for universal knowledge to be caused in us from sense-apprehension (emphasis added). (*In II Post. Anal.*, lect. 20, nn. 594-595).[18]

So the respective objects of sense and intellect manifested continuity as regards the universal.

But human perception revealed an even more intimate unity of sense and intellect than continuity in their respective objects. Human perception was itself both intellectual and sensory (Aquinas, 1266-1274c):

> One and the same man perceives himself both to understand and to have sensations (*Summa*, I, q. 76, art. 1).[19]

Hence, both understanding and sense are factors in complete human perception. This total complex unity of human perception Thomas usually calls "experiential knowledge" (*Scientia experimentalis*: cf. *Index Thomisticus*, Sectio II, Volumen 8, p. 769). For example (Aquinas, 1266-1274e), even Adam and Eve in Paradise needed animals:

> What they needed them for was to acquire an experiential knowledge of their natures.
>
> Indigebant tamen eis ad experimentalem cognitionem sumendam de naturis eorum. (*Summa*, I, q. 96, art. 1 ad 3).

Though in general the universal nature of bodies was the object of the intellect, only *one universal nature* was the first, the direct, the only one naturally given in all others, and naturally known to everyone. That universal nature Aquinas called *Ens*. This term is frequently translated "being." However, for many modern philosophers "being" does not primarily signify extramental reality, as it does for Aquinas (1252-1256):

> Some things such as a man or a stone have their total and complete existence outside of the soul . . . The words *ens* originally named (such an) existence. (My translation of *In I Sent.*, dist. 19, q. 5, art. 1).[20]

Hence *ens* is best translated "mind-independent reality"—further in Deely, 1982: III.C.2.(c) and III.D.2.(b).

What was naturally known could not be denied by anyone. These were truths immediately evident to everyone and whose terms were immediately evident to everyone:

> Boethius says: *There are some axioms or self evident propositions generally known to all*, such as "The whole is greater than the part" or "Things equal to a third thing are equal to one another." (Aquinas, 1266-1274f: *Summa*, I-II, q. 94, art. 2).[21]

These naturally known axioms and their naturally understood terms were immediately known in sensible things by the light of the agent intellect. These terms were being (i.e., reality), one, and so on. All other knowledge was only potentially known in these naturally known axioms and terms. Getting beyond what is naturally known required acquiring new knowledge (Aquinas, 1256-1259):

> Certain seeds of knowledge pre-exist in us, namely, the first concepts of understanding, which by the light of the agent intellect are immediately known through the species abstracted from sensible things. These are either complex, as axioms, or simple, as the notions of being, of the one, and so on, which the understanding grasps immediately. In these general principles, however, all the consequences are included as in certain seminal principles. When, therefore, the mind is led from these general notions to actual knowledge of the particular things, which it knew previously in general and, as it were, potentially, then one is said to acquire knowledge. (*De Veritate*, q. 11, art. 1).[22]

The "one" mentioned here as naturally known was as universal as being itself, since it was common to substance and accidents like being (reality) itself. Because they extended to all categories of substance and accidents, "one," "many" and other similar concepts were called transcendentals (Aquinas, 1266-1274b):

> The other [type of] division is formal division, which comes about by the opposition or diversity of forms: from this results that kind of plurality which is in none of the categories but is one of the transcendentals, in the sense that being itself is diversified by the 'one' and the 'many.' (*Summa*, I, q. 30, art. 3).[23]

All our concepts reduced to "reality." So the transcendentals and the categories of substance and accidents added content to the original concept of reality. But the additions made by the transcendentals to the concept of reality added no new content *from the real*. The additions made by the transcendentals:

> add to something in concept only. This occurs when something which is nothing in reality but only in thought belongs to the notion of one thing and not to the notion of another . . . Thus to 'being,' the first intellectual conception, *one* adds what is merely conceptual—a negation; for it means undivided being . . . (Aquinas, 1256-1259: *De Veritate*, q. 21, art. 1).[24]

But the categories of substance and accidents add something from reality to the naturally known concept of being. The ten categories explicate (*ibid.*)

determinately and actually [what] is only implicitly and as it were potentially contained [in the concept of being] . . . ; not, of course, an accident of difference which is outside the essence of being, but a definite manner of being founded upon the very existence of the thing.[25]

Hence, the categories of substance and accidents add new knowledge of reality to the naturally known concept of reality. So it is impossible to demonstrate about the categories merely from the common principles whose terms are reality and the transcendentals. The categories or genera are the "definite manners of being" mentioned above (Aquinas, 1269-1272b):

> It is impossible that all things be syllogized exclusively from such common principles, because the genera of beings are diverse. Thus, the principles which pertain only to quantities are diverse from those which pertain exclusively to qualities. Such principles must be co-assumed with common principles, if one is to reach a conclusion in each matter. For example, if one wishes in quantities to syllogize from the aforesaid common principle, it is necessary to admit that since it is false that a point is a line, it must be true that a point is not a line; in like manner, in qualities, it is necessary to co-assume something peculiar to quality. Hence what remains is that it is impossible that the principles of all syllogisms be the same. (*In I Post. Anal.*, lect. 43, n. 386).[26]

This text needs a little further exegesis. Thomas' "common principle" here is that it is impossible to affirm and deny the same about the same at the same time. But to this common principle something distinctively new from reality must be added about quantity in order to demonstrate about the accident of quantity. For example, something about points and lines must be added from the reality of the accident of quantity.

Nothing new from reality was added to natural knowledge by the transcendentals and common principles made up of the transcendentals, such as the impossibility of affirming and denying at the same time. But naturally known reality became progressively better understood thanks to their mere conceptual additions. Thus the unity of each reality and the multiplicity of real beings could only be understood thanks to the opposition of the real and unreal in the principle of contradiction (Aquinas, 1266-1274f):

> Now we discover that the things which enter into our apprehension are ranged in a certain order. That which first appears is real, and some insight into this is included in whatsoever is apprehended. This first indemonstrable principle, 'There is no affirming and denying the same simultaneously,' is based on the very nature of the real and the nonreal: on this principle, as Aristotle notes, all other propositions are based. (*Summa*, I-II, q. 94, art. 2).[27]

This necessary order of the transcendentals continues through the principle of contradiction to "unity" and "multiplicity" (Aquinas, 1266-1274a):

> Even in our minds, the many is subsequent to unity, for we only conceive divided things as many by ascribing unity to each of them. So unity enters the definition of the many, but the many does not enter the definition of unity. Now division arises in the mind simply by negating existence. So that the first idea to arise in the mind is the existent, then that this existent is not that existent and so we grasp division, thirdly unity, and fourthly the many. (*Summa*, I, q. 11, art. 2 ad 4).[28]

In Thomas' philosophy of experience, the intellectual and the sensory were factors of total human perception, as seen above. But furthermore, as just shown, within human perception of many real things, the real and the unreal were distinguished. Such perception of many real things fell within the scope of what is naturally known to everyone. For such knowledge required no new information about reality beyond what is naturally known.

Natural knowledge extended to sensory-intellectual perception of many real things. But it did not extend to perception of the real distinction of substance and accidents. The reason was that substance could only be known by the intellect and so could not be perceived at all. Once intellectual knowledge of substance was added to natural perception of many realities, it was understood that naturally perceived realities were *real accidents*. But knowledge of substantial nature existed only in the intellect, not in imagination or external sense. Substantial nature was not known except potentially in natural perception (Aquinas, 1256-1272):

> Certain first principles composed of concepts and known to everyone are naturally given to us. From these first principles reason proceeds to actual knowing of conclusions only potentially contained in the principles . . . Similarly certain concepts known to everyone are naturally given us in the intellect: such are the concepts of reality, the one, the good and the other [transcendentals]. From these the intellect proceeds in the same manner to learn the nature of each kind of thing as when it reasons from self-evident principles to conclusions [potentially contained in the principles]. This process is twofold. It is either through what one perceives with his senses as from sensible properties of something I understand the nature of that thing: or it is through what one hears from others . . . Now sense and imagination never attain knowledge of the nature of a thing but only reach to the accidents surrounding the nature. So the representations in the senses and imagination represent not the nature of the thing but its accidents alone. For example, our senses represent a man's accidents, but our intellect knows his very substantial nature.

> So the intelligible representation is the likeness of the essence of the thing. It is somehow the very quiddity and nature of the thing existing

intelligibly by contrast with its natural existence in the thing. *Hence whatever does not fall under sense and imagination but under intellect alone* is known by the fact *that its quiddity or nature is somehow in the intellect* (emphasis added: my translation of *Quaestiones Quodlibetales*, Quodlibet VIII, q. 2, art. 2).[29]

In this text Thomas repeats that the "nature of each kind of thing" is only potentially contained in the naturally known realm of reality and the transcendentals. Moreover he gives the *reason why* substance cannot be in that realm: namely because substance does not fall under either sense or imagination. For in natural knowledge, *by sense, imagination and* intellect *we perceive* a multitude of real things.

According to Aquinas, the reality of material things was the naturally known object of the intellect. The reality (*ens*) of material things was its proper object through which it knew all other things. But the reality of material things as direct object always included two reflex objects. First, as we have seen, it included perception of that reality (*ens*) in sensory or imaginary objects in which alone that reality existed. Secondly, it included a perception of the act of intellect itself. Now the act of intellect was in fact a spiritual reality: it was not a material reality (Aquinas, 1266-1274d: *Summa*, 1, q. 86, art. 1 ad 3). But the mere perception of the act of intellect did not show "how it differs from other things, which is to know its whatness and nature" (*ibid.*, q. 87, art. 1). So reflex perception of the act of understanding manifested it as a reality indistinguishable in nature from material realities directly understood. Its distinctive spiritual nature whereby it differed from matter was not naturally known. Thus the reality of material things was nevertheless the proper object of intellect despite perception of what *could be proved to be* a spiritual reality (Aquinas, 1266-1274c: *Summa*, I, q. 75, art. 2). So, as naturally known, the different acts of intellect (apprehension, judgment and reasoning) were perceived merely as many real things. These realities were perceived along with innumerable material realities, but their distinctive nature was not perceived.

Section 4. Duns Scotus: the distinction of substance and accidents is not immediately experienced.

Representative medieval and renaissance Aristotelians held that at the origin of intellectual knowledge the existence of substance remained unknown. Moreover, they held that the distinction of substance and accidents is never given in sensory experience.

Duns Scotus (d. 1308) placed the origin of intellectual knowledge in what he called "knowing actually and confusedly." This "actual" knowing he distinguished from mere habitual knowledge. Confusedly knowing was knowing prior to defining the object known. Scotus (1302-1303) writes:

> These things being preestablished, I hold that the order of origin in actual knowledge of things confusedly understood (and I mean what is actually confusedly understood) is the following. What is first understood by the intellect is any determinate species of sensory quality in which a singular more effectively and forcefully produces sensation, presupposing that it is present to sensation in due proportion. (My translation of *Ordinatio*, lib. I, dist. 3, la pars, q. 2, n. 73).[30]

So, for Scotus, experiential knowing of such sensible qualities as red and green are the origin of all intellectual knowledge.

Only in distinct knowing (i.e., respecting defined objects) does the distinguishing of substance from accidents occur. Even then substance is never known directly; it is only indirectly known through its accidents. Its accidents are themselves not first known as accidents but only as beings. To grasp Scotus' doctrine on this point requires a preliminary grasp of some of his definitions.

"Substance" and "accidents" are examples of what Scotus called "quidditative" concepts. A quidditative concept is a universal concept. Because the quidditative concept is universal it needs to be supplemented by the concept of "this-ness" (*haecceitas*) in order to be individivated. The concept of thisness is the determining concept that ultimately determines quidditative concepts respecting an individual essence (Scotus, 1302-1303: 82-83). All quidditative concepts are derived from experience (*ibid.*, pp. 88-89). So the quidditative concepts of substance and accidents are derived from experience (Gilson, 1952: 462-464).

However, for Scotus, substance cannot be directly experienced. Accidents are directly experienced. Substance is a quidditative concept, yet it cannot be directly experienced; it can only be acquired by abstraction from accidents. For accidents alone are directly experienced. Now these directly experienced accidents are conceived as beings. Scotus uses experience of the consecrated host as proof that we do not experience the *absence* of substance; and that hence we *do not experience its presence*. Scotus takes the fact that substance can only be experienced indirectly through accidents as proof that being is univocal to substance and accidents. He writes (1302-1303):

> The second reason I explain as follows: We argued that God cannot be known naturally unless being is univocal to the created and uncreated. We can argue in the same way of substance and accident, for substance does not immediately move our intellect to know the substance itself, but only the sensible accident does so. From this it follows that we can have no quidditative concept of substance except such as could be

abstracted from the concept of an accident. But the only quidditative concept of this kind that can be abstracted from that of an accident is the concept of being.

Our assumption that substance does not immediately move our intellect to know the substance itself, we prove thus: If something moves the intellect when it is present, then whenever the intellect is not so moved, it will be able to know naturally that this object is absent. This is clear from the *De anima*, Bk. II, according to which the sense of sight can perceive darkness when, presumably, light is not present, and the sense, in consequence, is not moved. Therefore, if substance immediately moved the intellect naturally to know the substance itself, it would follow that when a substance was absent, the intellect could know that it was not present. Hence, it could know naturally that the substance of bread does not exist in the Consecrated Victim of the Altar, which is clearly false. Naturally, then, we have no quidditative concept of substance caused immediately by substance itself. Our only quidditative concept thereof is that caused by, or first abstracted from, an accident, and this is none other than the concept of being. (Scotus, *Ordinatio*, lib. I, dist. 3, la pars, q.3).[31]

Hence, *the distinction of substance and accidents is not itself immediately experienced according to Scotus*. Accidents alone are immediately experienced, since only accidents immediately move the intellect. Substance, whether as a universal (quidditative) concept or as an individual (thisness) concept, is not directly experienced.

Section 5. Francis Suarez: the impossibility of distinguishing substance and accidents at the origin of intellectual knowledge.

Francis Suarez (d. 1617) writes a lucid passage on reality as known at the origin of intellectual knowledge (Suarez, 1597):

Hence I infer that though things first and directly known are in fact accidents, however in virtue of that concept they are not known precisely as accidents. That is, they are not known under the rationale of inhering in something but only under the rationale of this real and material being. Indeed in virtue of this first concept we do not discern whether that object is composed of an accidental form and a subject. It is merely conceived precisely and abstractly as a unit. That is clearly shown by the mystery of the Eucharist. For we no more conceive the substance of the bread when it is present than when it is absent. Therefore the formal concepts of accident as inhering and of substance as sustaining, actually standing by itself, are acquired subsequently by reasoning, and especially through reasoning about things changing. For when we see accidents change in a subject, we understand that the subject itself is changed.

If we compare the expressed formal concepts of accident as accident and substance as substance, we find no constant order among them as objects known. For in our original knowing of them we surely conceive them as correlatives, since we cannot distinguish them except as correlatives. But subsequently we can be indifferently stimulated to knowing directly either one, though indirectly, i.e., obliquely, knowledge of one always somehow points to the other. For as I have said, each concept is a correlative of the other. (My translation of *Disputationes Metaphysicae*, disp. 38, sect. 2, n. 12).[32]

This whole passage closely follows the cited passage of Scotus, including the argument from the Eucharist. Suarez' analysis amounts to a commentary on and an assent to Scotus' doctrine. But Suarez brings new light to Scotus. Accidents are first known not *as accidents* but merely as material beings. For since the distinction of substance and accidents is still unknown, the accidents' correlative definition as "inhering in" as opposed to substance's "sustaining" remains unknown. Suarez holds that the distinction of substance and accidents is subsequently acquired by reasoning (*discursu*). His position agrees with Aristotle's and Aquinas' argument against Parmenides that this distinction is one grasped by reason alone (*logos, ratio*).

Suarez (1597) thus explains why substance cannot be understood as actually contained in sensory experience:

Our intellect is not affected except by impressed sensible 'species.' However 'species' of substance are not impressed in the senses but only 'species' of accidents. Therefore accidents are what first affect the intellect: therefore they are known prior to substance . . . This latter argument seems to me absolutely true. But it is to be understood so that substance is not absolutely excluded from the first concept of the intellect . . . The intellect, although it is first affected by knowing some immediately sensible accident, conceives it concretely and not abstractly. Thus in that first concept substance is not entirely excluded. For in that objective concept of concrete accident substance is involved, as it were covered and wrapped in accidents. So we can say that the thing first known directly and formally is an accident. But the thing adequately and materially known is substance, actually the composite of substance and accidents. For it is conceived as subsisting in such an accidental form. (My translation of *Disputationes Metaphysicae*, disp. 38, sect. 2, nn. 8-9).[33]

Suarez says substance is "materially" conceived in the "adequate object" of sensory experience. He means that substance is de facto present as that experience is subsequently understood by reasoning, e.g., about change.

Thus for Suarez, at the origin of intellectual knowledge it is impossible to distinguish between substance and accidents. And substance can never be understood explicitly in sensory experience because the "species" impressed in the senses are of accidents only. These accidents are known as material realities.

Section 6. John Poinsot ("Joannes a Sancto Thoma"): the impossibility of distinguishing substance and accidents in the experiential origin of intellectual knowledge.

John Poinsot (d. 1644) studied the cited doctrine of Scotus and accepted it while giving it a Thomistic twist. He adjusts Scotus' doctrine to the Thomistic doctrine that the quiddity of material things is the proper formal object of the intellect. He writes (Poinsot, 1633: 22-23):

> So be it: the intellect first knows the quiddity of its object not in its essence but only as 'real' (*an sit*). Hence neither respecting the object's singularity nor respecting its nature does it attain any predicate but that of 'real.' Nevertheless the singular as singular is not known except under the confused and most common rationale of 'being.' That means knowing something common to the singular and to the nature. For respecting each, knowledge is had as to factual existence (*an sit*). And this existence, factual concrete existence found in the concrete sensible, will be what is first known to the intellect.

> Now it should be noted carefully that when the intellect knows something merely as real, it does not prescind from its formal object, the *quiddity* or *whatness* which is the primary intelligible. That is impossible. It merely does not proceed into the essence by penetrating the proper constitution of the quiddity and its causes of being. It merely attains a very common and confused predicate of the quiddity: namely its reality. That is what it knows as quiddity at the origin of knowing . . .

> Now something is the more confused to the degree that fewer of its characteristics are discerned, so that its proper differences and predicates are not distinguished. Therefore the most confused of all objects is that in which substance and accidents are not distinguished. For these are the most general genera and most common predicates. And that object we call concrete being applied to the sensible quiddity found in some sensible nature, and not as undergoing a state of abstraction and universality. (My translation).[34]

For Poinsot, intuition is had only of a physically present object known as physically present (Poinsot, 1633: 733-734). Hence intuitive knowledge for him is what we call today experiential knowing. Now the origin of intellectual knowledge for him is an imperfect form of experiential knowing.

> Degrees are found in experiential knowing and one case is more imperfect than another. Thus when we see something at a distance, we can in no way discern what it is in particular. Only intuitive knowledge of its reality is had. So the intellect in its original knowing sees what is proposed to it as if it were far off in the genus of intelligibles, though the object is in fact physically present. And so its intuitive experience only attains the object as 'real.' That constitutes imperfect intuitive experience clouded by total confusion respecting the nature and its distinct predicates. (My translation of Poinsot, 1633: 29a22-38).[35]

Finally for Poinsot, the intellect knows *accidents only* in sensory experience, and it knows substance only by sensory experience of accidents. For substance can change without sensory experience being able to discern any change whatsoever. Substance cannot be sensed by any sense powers whatsoever, whether external senses or internal senses.

According to Poinsot, substance is "sensible accidentally." The "sensible accidentally" is a peculiar Aristotelian concept. Aristotelian tradition distinguishes three kinds of sensibles. First, the "proper sensibles." These are what are specifically sensed by each of the several senses uniquely, as color by sight alone and sound by hearing alone. Secondly, the "common sensibles" which are sensed by more than one sense power: e.g., motion, rest, and magnitude are sensed as modifications of color and tactile qualities by sight and touch respectively. Finally, the "sensible accidentally" (*sensibile per accidens*) is what is not at all sensed by a given sense power but is known by some other faculty of the soul. For example, sweetness of candy is not at all visible to sight; but the candy as visible is "sensible accidentally" as sweet to taste (Poinsot, 1635: 111-116).

Now substance is "sensible accidentally" respecting all sense powers:

> In order for something to be 'sensible accidentally' respecting all sense powers, it is required that it not be sensed at all by any sense, [whether by external or internal sense]. That can only be substance as the subject in which inhere the accidents that are sensed. Substance is sensed not because it itself constitutes the content of the object sensed as 'proper sensibles' do: nor because it contributes to the object sensed as the common sensibles do. Substance is sensed only because it receives and sustains in existence that accidental reality which is objectified in vision or in another sense power. So substance is sensed as connected in this fashion with what is objectified but not as constituting it or contributing to it as an object. The manifest sign of this is that an accident can affect the sense power in the same way before and after a substantial change has occurred, and even if the substance is entirely removed [as in the case of the Eucharist]. For the proper and common sensibles that are necessarily required for sensation may remain the same despite change of substance. (My translation of Poinsot, 1635: 115).[36]

Thus for Poinsot, the origin of intellectual knowledge is experiential knowing of reality that cannot distinguish between substance and accidents. And the intellect cannot distinguish substance and accidents in sensory experience because substance can change without sensory experience discerning any change. He objects to himself that if substance is not found in sensory experience it can never be known by the intellect: for nothing is in the intellect that was not in the senses. He replies (1635: 119): "Substance is in sensory experience not in itself and separately from the proper sensible but under it and clothed in that external sensibility."

In these matters Scotus, Suarez and Poinsot are in remarkable agreement.

Section 7. Locke: no experience of substance, but its existence is a certain conclusion.

John Locke (d.1704) held that all human understanding had its origin in simple ideas derived from experience. Locke admitted two sources for simple experiential ideas. First, sensation which furnishes such simple ideas as yellow, white, heat, cold, hard, bitter, sweet and similar sense qualities. Secondly, reflection on our own psychological operations which furnishes such simple ideas as perception, thinking, doubting, believing, reasoning, knowing, willing. These latter ideas belong to what he calls "internal sense." Locke recognizes no distinction between a faculty of intellect and a faculty of sense. All other ideas originate from these two sorts of simple ideas (Locke, 1690: I, 124):

> These two, I say, viz. external material things as the objects of SENSA-TION, and the operations of our own minds within, as the objects of REFLECTION, are to me the only originals from which all our ideas take their beginnings.

Locke finds that the idea of substance cannot be found in either experiential source (*ibid.*: 107):

> [We have] the idea of substance which we neither have nor can have by sensation or reflection.

Our idea of substance arises because many simple experiential ideas are found to go constantly together. So (*ibid.*: 390-391):

> because as I have said, not imagining how these simple ideas *can* subsist by themselves, we accustom ourselves to suppose some *substratum* wherein they do subsist, and from which they do result, which we call substance.

Edward Stillingfleet, Bishop of Worcester, in Locke, 1697-1698: IV, p. 5, took Locke to task for having "almost discarded substance out of the reasonable part of the world." Locke protested his innocence of the charge (*ibid.*, p. 18):

> I ground not the being, but the idea of substance, on our accustoming ourselves to suppose some substratum; for it is of the idea alone I speak there, and not of the being of substance.

> And having every-where affirmed and built upon it, that a man is a substance; I cannot be supposed to question or doubt of the being of substance, till I can question or doubt of my own being.

Furthermore (*ibid.*, pp. 8, 449), Locke protested that his understanding of substance was the same as that of Burgersdicius. Burgersdicius, or

Francis Burgersdyk (d.1635), was a prominent Protestant scholastic philosopher who taught at Leiden University in Holland. His handbooks were used for more than two hundred years.[37] From what we have seen of Scotus, Suarez and Poinsot, Locke's claim for support in Burgersdicius was probably well founded.

In any case, Locke's position on the origin of understanding in experience is basically the same as that of the influential Aristotelians Scotus, Suarez and Poinsot. They agree with Locke that what are first experienced are realities that subsequently are understood as accidents. These realities only become known as accidents when it becomes evident to reason that such realities must inhere in some substance.

Locke is well known for rejecting the doctrine of really distinct faculties in the soul: intellect, will and sense faculties (Locke, 1690: 314, 323-324). That was common Aristotelian doctrine taught by a Scotus, a Suarez, and a Poinsot. But Locke's doctrinal divergence from Aristotelians does not arise in analysis of the situation at the origin of knowing. In the origin of knowing the distinction of substance and accidents is still unknown, and the faculties are accidents for the Aristotelians. Moreover, the distinction of the various faculties of the soul demanded a prolonged philosophic study modelled on the *De Anima* of Aristotle. The discovery of the several accidental faculties of internal sense (imagination, memory, etc.) as distinguished from external senses (sight, hearing, etc.) was already very difficult. But the discovery of the distinct accidental faculty of intellect was reputed most difficult. According to Aquinas (1266-1274d), one can have perceptual awareness of his intellectual activity just by thinking. But for the philosophic understanding of the intellect as a distinct accidental faculty of the soul,

> a diligent, subtle inquiry is needed. Many, for this reason, are simply ignorant of the soul's nature and many are positively mistaken about it (*Summa*, I, q. 87, art. 1).[38]

And Suarez (1597: 504) says that we cannot distinguish "intellectual awareness from sensitive awareness." This distinction can only be drawn "after lengthy argument and reflection." And this would not be the case if we could experience the distinction of substance and accidents (*ibid.*). Hence, for any time prior to undertaking prolonged special study of matters treated in Aristotle's *De Anima*, Locke and the Aristotelians would not differ about reflex psychological experience because of differing doctrines on faculties of the soul. For prior to that special study, the Aristotelians would understand reflex experience without any doctrine of faculties.

But Locke (1690: 230) is more explicit than these Aristotelian predecessors that the distinction of substance and accidents is a contingent historical discovery:

> They who first ran into the notion of *accidents* as a sort of real beings that needed something to inhere in, were forced to find out the word *substance* to support them.

Here Locke reminds us of Aristotle and Aquinas who also looked back to a time, that of Parmenides, when the distinction of substance and accidents had not yet been discovered.

Locke, when thinking as an empiricist exclusively bound to experiential knowing (1690: 230-231), finds the idea of substance confused and obscure, and consequently of little use in philosophy:

> Of substance we have no idea of what it is but only a confused obscure one of what it does . . .

Satirically, he adds:

> Were the Latin words, *inhaerentia* and *substantio*, put into the plain English ones that answer them, and were called *sticking on* and *under-propping*, they would better discover to us the very great clearness there is in the doctrine of substance and accidents, and show of what use they are in deciding of questions in philosophy.

Locke means to say that the doctrine of substance and accidents is of no use in determining questions of experiential knowing.

But when confronted by the Bishop of Worcester (Locke, 1697-1698: IV, p. 5) for having "almost discarded substance out of the reasonable part of the world," Locke responds (*ibid.*, p. 18) as a moral and political philosopher who has "everywhere affirmed and built upon" substance since he is as certain of it as he is of his own existence. Moreover, the Bishop (*ibid.*, 443) is as certain "that substances are and must be, as that there are many beings in the world." Locke replies (p. 445) that his certitude about pluralism of substances is just as great: "I conclude the same thing because we cannot conceive how sensible qualities should subsist by themselves." Thus Locke, writing in 1697-1698 as a moral and political philosopher, agrees with the Bishop that the doctrine of substance is the contrary opposite of Monism. Already in his unpublished manuscript of 1693, Malebranche's occasionalism was seen by Locke (1693: 255-256 par. 10) as coming down to

> the religion of Hobbes and Spinoza, by resolving all, even the thoughts and will of men, into an irresistible fatal necessity. For whether the original of it be from the continued motion of eternal all-doing matter, or from an omnipotent immaterial being, which, having begun matter and motion, continues it by the direction of occasions which he himself has also made: as to religion and morality, it is just the same thing.

Hence as moral and political philosopher Locke sets the doctrine of substance over against the Monism of Spinoza and Hobbes. Substance (Locke, 1690: 321) is the moralist's *interpretation* of the experiential fact of freedom:

> So that this way of putting the question (viz. whether the will be free) is in effect to ask, whether the will be a substance, an agent, or *at least to suppose it*, since freedom can properly be attributed to nothing else. (My emphasis.)

By saying "at least to suppose it," Locke means that human substance is the rational conclusion from the experiential reality of human freedom.

Some contemporary commentators of Locke explain his doctrine of substance as contrary to his empiricism. For Jonathan Bennett (1968: 88-89), the substance-accident doctrine rightly understood enables Locke to explain that all prediction involves a thing-concept. But Locke, according to Bennett (p. 98), confused this truism with his false claim to having discovered how "things subsist by themselves . . . independently of any percipient." For Antony Flew (1968: 176), Locke's doctrine of substance involved:

> abandonment of his greatest insight and a betrayal of the glorious revolution he was leading against the superstition of real senses and natural kinds.

These commentators do not account for Locke's statement (1697-1698: IV, p. 5) that he "everywhere built upon" the doctrine of substance because he could not doubt his own existence and the plurality of real individuals in the world. His substantial existence is precisely required to explain the experiential reality of his freedom: "to ask whether the will be free . . . is to ask whether the will be a substance." For Locke, denying substance dissolves man into the cosmic process and so annihilates human freedom. Locke could not agree with B.F. Skinner's dictum (1971: 200-201): "To man *qua* man we readily say good riddance." These commentators do not understand Locke's doctrine of human substance for what it is: a reasoned interpretation of the experienced reality of freedom that refutes the Monism of Hobbes, Spinoza and Malebranche. Aristotle and Aquinas, who had faced Parmenides' Monism, would have understood Locke's pages.

I understand Locke's reasoning in the following fashion. His freedom is a reality experienced as an "idea of reflection." Now it is not possible that a free reality be merely either a part of Hobbes' unfree material environment or a part of Spinoza's infinite substance, both of which would render his free reality impossible. Therefore his free reality is an independent existent; that is to say, his experienced freedom *inheres in* his individual substance that he cannot experience. Similarly, for the Aristotelians, substance in the fullest sense is an individual subsisting in itself so that it cannot be a part of something else. The subsisting individual substance is contrasted both with the accidents which exist in it and with its own parts such as hands and feet which exist in it as incomplete substances. Since subsisting substances are independent real existences, the discovery of the substance-accident distinction refutes Parmenides' Monism, according to Aristotle and Aquinas. Similarly, Locke reasons from his freedom as experienced to its being a real accident in his independent substance in order to refute the Monism of Hobbes, Spinoza and Malebranche. He reasons that his freedom, at first experienced only as real, must also be an accident inhering in his substance.

A certain reading of the history of philosophy reifies schools of philosophy into irreducible opposition. We have quoted Antony Flew on Locke as ''betraying [his] glorious revolution'' by retaining the doctrine of substance. Regis Jolivet (1929) sees empiricism not as a revolution but as the slow outcome of centuries of complex cultural factors: the Humanism of the renaissance, the new scientific methods and the late scholasticism. But Jolivet (*ibid.*, 110) also sees empiricism as irreducibly opposed to the doctrine of substance. However, what we have already seen indicates that the opposition of schools may be more apparent than real.

From our twentieth century viewpoint, Locke does present a watershed in the history of philosophy. For him, the understanding of nature is now given over to the new sciences in which the real is exclusively defined by experiential knowing. The doctrine of substance, consequently, is useless for the understanding of nature since it is not given in experiential knowing. Substance functions only in Locke's moral and religious philosophy. By contrast, once the Aristotelians had discovered substance, all experience was interpreted in terms of individual substances. For substance existed only in individuals, and all individuals were substances. By contrast with them, Locke presents a watershed. But it is a socio-cultural watershed, not a watershed in philosophical understanding. Locke's doctrines, both about experiential knowing and about how one concludes to the distinction of substance and accidents, are the same as those of the Aristotelians. But Locke witnesses to a socio-cultural watershed: the socio-cultural shift by naturalists to exclusive defining in terms of experiential knowing.

The foregoing analysis of experiential knowing by these philosophers gives us a partial answer to the question: can philosophers think reality at the level of political scientists who understand human freedom in terms of real relations only? For these philosophers hold that the substance of things is not knowable experientially. And so they cannot expect political scientists to encounter substance since their discipline is exclusively bound to experiential knowing. Moreover, for Locke, freedom is experientially known as a reality subsequently interpreted as inhering in human substance. Were this experiential reality manifesting human freedom found to be *real relations*, we would have the full affirmative answer to our question: can philosophers think reality at the level of political scientists who understand human freedom in terms of real relations only? The answer would be: yes, they can.

Section 8. Kant. Kant's philosophy of experience: ancient tradition put in novel language.

Now we find some philosophers for whom the experiential fact of communication is the fundamental presupposition of philosophy. Moreover, communication manifests the coordinated perceptions of those who communicate. Inasmuch as these perceptions are coordinated, they are *related* to each other. Inasmuch as for each the other is coordinated to it *independently of its own perceiving*, this relation is a *real relation*. For in actual communication the message must be an object for each not merely *thanks to each's own perceiving*, but also *because the other perceives*. Hence philosophers for whom the fact of communication is the fundamental presupposition of philosophy *make philosophy begin with real relations only*. Now in the Aristotelian tradition real relations are real accidents. Hence these philosophers begin philosophy with experiential realities that Aristotelians would subsequently prove to be accidents inhering in a substance. Moreover, these philosophers who start philosophy with real relations think reality at the level of those political scientists who understand human freedom in terms of real relations only. Obviously, these are the philosophers for whom we have been looking.

The reader may be surprised to learn that what we have just described resembles Immanuel Kant's position on the fundamental presupposition of philosophy. Kant (1790: 83-84) writes:

> Cognitions and judgements must, together with their attendant conviction, *admit of being universally communicated; for otherwise a correspondence with the Object would not be due to them.* They would be a conglomerate constituting a *mere subjective play* of the powers of representation, just as scepticism would have it. But if cognitions are to admit of communication, then our mental state, i.e. the way the cognitive powers are attuned for cognition generally, and, in fact, the relative proportion suitable for a representation (by which an object is given to us) from which cognition is to result, must also admit of being universally communicated, as, without this, which is the subjective condition of the act

of knowing, knowledge, as an effect, would not arise. *And this is always what actually happens* where a given object, through the intervention of sense, sets the imagination at work in arranging the manifold, and the imagination, in turn, the understanding in giving to this arrangement the unity of concepts . . . *The universal communicability of our knowledge . . . is presupposed in every logic and every principle of knowledge that is not one of scepticism.* (Emphasis added).[39]

Hence "an object [of experience can never be and is never] given to us" except as "universally communicable" to others. So *communication to others belongs to the conditions of the possibility of objects of experience.* This communicability consists in the a priori proportioning of the powers of individuals to one another. This a priori mutual proportioning is a *real relation* between those who communicate because it is independent of and prior to any actual experience.

According to Kant (1793: 129), communicability is a criterion that manifests theoretical objects of reason as better grasped by reason than knowledge of mysteries:

> Investigation into the inner nature of all kinds of faith which concern religion invariably encounters a mystery, i.e., something holy which may indeed be known by each single individual but cannot be made known publicly, that is, shared universally. Being something holy, it must be moral, and so an object of reason, and it must be capable of being known from within adequately for practical use, and yet, as something mysterious, not for theoretical use, since in this case it would have to be capable of being shared with everyone and made known publicly.[40]

Now reason has its own natural mysteries quite apart from any question of divine revelation. Kant calls them objects of "pure rational faith" (*ibid.*). The cause of gravity is a rational mystery, though gravity itself is an object of theoretical reason because (*ibid.*, 129-130 note) it "can be made public to all, for its *law* is adequately known."

Freedom is no mystery,

> because the knowledge of it can be shared with everyone; but the ground, inscrutable to us, of this attribute is a mystery because this ground is not given us as an object of knowledge (Kant, 1793: 129).[41]

Indeed, for theoretical reason a mysterious free cause seems contrary to the law of nature, and so contrary to all possible experience:

> [The fact of] practical freedom can be proved through experience. For the human will is not determined by that alone which stimulates, that is, immediately affects the senses; we have the power to overcome the impressions on our faculty of sensuous desire, by calling up representations of what, in a more indirect manner, is useful or injurious. But these considerations, as to what is desirable in respect of our whole state, that is, as to what is good and useful, are based on reason . . . While

we thus through experience know practical freedom to be one of the causes in nature, namely, to be a causality of reason in the determination of the will, transcendental freedom demands the independence of this reason—in respect of its causality, in beginning a series of appearances—from all determining causes of the sensible world. Transcendental freedom is thus, as it would seem, contrary to the law of nature, and therefore to all possible experience; and so remains a problem (Kant, 1787: 663-664).[42]

The grounds of freedom will ever remain a rational mystery (Kant, 1793: 45 note):

What we wish to understand, and never shall understand, is how predeterminism, according to which voluntary actions, as events, have their determining grounds in antecedent time (which, with what happened in it, is no longer within our power), can be consistent with freedom, according to which the act as well as its opposite must be within the power of the subject at the moment of its taking place.[43]

So the cause of gravity is a rational mystery of theoretical reason. The cause of freedom is a mystery of practical reason. Hence, communication manifests certain objects of theoretical and practical reason to be better understood than objects known as rational mysteries. *Therefore public communication is a criterion of rational understanding, according to Kant.*

The *Critique of Pure Reason* sets out as its problem the explaining of certain facts of communication, though it does not use the express term "communication." The Preface to the Second Edition (1787: 17) maintains that logic had reached its definitive state as "a closed and completed body of doctrine" by the time of Aristotle. From that time it has never been forced to retrace its steps. It is the immutable vestibule of science communicated to all subsequent generations, basically unchanged. Mathematics is a science, and it also has been communicated basically unchanged since the time of the Greeks. Natural science had been a science for a century and a half before Kant's time, and it too has been communicated basically unchanged since then. Hence long ago, "mathematics and natural science by a single and sudden revolution have become what they now are" (*ibid.*, pp. 19-20), never needing to retrace a step. Consequently, Kant places the problem of the *Critique of Pure Reason* in the following words (1787: 56):

Since these sciences actually exist, it is quite proper to ask how they are possible; for that they must be possible is proved by the fact that they exist.[44]

"*Proved by the fact that they exist*": the fact of their existence is their being communicated basically unchanged for many generations. Hence the *Critique of Pure Reason* presupposes the fact of communication.

I have tried to show that communication includes real relations. So I can argue that anyone who admits communication admits real relations. Now Kant did not so argue explicitly but only implicitly. However, Kant did *argue against idealism* which holds that we can know only our own representations. His argument against idealism is that he experiences relations to things "bound up with [his] existence" but outside his existence. Consequently he is as certain of the *relation* of things outside his existence *to his outer sense* as he is of his own existence. Kant writes (1787: 34-36 note):

> But through inner *experience* I am conscious of *my existence* in time (consequently also of its determinability in time), and this is more than to be conscious merely of my representation. It is identical with the *empirical consciousness of my existence*, which is determinable only through relation to something which, while bound up with my existence, is outside me. This consciousness of my existence in time is bound up in the way of identity with the consciousness of a relation to something outside me, and it is therefore experience not invention, sense not imagination, which inseparably connects this outside something with my inner sense . . . I am just as certainly conscious that there are things outside me, which are in relation to my sense, as I am conscious that I myself exist as determined in time.[45]

Kant's opinion is clear. This relation is identical with his consciousness of his empirical existence; and his empirical existence is "more than" his mere representation. Hence this relation to things outside his existence is "more than" his mere representation. So the "more than" his representation means *real relation*. In this essay, any relation that does not totally reduce to being an object of consciousness (i.e., does not totally reduce to what is termed "objective being"), is called a real relation. Therefore consciousness of real relations is what refutes the idealist position that we can only know our representations. And so it is not contrary to Kant's philosophy to find real relations in communication. For he admitted both actual communication and real relations.

Kant concludes his refutation of idealism thus (1787: 245):

> In other words, the consciousness of my existence is at the same time an immediate consciousness of the existence of other things outside me.[46]

Yet according to Kant, we experience things outside us only as terms of real relations. This real term is called the transcendental object (Kant, 1787: 137). But the intrinsic nature and intrinsic powers of this real term cannot be experienced in any way (*ibid.*, p. 279). As beyond experience in its intrinsic nature and properties it is called *noumenon*. It is likewise called *noumenon* as it might be the object of an experiential intuition that is impossible for us: but we have no positive reason to believe that such an intuition is in fact possible for any being (*ibid.*, p. 268). Transcendental object and *noumenon* are therefore the same reality existing independently of our experience; Kant once uses one for the other (*ibid.*, p. 339). But as term of *experienced real relations* it is the transcendental object, whereas as beyond experience in its intrinsic nature it is called *noumenon* (*ibid.*, p. 514). The *noumenon* is certainly real; but since it is beyond experience in its intrinsic nature, we cannot say whether its reality is outside us or inside us, or even whether it would disappear if our sensibility disappeared (*ibid.*, p. 293). As the *noumenon* cannot be experienced in its intrinsic nature, it forms one and the same transcendental object for all our experienced real relations to it (*ibid.*, p. 137), since we cannot experience distinctions intrinsic to it (*ibid.*, p. 288).

When we examine these doctrines of Kant against the background of the Aristotelians and of Locke, how striking is the similarity of his account of experiential knowing to theirs! 1. No experience of the intrinsic natures of things. 2. Experience of many realities that could belong to one single reality, as Parmenides and Spinoza held. 3. What realities we do experience (for Kant, real relations), cannot be ultimately real because they cannot exist in themselves. *Kant's account of experiential knowing is ancient tradition put in novel language.*

Kant built a unique philosophical system on a traditional account of experiential knowing. His system is a rational construct that explains experiential knowing of communication and real relations. His system as such does not concern the question of whether philosophers can think reality at the level of the aforementioned political scientists. But I must recall that for Kant we can have no experience of real human freedom. Now these political scientists claim to discover real human relations that *are free*. Hence according to them, human freedom is an object of experiential knowing. Therefore, if they are right, then experiential knowing of real relations would lead us to conclude to human substance. For as Locke rightly said, human freedom *as a reality* cannot be resolved into its environment. Hence if these political scientists prove right, we would be forced to reply to Kant in these words. Real relations *in general* do not suffice to prove real plurality in the transcendental object. But *free* real relations do prove real plurality in the transcendental object. For free real human relations prove the reality of human substances.

Section 9. Hegel. Hegel's philosophy of experience: the intrinsic nature of things cannot be a matter of experience.

Hegel's philosophy of experience is chiefly found in his philosophy of nature. First of all, sensory experience does not manifest the necessity of nature (1830a: 82 par. 39):

> If perception, therefore, is to maintain its claim to be the sole basis of
> what men hold for truth, universality and necessity appear something
> illegitimate.[47]

Experimental physics provides "universalized understanding" of experience. But its universalized experienced determinations of things lack the intrinsic bond of necessity that constitutes them into concrete natures. The universals of experimental physics (1830b: 202 par. 246) are "split up, dismembered, particularized, separated and lacking any necessary connection."[48]

So Hegel's philosophy of nature aims at manifesting experience as an appearance of the intrinsic necessity of nature. But (1830b: 197 par. 246) "this is not an appeal to experience in regard to the necessity of the content [of nature]."[49] Rather:

> the material prepared out of experience by physics is taken by the philosophy of nature at the point where physics has brought it, *and reconstituted without further reference to experience as the* basis of verification. (My emphasis.) (1830a: par. 246, addition p. 201).[50]

Hence, for Hegel, philosophy of nature seeks the necessary connection between physics' experiential determinations. That necessary connection constitutes the intrinsic necessity of natures. But physics' experiential understanding itself cannot attain to this necessary connection. Therefore Hegel's philosophy of experience agrees with that of the Aristotelians, Locke and Kant in this respect: the intrinsic natures of things cannot be a matter of experiential understanding.

However, Hegel's agreement even with such an ancient and continuous philosophic lineage may seem a meager result from this difficult study. The result consists in the mere negative agreement for some kind of "Positivist agnosticism" as their philosophy of experience: namely, we *do not directly experience* the nature of things. It is time to ask whether any positive agreement exists as to *what reality* is the direct object of experience.

Section 10. Philosophers proposing experience of real relations as first known reality.

Let us begin with an overview.

Two philosophers have seen experience of real relations as the first known feature of mind-independent reality. These two are Kant and Bertrand Russell. Merleau-Ponty made what must be understood as real relations serve the same function; but he did not name them "real relations."

We have already considered Kant's refutation of Idealism thanks to experience of real relations. Now let us examine the validity of his argument.

Kant has a section in the second edition to the *Critique of Pure Reason* called *Refutation of Idealism* (1787: 244-247). In a note to the Preface of the second edition, he added a note to his refutation. Kant began by rejecting what can be called fideist indirect Realism, calling it (1787: 34) a "scandal to philosophy and to human reason in general that the existence of things outside us—must be accepted on faith." Then he gave his own account of direct experience in real relations:

> It will probably be objected, that I am immediately conscious only of that which is in me, that is, of my representation of outer things; and consequently that it must still remain uncertain whether outside me there is anything corresponding to it, or not. But through inner experience I am conscious of my existence in time (consequently also of its determinability in time), and this is more than to be conscious merely of my representation. It is identical with the empirical consciousness of my existence, which is determinable only through relation to something which, while bound up with my existence, is outside me. This consciousness of my existence in time is bound up in the way of identity (*identisch verbunden*) with the consciousness of a relation to something outside me, and it is therefore experience not invention, sense not imagination, which inseparably connects this outside something with my inner sense . . . I am just as certainly conscious that there are things outside me, which are in relation to my sense, as I am conscious that I myself exist as determined in time . . . This latter (permanent X) must therefore be an external thing distinct from all my representations, and *its* existence must be included in the *determination* of my own existence, constituting with it but a single experience such as would not take place even inwardly if it were not at the same time, in part, outer (1787: 34-36).[51]

So according to Kant, he directly experiences a relation of some permanent X to his empirical existence. And that directly experienced relation is "more than" his representations within him. This "more than" is what does not reduce to objective being, according to the terminology I am using. So that relation is directly experienced as real. Kant thus claims to refute Idealism by direct experience of a real relation alone. For he does not directly experience the intrinsic nature of the permanent X.

This doctrine of experience of a real relation does not conflict with Kant's doctrine of total ignorance of noumena. Noumena are hypothetical objects of intuitions that we do not have; they are purely hypothetical objects, in no way experienced (1787: 292). The term of the experienced real relation is the transcendental object. This object is experienced but only extrinsically through real relation to it. In the cited text Kant says: "*Its* existence must be included in the determination of my own existence constituting with it but a *single experience''* (my emphasis). But it is only experienced as a term of reference (Kant, 1787: 36 note).[52]

This doctrine is not easy to understand. Aristotle can help elucidate Kant on this point. Aristotle says (335-322BCa):

> All relatives are referred to their correlates provided they are rightly defined (*Categories*, 7a23-25).[53]

Aristotle explains that the properly named correlate of *wing* is not *bird* but *the winged*. For wings as such do not belong only to birds but also to many other creatures. So the properly named correlate is not what is named intrinsically by its intrinsic nature (bird). The properly named correlate is what is extrinsically named as correlate properly speaking (the winged). Hence Kant needs no more than experience of his real relation to X as determining his empirical existence in order to experience X's real relation to him. X's real correlation to Kant's empirical existence is properly named extrinsically as correlated to Kant's experience of it. Its correlation is not properly named intrinsically thanks to what is intrinsic to X, its intrinsic nature. So Kant can quite rightly say: he experiences a real relation to an X of unknown nature and the real relation of the X to his empirical existence.

But it can be objected to Kant that the intelligible object determines the intellect in its existence, yet the intelligible object is not really related to the intellect. For the intelligible object is merely sensible and only intelligible in potency. So the relation is not reciprocal. The intellect is really related to sensible objects, but sensible objects are not really related to the intellect. However, Kant is speaking of directly experienced objects. But the objection does not hold for objects directly experienced. For in direct experience the intelligible and the sensible are not distinguishable. Hence the objector must maintain that Kant cannot experience real relation to sensory environment of unknown nature and sensory environment as really related to his experience of it. But then the objection is unreasonable.

Bertrand Russell (1944: 16) holds that the data of epistemology are egocentric. But he proves the reality of the world of sense by manifesting the reality of relations. Having manifested the reality of relations, he writes (1914: 52-53):

> And in fact there is no reason except prejudice, so far as I can discover, for denying the reality of relations. When once their reality is admitted, all logical grounds for supposing the world of sense to be illusory disappear.

He manifests the reality of relations (1914: 50-53) thus. He prepares his argument for real relations by dividing known relations into two general kinds, each with three subdivisions. 1. A *symmetrical* relation is one be-tween terms which are referred to each other in precisely the same way. Thus the relation of sibling to sibling is symmetrical. A non-symmetrical relation is one that *sometimes* is not symmetrical. Thus the relation of "brother of B" is non-symmetrical since B is *sometimes* sister of A. An asymmetrical relation is one that is *never* symmetrical. Thus, *before, after, greater, above, to the right of* are *never* symmetrical. All relations that give rise to series are asymmetrical. 2. *Transitive* relations are such that if a rela-tion holds between A and B, and also between B and C, a relation also holds between A and C. *Before, after, above, greater,* which are asymmetric relations giving rise to series, are transitive. But symmetric relations such as *equal* are also transitive. A relation is *non-transitive* if it may *sometimes* not be transitive; e.g., "brother of" is non-transitive because sometimes the "brother of" one's brother is one's self. A relation is intransitive if it is never transitive: thus if A has a relation to B, and B to C, but A never has a relation to C. For example, *father, one inch taller* and *one year later* are intransitive.

After classifying relations in this way, Russell (1914: 52) argues as follows. Symmetrical relations such as *equality* might be explained as men-tal constructs by saying they are nothing more than the common property of magnitude possessed by their two terms. Similarly, non-transitive rela-tions such as *inequality* might be explained away by saying that their terms have dissimilar properties such as unequal magnitude. But an asymmetri-cal relation such as *greater* cannot be explained away by *mere difference* of magnitude since "there would be no difference between one thing being greater than another, and the other being greater than the one" [e.g., to say 5 is greater than 3 cannot be reduced to the mere difference 2, since 3 also *differs* from 5 by 2, but it is not *greater* than 5]. Hence, asymmetrical relations are real relations.

Merleau-Ponty (1960) defends the reality of relations in his effort to escape what he regards as the solipsism of the Cartesian *cogito*. This break-ing out of solipsism, he believes, can occur through bodily gestures in two stages. First, *privately*, when I touch one of my hands to the other; thus, my hands become reciprocally subject and object to each other, and so I escape solipsism (Merleau-Ponty, 1960: 170). Secondly, *publicly*, by the gaze of one face meeting the gaze of another face. The two gazes adjust to each other and thus each gazer completely escapes solipsism. Merleau-Ponty holds that these two adjustments are inexpressible in thought since the *cogito* is inevitably solipsistic (Merleau-Ponty, 1960: 16-17).

In my terminology, Merleau-Ponty argues for real relations. Put in the terminology of this essay, real relations are ones that do not totally reduce to mere objective being. His argument is as follows. Where a multiplicity of subjects is experienced not all objects totally reduce to mere objective being for any one of them: i.e., each relates to the other subjects experienced as to that which does not totally reduce to mere objective being for one's self. Hence, the relations experienced are real relations.

Section 11. Experience of real relations as common epistemological ground for philosophies of experience.

We have already seen that philosophers as diverse as Kant, Russell and Merleau-Ponty hold a common doctrine. That doctrine is: direct experience of real relations is the first known mind-independent reality. Now it will be shown below that a Process philosopher such as Whitehead, Phenomenalists such as Hume and Ayer, an Objective Idealist such as Lachelier, also hold the same doctrine. Moreover, it will be shown that Hegel and Aquinas base their systems on an original experience of reality as real relations.

I shall also restate Kant's philosophy of science by contrasting his a priori elements of experience (e.g., substance, accidents, cause) with the real relations that he admits as the only realities directly experienced. This is a legitimate procedure from Kant's point of view; first, since for him a priori elements of experience are mind-dependent representations, while the real relations are not reducible to mere mind-dependent representations; secondly, since for him knowledge of real relations is derived from experience, whereas the a priori elements are not derived from experience. In this way, Kant's support for the thesis of real relations as first known realities will be contrasted with his anachronistic doctrine of absolutely necessary (mind-dependent) scientific laws.

Since, concerning experience of real relations, no historical dependence is discernable among them, I shall treat these philosophers according to the order of the explicitness of this doctrine in their texts: Whitehead, Ayer, Kant, Lachelier, Heidegger, Hume, Hegel and Aquinas.

My position coincides almost entirely with Whitehead's philosophy of experience (1925, 1929, 1948), allowing for different terminology. Whitehead described his philosophy of experience as "provisional realism." "Provisional realism" is "Objectivism." It is the doctrine that "the world disclosed in sense perception is a common world, transcending the individual recipient" (Whitehead, 1925: 132). According to Whitehead, this doctrine is common to Realists and Objective Idealists. These two schools differ on whether "the reality of this world involves . . . cognitive mentality . . . in every detail" (ibid.).

That is "the ultimate problem of metaphysics" (ibid.). But the two schools of Objectivists have a common doctrine on direct experience of a common public world irreducible to individual experience. Objectivism is counterdistinguished on the one hand to Subjectivism, which holds that "immediate experience is the outcome of the perceptive peculiarities of the subject enjoying the experience" (*ibid.*, p. 128). And on the other hand Objectivism is opposed to Intermediate Subjectivism, which holds that "things experienced only indirectly enter into the common world by reason of their dependence on the subject who is cognizing" (*ibid.*, p. 129). Whitehead's "ultimate appeal" [for his provisional realism] "is to naive experience" (*ibid.*, pp. 129-130). His "provisional realism" eschews ultimate metaphysical explanations and sticks to direct experience. This is what I call Direct Realism in epistemology of experience. What he calls Subjectivist is usually called Subjective Idealist: what he calls Intermediate Subjectivist is usually called Indirect Realist.

According to Whitehead (1929: 187), what is directly known is extremely meager. It is only extension and quantitative relations:

> All that is perceived is that the object has extension and is implicated in a complex of extensive relatedness with the animal body of the percipient. Part of the difficulties of Cartesian philosophy, and of any philosophy which accepts this account as a complete account of perception, is to explain how we know more than this meagre fact about the world *although our only avenue of direct knowledge limits us to this barren residium*. (My emphasis).

Moreover, extension itself is not an actual existent. It is merely a *real potentiality* for subdivision. But the *real actualities* de facto subdividing the extension are not themselves perceived. Perception manifests (*ibid.*, p. 188):

> the contemporary world in respect to its potentiality for extensive subdivision into atomic actualities and in respect to the scheme of perspective relationships which thereby eventuates. But it gives no information as to the actual atomization of this contemporary 'real potentiality.'

He calls these relations not only "extensive" and "perspective", as in the two above texts, but also "mathematical." These mathematical relations are actual facts in nature (1929: 499):

> Sounds differ qualitatively among themselves, sounds differ qualitatively from colours, colours differ qualitatively from the rhythmic throbs of emotion and of pain; yet all alike are periodic and have their spatial relations and their wave-lengths. The discovery of the true relevance of the mathematical relations disclosed in [perception] . . . was the first step in the intellectual conquest of nature. Accurate science was then born. Apart from these relations as facts in nature, such science is meaningless, a tale told by an idiot and credited by fools.

Hence, these relations are real actual relations. They are the only actual realities directly experienced, according to Whitehead. Real relations are "all alike periodic", i.e., *they are temporal relations.*

So the only mind-independent actuality perceived, according to Whitehead, is real temporal relations. He calls these real temporal relations "the space-time continuum" (Whitehead, 1948: 146, 147, 148). The actual terms of these real relations are not directly perceived; perception "gives no information as to the actual atomization of this contemporary 'real potentiality' [extension]" (Whitehead, 1929: 188). On the contrary, the terms we perceive as subdividing the real space-time continuum are mind-dependent projections (Whitehead, 1948: 147):

> Accordingly, our awareness of nature consists of the projection of sense-objects—such as colours, shades, sounds, smells, touches, bodily feelings—into a spatio-temporal continuum either within or without our bodies.

Whitehead adds to our previous account of philosophers the temporality of real relations. I disagree with his philosophy of experience only in minor particulars. First, since the terms of real relations are not directly experienced, he cannot say all real relations are mathematical. For relations must be named from the nature of their still unknown terms. Secondly, he proposes "actual occasions" as "the final real things of which the world is made up" (Whitehead, 1929: 27). Just how "actual occasions" are derived from direct experience of real temporal relations is an open question.

Lastly, for Whitehead (1929: 190), we perceive "the immediate present condition of the world." The present condition of the world is constituted by a mutual relatedness (*ibid.*):

> The immediate present thus establishes a principle of common relatedness. This is the principle of mutual relatedness in the 'unison of becoming'.

This mutual relatedness is a fact in the universe (*ibid.*, p. 189):

> One fact about the universe is that there is a 'unison of becoming' constituting a positive relation.

Hence the mutual relatedness in the immediate present is a real mind-independent relation.

Now according to Whitehead, such a real relation of immediate presence is completely independent of contemporary actualities (*ibid.*, p. 193):

> According to all the evidence it is completely independent of all actualities.

Here I must disagree. For if a real relation were independent of all actualities, it would be independent of the propagation of energy in the region. It would be independent of the time needed to propagate energy from extrabodily things to the body of the percipient, and independent of the time needed for the nerves of the brain to react. Now these time-lags are well established facts in our historical world.

In the context of our cited text, he admits that this view is not according to recent theories of time. But he protests (*ibid.*, p. 191):

> If the notion be wholly rejected, no appeal to universal obviousness can have any weight.

However, in another work (1948: 148), Whitehead himself spoke of "simultaneity whose temporal thickness depends on the specious present." Indeed this simultaneity (contrasting with the known time lag of energy) is a "specious present": i.e., *it is an unreal present*. It is part of the object constancy of moving objects which is a biologically determined illusion. But apparent simultaneity no more militates against direct experience of real relations than do the unreal psychological relations of figure and ground in perception and the unreal relations of differing cultures in our historical world. The relations of simultaneous presence are likewise unreal relations. But it is only by experiencing the distinction of unreal from real relations that we directly experience real relations as mind-independent. In our historical world, we can now experience apparent simultaneity as distinct from real temporal relations between things.

Whitehead is right that we do not directly experience actual things. We perceive actual things *only indirectly* through real relations directly perceived, of which the actual things are the terms. So the actual things in their intrinsic nature remain outside direct experience. Hence for direct experience their intrinsic nature remains indeterminate. Nevertheless, terms are experienced as terms of real relations; and hence the terms are *extrinsically experienced as actualities*, albeit of unknown intrinsic nature. So Whitehead is wrong in saying that we do not experience actualities at all.

By choosing to answer Phenomenalism as presented by A.J. Ayer, I can answer almost on his own terms. Ayer, in the second edition (1946) of his 1936 book *Language, Truth and Logic*, somewhat modified the phenomenalism of the original presentation. But in his later writings he continued to hold the doctrine as a valid theory. According to Ayer, what are directly experienced are *sense data*. Sense data are described as what is seen, touched, etc. But "seeing" and "touching" are not assumed to be "mental acts". For mental acts are not observable; Ayer (1963: 128 and 131) does not know "what it would be like to come upon an act of awareness.'' Sense data are *appearances* regardless of *what* appears and to *whom* it appears. Hence Phenomenalism denies that either *material* things or persons or mental acts of persons are directly experienced:

> Thus what we obtain by introducing the term 'sense-datum' is a means of referring to appearances without prejudging the question what it is, if anything, that they are appearances of, and what it is, if anything, that they appear *to*. (Ayer, 1963: 131).

In *Language, Truth and Logic* (1946: 124), Ayer held that *statements about* material objects could be entirely *restated* in statements about sense data. However, he never held the very different doctrine that material things themselves were *composed of* sense data (*ibid.*, p. 64). In the essay, ''Phenomenalism,'' twelve years later (1963: 138-140), he denied that statements about material things can be entirely restated in statements about sense data. For, on the one hand, no statements about sense data could definitively entail the existence of a material object since hallucination was always possible. On the other hand, the existence of a material object could never guarantee its being perceived because of possible obstacles to experience.

Ayer's Phenomenalism was never a doctrine of Idealism but always one of Indirect Realism. He conceded to Berkeley (1946: 140) that sense data could not exist unperceived. But we have good reason *to believe* that material objects exist unperceived (*ibid.*, p. 145):

> It has been argued that, even if things do in fact continue to exist when no one is perceiving them, we cannot have any good reason to suppose that they do. For it is plainly impossible for anyone ever to observe a thing existing unobserved. But this argument is plausible only so long as the notion of unperceived existence is left unanalysed. As soon as we analyse it, we find that there can be a good inductive ground for believing that a thing exists unperceived. For what we are asserting when we say of a thing that it exists although no one is perceiving it is, as we have seen, that certain sense-contents would occur if certain conditions relating mainly to the faculties and position of an observer were fulfilled, but that in fact the conditions are not being fulfilled. And these are propositions which we do frequently have good reason to believe.

However, Ayer has another side that does not perfectly fit with Indirect Realism. We directly experience relations between sense data. Because of these directly experienced relations we justly claim we perceive physical objects (Ayer, 1963: 142):

> The relations between sense-data in virtue of which we are justified in claiming that we perceive physical objects are contingent.

According to Ayer, material objects are not composed of sense data: in our terminology material objects do not entirely reduce to objective being.

Ayer did not ask whether these directly experienced relations do not totally reduce to objective being. Had he so asked and answered they do not so reduce, he would have been a Direct Realist. He would have been defending the position I am defending: neither *material things*, nor *persons*, nor *acts of persons* are directly experienced; real relations are directly experienced and indirectly, thanks to them, their real terms.

Kant's *Critique of Pure Reason* (1787: 54) aims at explaining the absolute necessity of the laws of natural science. The a priori forms of space and time are precisely aimed at what is a priori in the space and time factors of scientific laws (*ibid.*, p. 87). Now whatever is a priori is absolutely certain according to Kant (1787: 11). However, this ideal of absolute certainty has been completely abandoned in contemporary natural science (Wallace, 1974: 375):

> . . . certainty is an idol before which only the pure mathematician is now willing to torture himself.

So Kant's *Critique of Pure Reason* cannot be what it intends to be; namely, an explanation of experimental natural science.

Kant's philosophy of experience rightly stated (1787: 45) that substance and accidents are not found in experience:

> If we remove from our empirical concept of any object, corporeal or incorporeal, all properties which experience has taught us, we yet cannot take away that property through which the object is thought as substance or as inhering in substance (although this concept of substance is more determinate than that of an object in general). Owing, therefore, to the necessity with which this concept of substance forces itself upon us, we have no option save to admit that it has its seat in our faculty of a priori knowledge.

But his philosophy of science consists of structuring scientific experience with these non-empirical elements. Now the whole weight of philosophical tradition stands behind his doctrine that substances as distinct from accidents are not found in experience. But philosophical tradition also had a doctrine of experienced concrete realities of unknown nature. That other doctrine allows us to understand experimental science as concerned with many realities of unknown nature. Science is then understood as concerned about the real relations in nature. The structure of scientific experience is then real; namely, real relations. Kant admitted experience of real relations in order to refute Idealism. Real relations suffice to structure scientific experience now that science has abandoned absolutely necessary scientific laws.

Most contemporary philosophy of science omits substance and accidents as factors in experimental science. In Aristotelian philosophy, substance and accidents were held to be real constituents of things. Yet they were incomplete realities that could not exist except together. Ernan McMullin (1963: 174) calls them "*M*-principles". McMullin says "*M*-principles" are strongly opposed by philosophers closest to natural science and to logic. Philosophers close to natural science oppose "*M*-principles" because science produces a more concrete mode of explanation. The logicians oppose "*M*-principles" because they know how frequently names are taken for realities (McMullin, 1963: 203).

Causal transient activity is a typical case of substance and accident in the metaphysical tradition. The transient activity is the accident of the substance-cause. Max Jammer (1957: 229-230[54]) sees the elimination from science of causal transient activity as culminating the development since Newton.

According to William A. Wallace (1974: 326), the American philosophy of science "establishment" excludes from science insight into the nature of things. The nature of things is only verbally different from their "substance."

Hence, philosophy of science has sought to eliminate substance and accidents from the structure of scientific experience. It certainly was right to do so in order to structure scientific experience exclusively with experiential elements. Kant should have done the same.

Furthermore, we have seen that, according to Kant, communication with others is a condition of the possibility of objects of experience. Such an a priori proportioning is a real relation.

Moreover, Kant holds that all the facts of natural science are relations of attraction, repulsion, or impenetrability. He calls these relations (1787: 279) *realitas phaenomenon*.[55] He also holds that he experiences real relation to things outside himself and their real relation to his own empirical existence (1787: 34-36 note). It is difficult to see why that real relation that he experiences should be other than those relations of *realitas phaenomenon* that constitute the whole subject matter of natural science. Since our experience is both intellectual and sensory, that real relation to an unknown X must be experienced both as real and as apparent; i.e., as a real temporal relation identified by an unreal instantaneous relation of consciousness. If so, the real relation would be identified with the innumerable relations of attraction, repulsion and impenetrability experienced in outer sense and recorded in natural science. Real relation experienced would not be one and the same for all our knowledge, a general relation to reality, as Kant holds (1787: 137).

I have shown above that Kant rightly claims to experience a real relation to a permanent X and a real relation of that permanent X to himself. For correlatives are rightly named extrinsically and not by their intrinsic natures. But Kant's reason for natural science not considering real substance (*substantia noumenon*) is because its concept of material substance entirely consists of these relations of attraction, repulsion and impenetrability. But then the right conclusion is that natural science experiences real relations of attraction, repulsion, and impenetrability between things of unknown nature and properties. And that is the thesis of this essay.

Idealism as opposed to Realism needs to be distinguished from doctrines loosely defined as Idealist. Lalande's *Vocabulaire technique et critique de la Philosophie* (1962) urges that the term "Idealism" be used with caution because of its vagueness. The authority of the *Vocabulaire* on this term is great; for though it is Lalande's work, it reports discussions and contributions of the *Société Française de Philosophie*, then dominated by Idealists. Their discussion of this term eliminated from Idealism doctrines admitting the existence of matter, albeit only indirectly known. That eliminates from Idealism Whitehead, Ayer and Kant, to whom we have already replied. The *Vocabulaire* classifies Kant as an incomplete Idealist; more specifically (p. 443), as a merely formal Idealist who admits reality belonging to the sensory matter of knowledge. So a complete Idealist is one for whom the total object of knowledge is somehow relative to thought. Consequently, Lalande suggests it would be desirable if henceforth the strict definition of Jules Lachelier were to be accepted as defining Idealism. Lachelier's definition (Lalande, pp. 438-440; Lachelier, 1905: 112-113), runs as follows:

> I believe that a very precise meaning can be given to this term. It seems to me that *idealism*, in the philosophic sense, consists in believing that the world,—such at least as I am able to know and talk about it,—is made up exclusively of representations, even of my representations. Representations can be actual or possible, material or formal. By possible representations, I mean for example, the representation of the sun when it is below the horizon. By formal representation, I mean that of time or space and whatever else can be constructed a priori; I also mean the representations of laws (for which another name is needed, perhaps) which order all phenomena a priori, such as the laws of causality and finality.
>
> Do only my representations exist, however?—For me and for my world, the answer is yes. Yet there may be other systems of representations and other worlds, partly parallel to and partly identical with my own.—They are parallel with respect to what is sensible, i.e., representations of other feeling subjects differing from mine according to the difference in points of view as Leibniz suggested; identical in what is intelligible, that is, in what is mathematical or metaphysical, for the representation of time and space, of causality or of finality, cannot differ from one thinking subject to another.
>
> Thinking subjects are not different, even, except insofar as their thoughts are incorporated in different sensible representations,—or rather, properly speaking, there exist only feeling subjects who think

one and the same thought. From this point on nothing hinders our considering this unique thought as the common substance of which the different feeling subjects are the accidents. Thus at the start Idealism is presented in a psychological form, and then it becomes a metaphysical doctrine. My world becomes the world to the degree that my thought becomes true, and in this respect it becomes the unique and universal substance. In such a manner, it seems to me, the two meanings attributed to this word (Idealism) in the history of philosophy are reconciled.[56]

Now even though Lachelier's strictly defined Idealism admits of *nothing but representations*, it nevertheless held for real relations between sensible representations (Lalande, 1962: 911-912; my translation):

When I say 'Peter is son of Paul' I think of Paul as a real being really existing outside of Peter. When I say 'every man is mortal' I no wise think of *mortal* as some sort of reality existing on the same footing as the men and in relation to them. Indeed, for logicians, man is one notion and *mortal* is another notion in relation to the first. But that relation is a second intention, a thought about my primitive and objective thought. Class, genus, species, subject, predicate, comprehension, extension: all that exists only *in mente*. To assimilate the relation between subject and predicate to that of one man to another man is to put logical formalities on the same footing as real existences. It is truly to eat second intentions as imagined by Rabelais.[57]

Thus Lachelier held that the *sensory representations of feeling subjects* were really related to one another. Lachelier's doctrine on real relations recalls what we have already seen. His position on real relations recalls Kant's doctrine on mutual proportioning of different subjects' powers needed for communication. It also recalls the mutual proportioning Merleau-Ponty recognized in communication. Hence Lachelier's Idealist metaphysics of a unique thinking subject in all thinkers nevertheless admitted real relations experienced between Peter and Paul. So Lachelier's strictly defined Idealism *is Direct Realism at the level of experiential knowing*.

Lachelier entirely removed the grounds for Idealism from experiential knowing. These grounds are a priori: the a priori law of efficient causality regulating the mechanism of scientific phenomena; the a priori law of final causality; and several other a priori laws of pure intelligence. Lachelier rightly denied that these a priori laws can be given in experience.

What are directly experienced, many philosophers hold, are real relations between terms of unknown nature. Since the intellectual and sensory cannot be distinguished in experience, a priori laws cannot be experienced as distinct. Following the philosophers just cited, it is sufficient to argue thus against Lachelier's Idealism. What we directly experience are real relations (whose existence Lachelier admits) between terms of unknown nature. These terms are real because they are terms of real relations. But these real terms are experienced only indirectly through the real relations. Their intrinsic natures remain unknown: hence these terms are *not known to consist* exclusively of representations as Lachelier believed. Philosophy must *begin with experience of real relations between terms of unknown nature*, not with alleged a priori laws of intellect that cannot be experienced. Moreover, as we have seen, contemporary science and philosophy of science have abandoned claim to the absolute necessity of scientific laws. Such abandonment destroys the basis of Lachelier's Idealism (Powell, 1958: 15-18).

According to Heidegger, the problem of separating the real and unreal in judgment has made no headway "in over two thousand years." Traditionally, truth was held to be found in judgment. It was supposed to consist in agreement between something ideal and something real. Accordingly, Heidegger (1927: 259) asks:

Is this agreement Real or Ideal in its kind of Being, or neither of these?[58]

Our whole essay is written around an answer to this way of posing the question of Realism. We answer: I experience the identity and distinction of a certain real and a certain unreal relation, e.g., the real relation and the unreal cultural relation between a man and his wife. In this experience of identifying and distinguishing, the agreement is ideal (unreal). But the real relation exists only as ideally identified with the unreal public object, the unreal cultural relation of marriage. Therefore, since we answer the question of Realism as posed by Heidegger, our philosophy of experience shares common ground with him.

As we shall see, Hume was a fideist Indirect Realist. Nevertheless he professed direct experience of real relations. His fideist Indirect Realism concerned the continued existence and the unity of bodies. Now, many philosophers hold "bodies" or "things" are not *directly* experienced *as real*, but only indirectly as terms of real relations. So direct experience of real relations does not directly contradict his mere belief in the permanence and unity of bodies. In fact, Hume (1739: 346) claimed direct experience of real relations of space and time:

The parts, into which the ideas of space and time resolve themselves, become at last indivisible; and these indivisible parts, being nothing in themselves, are inconceivable when not fill'd with something real and existent. The ideas of space and time are therefore no separate or distinct ideas, but merely those of the manner or order, in which objects exist.

The order between existing things is therefore what is meant by the ideas of space and time. But order between existing things is a real relation.

Furthermore, these real relations are given in sense experience (Hume, 1739: 341):

> The table before me is alone sufficient by its view to give me the idea
> of extension. This idea, then, is borrow'd from and represents some
> impression, which this moment appears to the senses. But my senses
> convey to me only the impressions of colour'd points, dispos'd in a cer-
> tain manner.

Hence the real relation of extension is given in sense experience.

Time is not a distinct sense impression but is given with objects sensed
as succeeding each other (*ibid.*, p. 343): Time, since it

> appears not as any primary distinct impression, can plainly be nothing
> but different ideas, or impressions or objects, disposed in a certain man-
> ner, that is succeeding each other.

The real relation of time is *experienced in objects succeeding each other*. The
Humean scholar Norman Kemp Smith comments on Hume's concept of
the *relations of place and time*, as follows (Smith, 1941: 355):

> Independently of, and prior to, any act of comparison they force them-
> selves upon the mind with immediate assurance in perceptual ex-
> perience. These relations of time and place thus fall midway between
> Hume's two classes. They share in the character of knowledge, in that
> they are apprehended by direct inspection, and therefore with a certainty
> which does not permit of doubt.

Smith is showing relations of place and time are a third class of relations
irreducible to the two classes Hume had mentioned. But my point taken
from Norman Kemp Smith is: Hume claimed direct experience of real
relations.

According to Theodore H. Green, Hume was "constantly insisting"
on reducing mathematics to experience of relations between sense impressions. Being an idealist, Green found Hume's method unacceptable
(Hume, 1739: 222-223):

> The condition of such a method being acquiesced in is, that quantity in
> all its forms should be found reducible to ultimate units or indivisible
> parts in the shape of separate impressions. Should it be found so, the
> whole question indeed, how ideas of relation are possible for a merely
> feeling consciousness, would still remain, but mathematics would stand
> on the same footing with the experimental sciences, as a science of rela-
> tions between impressions. Upon this reducibility, then, we find Hume
> constantly insisting.

In fact, Hume says relations between impressions are perceived (*ibid.*, p.
526):

> Every idea of a quality in an object passes thro[ugh] an impression; and
> therefore every *perceivable* relation, whether of connexion or repugnance,
> must be common both to objects and impressions (Hume's emphasis).

Now according to Hume, impressions are distinct existences (*ibid.*, p. 540):

> 'Tis still true, that every distinct perception, which enters into the com-
> position of the mind, is a distinct existence, and is different, and distin-
> guishable, and separable from every other perception, either contem-
> porary or successive.

Using the terminology of this essay: since perceptible relations obtain between distinct existences, they do not reduce to mere objective being. Such
perceptible relations are *real relations*. This conclusion seems surprising.
But it surprises only because one forgets that for Hume, impressions are
not *images or signs of something other than themselves* (*ibid.*, p. 479):

> That our senses offer not their impressions as the images of something
> *distinct*, or *independent*, and *external*, is evident; because they convey to
> us nothing but a single perception, and never give us the least intima-
> tion of anything beyond.

So impressions are distinct existing things between which real relations
are perceived. However, concerning the continued existence and unity
of bodies, Hume is a fideist Indirect Realist.

Despite claiming direct experience of real relations, Hume held that
we could only have natural belief in the permanence and unity of bodies
(fideist Indirect Realism). My sole comment is as follows. This fideist Indirect Realism at least does *not apply to the reality of terms of real relations*.
For we indirectly experience these terms *as real* through the real relations
directly experienced. The reality of the terms of real relations is indirectly and extrinsically experienced through their real relations.

As we have already seen, Hegel's natural philosophy is a philosophy
of experience. In philosophy of nature:

> philosophy must accord with [übereinstimmend] the experience nature
> gives rise to. (1830b: I, 197 par. 246).[59]

But natural philosophy does not "accord" with experience as the ultimate
"basis of verification." It "translates" the experiential universals of natural
science into immanent "moments" of the necessary development of the
intellectual Notion (*ibid.*, p. 201):

> The material prepared out of experience by physics is taken by the phi-
> losophy of nature at the point to which physics has brought it, and recon-
> stituted without any further reference to experience as the basis of ver-
> ification. Physics must therefore work together with philosophy so that
> universalized understanding which it [physics] provides may be trans-
> lated into the Notion, by showing how this universal, as an intrinsically
> necessary whole, proceeds out of the Notion.[60]

Lacking immanent necessity as moments of the Notion, the universal of physics is:

> split up, dismembered, particularized, separated and lacking in any necessary connection within itself . . . (*Ibid.*, 202).[61]

However, the experiential universals of physics must fully conform to existents that "cause themselves to be noticed" (Hegel, 1830b: II, par. 286, addition p. 47):

> That which is not subject to observation does not exist in this field however, for existence is just that being-for-other which causes itself to be noticed.[62]

Thanks to the translation of experiential universals into the Notion, the Notion itself appears in experiential existents. This appearance of the Notion first occurs when experiential universals are shown to be related "moments" of the Notion.

When gravity as empirical universal is translated into the Notion, attraction and repulsion become related "moments" of existent motion. Thus the Notion itself appears in existent motion thanks to the "ideal intro-reflexion" manifested by real relations between several determinate bodies:

> This Idea [of gravitation] is the Notion disclosing itself *in external reality in the particularity of bodies, and at the same time, in the ideality and intro-reflection of these bodies, displaying itself in motion.* This contains the rational identity and inseparability of the moments, *which* are otherwise taken to be independent. *In general, motion, as such* only has significance and existence, where there is a system of *several* bodies which are variously *determined* and so stand in a certain relationship to one another (emphasis by Petry). (Hegel, 1830b: I, 261 par. 269).[63]

So thanks to the Notion, the split up, independent empirical universals, attraction and repulsion, are reduced to real relations between several determinate bodies. Motion lacks both "significance and existence" except as real relations between several determinate bodies. Empirical universals give the quantitative law of falling bodies. But empirical universals (*ibid.*, p. 260):

> lack the significance of the Idea [of gravitation] developed into its reality which is given in this paragraph [par. 269].[64]

So, in this paragraph 269, Hegel shows how the Notion *first appears in reality* as the Notion of existent motion. The Notion of existent motion is: real relations of several determinate bodies.

In sum, for Hegel, natural philosophy translates empirical universals into the intellectual Notion. Empirical universals arise from "existents that cause themselves to be noticed." The first empirical universal to be translated into the Notion is universal gravitation. Universal gravitation is translated into the Notion as real relations of several determinate bodies.

It seems that, for Aquinas, direct experience of real relations was the first known reality. For him, as we have already seen, "reality" is what is naturally first known. Moreover, natural knowledge extends to a whole experiential realm of "reality" understood in terms of the transcendentals: "one," "many," "true," etc. This realm presents us with many realities, but their nature remains unknown. Subsequent knowledge, however, reveals what was naturally known to have been "accidents" by their intrinsic nature. It seems these accidents are always real relations according to Aquinas, as I now show.

Among what belongs to the realm of the naturally known is the principle, "This existent is not that existent" (*Summa Theologiae*, I, q. 11, art. 2 ad 4).[65] Commenting on the *Posterior Analytics* (1269-1272b), he explains how such "first common principles come to be known." And he explains:

> Just as from memory is formed experience, so from experience or even from a universal already in the mind . . . from that experience and from such a universal itself formed from experience, is formed a [first common] principle of art and science. (My translation of *In II Post. Anal.*, lect. 20, par. 592).[66]

This origin of the first naturally known principles in experience needs explanation. Accordingly, Aquinas writes (1269-1272b):

> It is clear that sensing is properly and per se of the singular, but yet there is somehow even a sensing of the universal. For sense knows Callias not only so far forth as he is Callias, but also as he is this man; and similarly Socrates, as he is this man. As a result of such an attainment pre-existing in the sense, the intellective soul can consider man in both. But if it were in the very nature of things that sense could apprehend only that which pertains to particularity, and along with this could in no wise apprehend the nature in the particular, it would not be possible for universal knowledge to be caused in us from sense-apprehension. (*In II Post. Anal.*, lect. 20, par. 595).[67]

Now the distinction of many realities in the naturally known realm comes about from the principle "this existent is not that existent":

> Even in our minds, however, the many is subsequent to unity, for we only conceive divided things as many by ascribing unity to each of them. So unity enters the definition of the many, but the many does not enter the definition of unity. Now division arises in the mind simply by negating existence. So that the first idea to arise in the mind is the existent, then that this existent is not that existent and so we grasp division, thirdly unity, and fourthly the many. (1266-1274a: *Summa*, I, q. II, art. 2 ad 4).[68]

As shown above, that principle itself arises from experience, according to Thomas. So if experience itself has any determinate type of content, it will determine the content of the many realities of the naturally known realm. Specifically, is that determinate content always a real relation?

Experience is the object of a specific sense power, according to Aquinas (1269-1272a); namely, it is the object of the "cogitative power":

> Experience arises from the association of many singular [intentions] received in memory. And this kind of association is proper to man and pertains to the cogitative power (also called the particular reason), which associates particular intentions just as universal reason associates universal ones. (*In I Met.*, lect. 1, n. 15.)[69]

But what "associates particular intentions" precisely constitutes *experience*. Moreover, it is the *specifying formal object* of the cogitative power. For this is "proper to man and pertains to the cogitative power." Now, the phrase: "proper to man and pertains to the cogitative power," signifies for Thomas that the cogitative in man and instinct in animals have *fundamentally the same specifying formal object*, though the cogitative has something unique. The cogitative in man associates *into an experience* what comes ready made as the specifying object of animal instinct (Aquinas, 1266-1274a):

> But an animal has to seek and shun things not only because they suit or do not suit its senses but also because they are in other ways fitting and useful or harmful. Thus a lamb, when it sees a wolf approach, flees, not because it does not like the colour or shape, but because it is its natural enemy. And likewise a bird collects straw, not because it pleases its senses, but because it needs it for building its nest . . . What we call natural instinct in other animals in man we call cogitation, which comes upon intentions of the kind in question through a process of comparison. (*Summa*, I, q. 78, art. 4).[70]

Thus the cogitative in man is more perfect than animal instinct. So also is man's sense memory more perfect than that of other animals. Nevertheless, despite these differences the cogitative and sense memory in man are specifically the same powers of the sensory soul as instinct and memory in animals:

> Cogitation and memory reach so high in man through their similarity to and connection with abstract reason by a kind of overflow, not through anything belonging to the sense-soul as such. So they are not new powers but the same powers, more perfect than they are in animals. (*Summa*, I, q. 78, art. 4 ad 5).[71]

Hence, experience is the specifying formal object of the cogitative, despite its difference from the objects of animal instinct.

Thus the cogitative's specifying formal object is "associating" particular intentions into one experience that animal instinct innately perceives as already "associated." "Associated" here translates "collativa". Aquinas habitually defines the specifying formal object of the cogitative as *collativa intentionum individualium* (cf. *Index Thomisticus*, Sectio II, Vol. 4, p. 564). *Collativa* ordinarily means *discursive knowledge* as opposed to simple vision (*ibid.*). Thus he writes (1266-1274h):

> The characteristic activity of the rational soul is putting things together and proceeding from one idea to another. Christ, therefore, had discursive articulated [*collativa*] knowledge. (*Summa*, III, q. 11, art. 3, *sed contra*).[72]

But to put together and proceed from one another is *to relate things*. Hence *collativa intentionum individualium* means: interrelating individual intentions. Thus in a passage above quoted (1269-1272b), Thomas shows

> how from experience of singulars the universal is formed in the mind . . . For sense knows Callias . . . as . . . this man and similarly Socrates as . . . this man. As a result . . . the intellective soul can consider man in both. (*In II Post. Anal.*, lect. 20, nn. 594-595).[73]

Hence the cogitative's specifying formal object *is to relate individual intentions into one experience*. For example, its formal object is to relate into one experience "this man" and "that man," or "this white" and "that white"—to take Aquinas' examples (*ibid.*).

Now according to Aquinas, this sensory experience is the datum in which the intellect finds its natural object "reality" and the principle "this existent is not that existent." Hence intellect first naturally knows these "related intentions" as "reality" and as "many realities." But once one has passed beyond natural knowledge, such data *experienced as related* are understood as *real relations*. For once one has passed beyond the naturally understood realm by distinguishing substance and accidents, realities *experienced as related* are understood to be related by real accidents in the category of relation.

Furthermore, for Aquinas (text cited at note 70 above), the cogitative and sense memory have the same content except that the sense memory conserves as "past" what the cogitative perceived as "present." Now recall (*reminiscentia*) is the process of remembering such a past thing (Aquinas, 1260-1272: lect. IV: "*Reminiscentia est quidam motus ad memorandum*").[74] Now Aquinas lists as means of recall: similarity, contrast and propinquity; and propinquity is either social (father-son) or spatial or temporal (*ibid.*, lectio V).[75] But these "intentions" are all relations in the understanding of the intellect. Hence *through relations* we remember *things remembered*. But save for the difference of past and present, sense memory has the same content as the cogitative. Hence the cogitative perceives things related through present intentions that intellect later finds to be real relations.

Thomas V. Flynn (1953: 563) summed up thus his research on the cogitative in Aquinas and the Thomistic commentators:

> We can sum up our findings in the following manner. The Cogitative Faculty is the highest of all sense faculties in man and is only modally distinct from the Estimative Power in brutes. Its formal object is the material singular as containing something similar to others, and its proper act is to compare such objects. In relation to intellectual abstraction, its act is to give phantasms their ultimate remote preparation. This preparation is in the order of material causality. [The Estimative Power is what we call animal intelligence: see Deely, 1971].

Now, the material singular as something similar to others is *really related* to that other. As ultimate remote preparation for intellectual abstraction, such data lie at the origin of intellectual knowledge. So Flynn's findings support my own on these important points.

So experience of real relations is the first mind-independent reality according to those philosophies of experience. Real relations as first known reality is common epistemological ground for them. However different were the philosophies they drew from these data, their first mind-independent data were the same. Men whose philosophical destinations were so diverse seem to have been coerced by reality to begin their philosophy from real relations.

Philosophers of extremely different tendencies, and coming from very different cultures, have agreed at least on one point: namely, that although we do not have direct experience of natures, we do have direct experience of real relations. Hence, there is trans-cultural agreement on an experiential basis for philosophy. Therefore, from the *historical point of view itself,* historical relativism is *unconvincing*.

This concludes the historical part of our study. In Part II, we shall try to determine the philosophic truth of the matters to be considered.

Chapter II

WHY THE PROBLEM OF REALISM INVOLVES DIRECT EXPERIENCE OF PUBLIC OBJECTS

Section 1. The first task of this Part II: find the critical origin of philosophy and science needed to disprove complete historical determinism of experience.

We have found that complete historical determinism of philosophical experience is not credible even from the historical point of view. So many philosophers of disparate times and cultures and of opposed philosophical systems agree on experience of real relations that complete historical determinism seems *historically* improbable. But I have not yet manifested experience of mind-independent real relations that yields *philosophical refutation* of complete historical determinism; for mind-independent reality cannot be historically determined. This is the first task of Part II. Part I has shown that many philosophers hold that real relations are the first experienced realities. I now turn to analyse experience in order to determine whether such is the case. In so doing I am looking for the critical origin of philosophy and science needed for philosophical disproof of complete historical determinism of experience.

Section 2. On describing "reality" by counterdistinction to public objects that totally reduce to objective being.

First I must clarify what I mean by publicly experienced reality. A publicly experienced reality is first of all a public object. But not all public objects are publicly experienced realities. Greek society lived for centuries with the Gods of Homer as public objects; but those gods were not publicly experienced realities. In our own society the supposed realities of science are but a small part of the public objects of even highly educated people. Many public objects exist among us that are not publicly experienced realities. Santa Claus is a public object for children, but Santa Claus is not a publicly experienced reality. Nevertheless, Santa Claus is a distinctive public object with distinguishing characteristics that set him off from any other public object. Moreover, he is readily re-identifiable year after year at Christmas time. But Santa Claus is not a publicly experienced reality. Santa Claus is not merely an object of cognition but also and especially an affective object, having unknown resonances in the subconscious life of children. But Santa Claus has no being except as an object of psychic life, whether that object be actual or habitual, cognitive or appetitive, conscious or unconscious. Santa Claus is a *public object whose being totally reduces to being an object of psychic life in this broad sense.*

For a philosophical understanding of direct experience alone (such as we are now pursuing), the understanding of the term ''reality'' is not without difficulty. By contrast, for a philosophy of substance, ''reality'' is easily understood: it means primarily individual substance and secondarily its accidents. But as we have seen, substance does not seem to be an object of direct experience. So we have no resource but to understand ''reality'' by counter-distinction to that whose total being reduces to being an object of psychic life in the broad sense just explained. For brevity's sake, ''reality'' means that whose total being is *not merely objective being.*

We need not fear falling into Phenomenalism by defining real being as irreducible to mere objective being. The Aristotelian John Poinsot has equivalently done as much. He tells us that intentional presence in knowledge is needed for all knowing. This required intentional presence is merely objective existence (*existentia objectiva*). Then he defines intuitive knowing as knowing the physical presence of the really existing thing. This real existence he calls ''outside the order of knowledge'' (*extra genus notitiae*). He counterdistinguishes mind-independent existence (*existentia realis*) from intentional and objective existence (*existentia intentionalis et objectiva*) which is not outside the order of knowledge:

> Intuitive awareness is the awareness of a thing in its presence, while abstractive awareness is the awareness of a thing in its absence. ''Presence'' and ''absence'' here must not be interpreted in the intentional sense of the presence of an object to or its union with the knower, for it hardly bears noting that no awareness can fail to have an object present in that sense, since indeed no awareness can occur at all without a union of object to knower. Therefore awareness in presence—so-called intuitive awareness—and awareness in absence—so-called abstractive awareness—are contrasted properly in terms of the dimension or element of physical presence or absence of an object in the environment as we are aware of it. Whence St. Thomas says [1256-1259] in q. 3 of his *Disputed Questions on Truth*, art. 3. reply to obj. 8, that the knowledge of vision (which is the same as intuitive awareness) adds to simple awareness something which is independent of the order of awareness, namely, the existence of things. Therefore it adds the element of mind-independent existence, for an intentional and objective existence is not independent of the order of awareness. And in the third book of his *Com-*

mentary on the Sentences of Peter Lombard [1252-1256], dist. 14, q. 1, art. 2, quaestiunc. 2, he says that "that very object which has an act of being independent of the perception is perceived in its independent being." Therefore the existence which intuitive awareness requires must be a mind-independent and physical existence. (Poinsot, 1632: Book III, q. 1, 722b27-723a5).[1]

Thus he has defined real being in terms of *existentia objectiva*, yet without falling into Phenomenalism.

In another text, the same author counterdistinguishes conceptual relations that have merely objective being (*esse objectivum*) in our apprehension from what has being in a thing when no mind is considering it (*nullo intellectu considerante*). This latter being is mind-independent or "real" (*realis*):

> The grounds for holding that relation is an intersubjective form or mode of mind-independent being rooted in but transcending as such the subjective characteristics of individuals are as follows. Relations merely consequent upon our ways of discoursing about the world express something subjective and not entirely toward another. Mind-dependent relations exist only in awareness. But we find existing in our physical environment, quite apart from the awareness we have of it, aspects and features having an existence or being exclusively toward something else. Therefore relations are found in the world which are not consequent upon our ways of discoursing about the world. These relations constitute a category of reality quite distinct from the categories of subjective being. (Poinsot, 1632: "Second Preamble," art. 1, 574b21-32).[2]

Here again, Poinsot is defining real being as what does not merely have objective being. Yet he does not fall into Phenomenalism.

The phenomenalist is one who holds that all objects *do reduce to mere objective being*. The solipsistic phenomenalist is a phenomenalist who recognizes no public objects. A solipsist of the present moment believes that all objects are such that their whole *esse* reduces to *percipi*. Descartes (1641a) in the IIIrd Meditation believed that his thought contained enough perfection to be the cause of all objects of his awareness and experience except the idea of God. But Descartes was *by no means* a phenomenalist. For he directly experienced his thinking as a real thing, a real *thinking* thing (Jolivet, 1929: 122).[3] But before he discovered his thought could not cause the idea of God, whatever he knew besides himself reduced to objective being for him. So he seemed (1641a: 163) "all alone in the world":

> And the longer and the more carefully that I investigate these matters, the more clearly and distinctly do I recognise their truth. But what am I to conclude from it all in the end? It is this, that if the objective reality of any one of my ideas is of such a nature as clearly to make me recognise that it is not in me either formally or eminently, and that consequently

I cannot myself be the cause of it, it follows of necessity that I am not alone in the world, but that there is another being which exists, or which is the cause of this idea. On the other hand, had no such an idea existed in me, I should have had no sufficient argument to convince me of the existence of any being beyond myself; for I have made very careful investigation everywhere and up to the present time have been able to find no other ground.[4]

Descartes here mentions "objective reality." "Objective reality" means for him the necessarily possible essences studied in mathematics and metaphysics, e.g., triangles and the attributes of God. In a word, necessary objects of thought have "objective reality" *whether or not* anything actually existing corresponds to them (cf. Cronin, 1966: 149).[5] Were it not for the idea of God all objective reality would reduce to mere objective being for Descartes' thinking. But Descartes' thinking would be *one reality that would not* reduce to mere objective being. Even had the idea of God been a mere idea produced by his thought, he would not have been a phenomenalist. For a phenomenalist, *all objects* whatsoever, including the thinking subject, reduce to mere objective being.

Section 3. Difficulties of contemporary philosophers in distinguishing between reality and mere objective being.

Today many empiricist philosophers find no direct experiential evidence that distinguishes experience itself from reality. Herbert Feigl (1958a: 464-465) writes thus concerning realist and phenomenalist interpretations of facts:

> There is no *testable* difference between these two interpretations of factual knowledge, but there are excellent reasons for the repudiation of phenomenalism and hence for the acceptance of a realist epistemology (emphasis added).

So for Feigl Realism is preferable to Phenomenalism because of the failures of Phenomenalism. But reality is not given in any testable experience as irreducible to mere objective being. Ernest Nagel (1961:151) finds the difference between the "real" and "mere appearance" to be

> an honorific way to express a value judgment and to attribute a "superior" status to things asserted to be real. There is perhaps an aura of such honorific connotation whenever the word is employed, despite explicit avowals to the contrary and certainly to the detriment of clarity. For this reason it would be desirable to ban the use of the word altogether.

So, for Nagel's Empiricism, "appearance" and "reality" are not distinguishable. W.V.O. Quine (1953: 44) thinks of science as a conceptual tool, ultimately for predicting future experience in the light of past experience. Physical objects are conceptually imported into the situation as convenient intermediaries—not by definition in terms of experience, but simply as irreducible posits comparable epistemologically to the gods of Homer.

So for Quine's Empiricism physical objects are reduced to mere objective being.

Heidegger's philosophy makes Realism and Phenomenalism into two *Geschicke des Seins*, leaving us incapable of even asking whether all objects are reduced to mere objective being. Even questioning about reality is a fatefully determined philosophical experience limited to some philosophers and excluded for others.

Yet all of these contemporary philosophers, unlike Descartes, are writing about public objects. The empiricists are philosophers of science, and science consists of public objects. Heidegger is a philosopher of historical experience; he writes about the different public historical worlds of different philosophies. Yet none of these philosophers of experience can tell us the difference between Santa Claus and a live horse as regards irreducibility to mere objective being. If such men failed, it must not be easy to experience the direct experiential evidence that distinguishes experience itself from reality.

Section 4. My description of 'publicly verified reality'.

Now finally I can say what I mean by a publicly verified reality. A *publicly verified reality* is: a public object that cannot be reduced to mere objective being, and is directly experienced as distinguished from what can be reduced to mere objective being. I clarify the description. *Public objects* means: something experienced by the public whether real or unreal. For example: a live horse, Santa Claus or scientific objects such as atoms or population species of animals. *That cannot be reduced to mere objective being* means: that cannot be reduced to an object of psychic life whether that object be actual or habitual, cognitive or appetitive, conscious or unconscious. *Directly experienced as distinguished from what can be so reduced* means: *the distinction* of what cannot be and what can be reduced *is itself directly experienced.*

I have direct experience of public objects. This is obvious from the fact that I describe all or almost all my experience in public language. But public language describes public objects. (Wittgenstein, 1936-1949: nos. 262-268). That is an extreme position if it is pushed to excluding notes and memoranda that a person makes to one's self and are understandable to one's self alone. But the overriding importance of public language in description of one's most private and intimate experience manifests direct experience of public objects. If I did not understand the public objects meant by the public language-words "chair," "table," "doors," "stairs," "mealtime," "bed," "street," "cars," I would not be able to use these objects when alone. Solitary use of the equipment of industrial society bespeaks understanding of that society's public objects.

The fact of direct experience of public language and public objects is commonly accepted today by empiricists of different varieties: by linguistic analysts and philosophers of science (not to mention Heideggerians who are not empiricists). For philosophy of experience, it is not too much to speak of *revolutionary change* from the assumption that all objects directly experienced are my individual private objects to the assumption that public objects are directly experienced. (Castañeda, 1967: 458-464). Descartes held that all objects directly experienced were one's private objects only, being modes of the individual's thinking substance. Leibniz' "monads without windows" express the assumption of individual private objects as sole objects of direct experience (1714a: par. 7). As recently as 1944, a philosopher of Bertrand Russell's stature maintained (1944: 16) that the theory of knowledge has a "certain essential subjectivity" . . . "its data are egocentric, and so are the early stages of its argumentation."

But the rush to public objects should not lead us to neglect possible private experience of reality. As we shall see, Merleau-Ponty moved from valid private experience to valid public experience. This essay shall follow him by beginning in private experience.

Philosophical learning need not distort experience. Primitive individual private experience of private objects may even need learned information in order to be described accurately. Allow me to illustrate from personal experience: when I was a small child I passed the dining room table, and to my amazement *it stood much lower* than I had ever seen it before. Only now as an adult do I understand that I had just then grown tall enough to see over the edge of the table, instead of being in my former situation of looking up to the edge. Without changing the cognitive content or the emotional tone of amazement at that experience, it is necessary to describe it philosophically in the light of subsequent knowledge that I had grown tall enough to see over the edge. Without this adult information, the childhood experience would not be faithfully described, even though as a child I could not have brought this information into that experience. Had I understood my change of height relative to the table I would not have been amazed. So likewise, I must describe my private individual experience with all the light that I can bring to bear from philosophy and science; but without changing the cognitive content or the emotional tone of my private individual experience.

Philosophy of experience does not return to some ignorant common sense analysis of experienced objects. It must bring to bear the hard won insights of Aristotle, Aquinas, Scotus, Suarez, Poinsot, Locke and Kant that we have seen. Let alone should philosophy of experience return to some presocialized time of life before one learned public language and public objects. Privately experienced objects of soliloquy must be carefully described in public language, as Shakespeare has shown.

However, neither can philosophy of experience forget that direct experience of the difference between experience itself (reducible to mere objective being) and reality is very difficult to elucidate. Recent radical empiricists such as Feigl hold that there is no experiential test for the difference between phenomenology and realism. Other radical empiricists such as Nagel and Quine have abandoned the search for the difference, as the quotations above show. Moreover, even direct experience of public objects does not necessarily yield direct experience of this difference characterized by me as what reduces to mere objective being as against what does not. Feigl, Nagel and Quine are all philosophers of the sciences' public objects and yet did not arrive at this difference. So too was Heidegger a philosopher of public historical objects, and he did not arrive at the difference between what reduces to mere objective being and what does not.

I have said that philosophy of experience must bring to bear the hard won insights of those classical philosophers. But their hard won insights *chiefly concerned the limits of experience*: that we do not directly experience the nature of things. According to them, we do directly experience many sensible realities. But we do not directly experience the nature of those realities. This was the chief insight of their philosophy of experience: the experience of many sensible realities and the exclusion from experience of the nature of things. However, these contemporary empiricists fail to account for how we can experience the real as such: i.e., as distinguishable from the merely objective.

In the description of *publicly verified reality* given above I included the condition: *that real being be directly experienced as distinguished from unreal being*. Now Aquinas held a similar position: he held for an experiential difference between real and unreal being, as I showed in the previous chapter. So the experience of "golden mountain" as unreal is had by discerning the unreal from the real, and the experience of Mt. Vesuvius as real is had in the same way.

No such direct experience of discerning the unreal from the real is found among the above mentioned empiricists. The lack of this experience is crucial for such philosophers who say they do not directly experience the real. All of them write much about such mind-dependent entities as linguistic terms. But with no description of the experience of the distinction of the unreal from the real, it is no wonder they have no doctrine on direct experience of the real. In their doctrine, the real and the unreal are experienced as confused and indistinguishable. That quite suffices to snuff out experience of the real.

Section 5. Social and cultural relational systems that exist only as objects of consciousness.

I have just asserted that linguistic terms are mind-dependent entities. The reason is that linguistic terms reduce to a system of mind-dependent relations. For some linguistic terms have *meaning*: they "stand for" singular terms whether concrete or abstract. Thus, for example, the concrete term "Peter" means, i.e., "stands for," a certain individual man. The abstract singular "9" "stands for" an abstract mathematical entity. Both kinds of meanings are mind-dependent relations to the things meant, as the synonym "standing for" clearly indicates. Some linguistic terms are general terms. General terms do not have meaning but instead they have *true extension*. This true extension relates to one, each of many, or to no entity. Manifestly true extension is a mind-dependent relation to the entities of which it is true. Other terms express the extension of the general term; these are quantifiers such as "all," "some," etc. They express the relations involved in extension of general terms. Finally some terms express truth functions; these are, for example, "not," "or," "but." These express mind-dependent relations between terms or statements. Hence linguistic terms reduce to a system of mind-dependent relations. I postpone the question of how to experience the distinction of these mind-dependent relations from real being.

Now if language is a system of mind-dependent relations, then the terms of language are *as such* mind-dependent. For example, in the reciting of a poem, the objects referred to in a language are mind-dependent objects by reason of the very fact that they are terms of mind-dependent linguistic relations. The objects described are *nothing but* subjects and predicates of mind-dependent relations. Subjects and predicates are terms of mind-dependent relations *as such*: and as such these objects are mind-dependent. (We shall see that mind-dependent relations are sometimes identified with and distinguished from real relations to real objects). Therefore, the whole of language and that which is described in language as such entirely reduces to objective being. For the same reason all cultural systems as described in language entirely reduce to objective being: i.e., the sciences, philosophies, literature, the communication-media, etc.

Social relations are organized in social systems indicating expected behavior. So social relations in systems such as the Western democracies and the People's Republics are "coated" with cultural relations comprising a social system are unreal relations prescribing future behavior that does not yet exist. Even in presently perceived behavior one discerns what *was* culturally expected behavior; so the unreal cultural relation is embedded in perceived interrelations between persons. The thrust of social systems into future relations totally reduces to objective being. Social systems likewise evaluate past behavior that no longer exists, otherwise crime would not be judged; and expected behavior would not be reinforced. This thrust into the past likewise totally reduces to objective being.

This unreal expected dimension of social systems such as the Western democracies and the People's Republics is especially manifest in their relation to foreigners. Foreigners are not expected to behave as members of the homeland, because they are not expected to understand or at least expected not fully to sympathize. Among foreigners, enemies in wartime are even expected to behave in a way hostile to one's countrymen. In Southern European countries, Catholics, Marxists, and Liberals constitute mutually opposed blocks disagreeing on which cultural values should coat social relations (Sanders, 1977: 12-22). In Northwestern Europe and the U.S., free elections that transfer government without violence are the expected behavior; the parties vying for power do not differ fundamentally in expected behavior. In economic organization, capitalist cultural relations are the expected behavior in most Western democracies. All these forms of expected cultural relations totally reduce to objective being.

Inasmuch as social relations are coated with unreal cultural relations, the terms of these unreal relations are *as such* unreal. In other words, to have U.S. citizenship, to be a property holder under U.S. law, to have constitutional rights under the U.S. Constitution, all these come to a person as expectancies under the U.S. legal system of unreal relations. To be the object of these expectancies reduces as such to mere objective being. Such a truth has been a theme of political philosophy and religious literature since ancient times. But though the expectancies in these social systems are as such unreal being, it does not follow that the people who happen to be American citizens, property holders, and possessors of constitutional rights are unreal beings. Moreover, it does not even follow that all human relations among these people are unreal. Part II of this essay will endeavor to contrast real and unreal relations within social relations.

We have seen that cultural systems (e.g., the sciences, philosophies, literature and the media of communication) constitute as such cultural relations that totally reduce to objective being. Likewise we now see political systems and economic systems are social systems coated with unreal cultural relations. Now these cultural relations and their respective unreal terms are public objects that pervade the whole of life. They constitute the expected background of people's experience. As providing this expected background of experience, they are rightly called the *Western World*, the *Free World*. The *Western World* is the total socio-cultural system of public objects habitually expected in experience. It reduces to mere objective being. The Western World is only one of the historical worlds now on the planet.

Human free choice is a prominent public object in the Western World. But free choice cannot be assumed to be a mind-independent reality. Free choice may perhaps be a mind-dependent object or belief that results from the mind-dependent historical world of the West. Free choice may be no more mind-independent than constitutional rights. As pointed out at the beginning of this essay, that is the contention of the prestigious Skinnerian school of psychology. But without mind-independent free choice the *human self* as believed in the Western World disappears as a mind-independent reality. As Skinner says: "To man *qua* man we readily say good riddance" (Skinner, 1971: 200-201). For the human self as believed in the Western World is the free self. If the self is totally reduced to conditioning by the natural and social environment as Skinner holds, then the Western self is merely a mind-dependent object resulting from the mind-dependent Western World. Hence we shall initially assume that it is nothing but an object of belief in the Western World, not a mind-independent reality. The purpose of this essay is to show that free choice is a mind-independent reality, and to do so from real human relations alone as experienced public objects.

Section 6. Why experience of real relations seems a credible fact.

This essay is devoted to philosophical study of direct experience. Now the experimental sciences after centuries of collective study of experiential data have never come upon the intrinsic natures of matter, life and mind. We have seen that the Aristotelians, Locke, Kant, Hegel, and others held the similar view that experiential knowing did not reveal the intrinsic natures of things. So our study will assume that the intrinsic natures of things are not revealed in direct experience.

But even were the natures of things directly experienced, these intrinsic natures would not solve the crucial epistemological problem. That crucial problem is to experience the difference between mere objective being and real being. Whatever object we experience has objective being. Now let us assume that the realist hypothesis is true; and that it is based on experiential knowledge of the intrinsic natures of things and of other such absolute properties as sensible qualities, extension, motion and rest. Let all these properties be assumed to be directly experienced intrinsic properties of the intrinsic natures that are also directly experienced. Let us take direct experience of a horse. The real horse with its nature, sensible qualities, extension, motion and rest have real existence. The experiential knowing of these realities has objective being. The *two kinds of existence* are radically different and they do not have the same meaning. It does not mean the same thing in the reality hypothesis to speak of the *real horse* and of *the experience of the real horse*. The real horse eats, jumps eight feet, etc.; the experience of the real horse does none of these things.

Now we experience knowing the same horse while it is living and after it is dead. And the knowledge experience is of the same concrete horse. But when the horse is dead it exists only as objective being. Even while the horse is still living but is out of one's presence, one can have this knowledge experience of it without knowing whether the horse has mere objective being or also enjoys real being somewhere outside one's presence. For if the horse has died since it left my presence, it now has only objective being in my knowledge experience. So despite the radical difference of existence and of meaning between the real and merely objective horse, one cannot experience this difference except in its physical presence. What is it about experience in physical presence of the horse that assures us that this knowledge experience is not just of the objective being of the horse but also experience of its real existence? What indeed but experience of the real relation of the horse as now *present to us*?

But cannot external sensation give us experience of the horse present to us? Why does one need experience of a new reality (that of a real relation) to supplement the already rich acquired stock of knowledge of the horse that I have generously provided to the realist hypothesis: its nature, sensible qualities, extension, motion and rest as intrinsic properties of its real nature? The answer is that did the external senses not yield experience of any mind-independent reality at all then they would not manifest the real presence of the horse to us. But why does not experience of the reality of its sensible qualities, its extension, motions and rest manifest its real presence to us? The answer is: the real presence of the horse *to us* is a real relation of those sensible qualities, extension, motions and rest *to us*. It is the *presence to us* of those intrinsic properties that proximately manifests the real presence of the horse. And that *to us* of those intrinsic properties is, for a realist doctrine, a real relation.

According to Heidegger (1943: 301), from the early times of Western philosophy "that which is" has always meant "that which is present":

> What is thus, and solely in the narrow sense, made manifest was experienced in the early stages of Western thought as "that which is present" and has long been termed "that which is" (*das Seiende*).[6]

Now Heidegger was a specialist on the history of the understanding of the real (*das Seiende*). He testifies that, since the Greeks, philosophers have understood the *real* as *that which is present to us*. Hence our conclusion, drawn from the requirements of direct experience of mind-independent reality, seems confirmed by philosophers' perception of reality since ancient times.

Here we find the reason why the experimental sciences and classical philosophers excluded the intrinsic nature of things from direct experience. The intrinsic natures of things do not consist in being *present to us*; the intrinsic nature of things is not to be *really related to us*. But it is only by real relations to us that we can distinguish in experience the real from the mere objective being of things, howsoevermuch we may know about the intrinsic natures and their intrinsic absolute properties. Hence the experience of the intrinsic natures of things must be excluded from our project of experiencing the difference between the real and the unreal. For the same reason the intrinsic absolute properties of things must be excluded from our project, namely, the sensible qualities, extension, motion and rest. For none of these intrinsic absolute properties is that peculiar reality *presence to us*; none of them consists of real relation to us. It is only as appearing within real relations to us that we shall be concerned about any intrinsic properties of things.

Moreover, the real relation alone can be an identical object of experience with an unreal one. When I point at the man in front of me and say "That is John," I seem to experience both a real relation of pointing at him and an unreal linguistic relation to him. Both relations signify the same experienced object but in different ways. I experience the unreal linguistic relation as meaning the same thing as the real relation (real in the realist hypothesis). Yet I distinguish the two relations. The real and unreal are brought together in experience by identity of meaning, and yet are distinguished in a single experience. In the realist hypothesis, we could never experience any absolute nature or property as identified in meaning with something unreal; we cannot experience a man real-only-from-the-belt-down but unreal from the belt up. We cannot experience a single extension that is part real and part unreal. Among intrinsic natures and properties the real and unreal are not experienced as a single meaningful object. Hence experience of their difference is not so simple because they do not constitute a single object of experience. But if real and unreal relations (may) have the same meaning, they (may) constitute one experiential object. The condition to be posited for that to be the case is that real relations exist. *And that remains to be manifested.*

Section 7. Alternative epistemological systems.

Idealism and Phenomenalism are epistemologies opposed to Realism.

The French Idealist Jules Lachelier defined Idealism as the doctrine that the world (at least knowable by me) is made up exclusively of representations. In the terminology of this essay, the world for the Idealist entirely consists of objective being. But intelligible representations (i.e., mathematical and metaphysical objects) are objects for a single identical thinking subject present in all thinkers. Multiplicity of subjects exists only at the level of feeling subjects and their sensory representations (Lachelier, 1905: 439).[7]

Phenomenalism holds that immediate experience is exclusively of private, transitory, probably mental existents that may also be called sensations, sense data, ideas, representations, or impressions. So in the terminology of this essay, all objects of immediate experience reduce to objective being. Phenomenalism holds that all material objects reduce to sets, patterns and successions of such transitory objective existents. Unlike Idealism, it cannot, in its pure form, admit an identical subject present to all human subjects (e.g., Berkeley's God). For it admits only observed phenomena, and God is not observed (Hirst, 1967b: 130-131).

Realist philosophers hold that not all objects of experience reduce to objective being. Realists are either Indirect Realists or Direct Realists.

Indirect Realists hold that *all direct* objects of experience reduce to mere objective being. But these direct objects of experience represent other indirect objects that do not reduce to mere objective being. Descartes' direct objects of thought are modes of his own thinking (i.e., reduce to mere objective being); but these objects represent a real God and real bodies. However Descartes was a direct Realist as regards himself; because the *cogito* supposedly reveals his own substance which has real existence. Descartes is not a thorough-going Indirect Realist. Herbert Feigl is a thorough-going Indirect Realist. *All* objects that we immediately experience are psychological states (Psis). But Feigl believes that these Psis are rigorously identical with neurophysiological processes in the brain. But this identity is not experienced and cannot be experienced; it can only be inferred (Feigl, 1958a: 380, 463-465). Hence, according to Feigl, all objects of experience entirely reduce to mere objective being. But these direct objects are grounds for inferring the existence of real objects.

According to Van Riet's history of Neo-Thomist epistemology during the past hundred years, all but very few among the innumerable authors were Indirect Realists (Van Riet, 1946: II, 289-290). For the vast majority of Neo-Thomist epistemologists what is directly known is objects that entirely reduce to objective being; either universal necessary principles, or being as possible being, or possible essences (Van Riet, 1946: II, 291-295). All these objects entirely reduce to objective being because no part of any one of them could exist except as an object of cognition. Real beings are known only indirectly through these merely objective beings.

David Hume is also an Indirect Realist. But Hume's Indirect Realism is not based on evidence whether directly experienced or proved from data. It is based on inexorable natural belief:

> Thus the sceptic still continues to reason and believe, even tho' he asserts, that he cannot defend his reason by reason; and by the same rule he must assent to the principle concerning the existence of body, tho' he cannot pretend by any arguments of philosophy to maintain its veracity. Nature has not left this to his choice, and has doubtless esteem'd it an affair of too great importance to be trusted to our uncertain reasonings and speculations. We may well ask, *What causes induce us to believe in the existence of body?* but 'tis in vain to ask, *Whether there be body or not?* That is a point, which we must take for granted in all our reasonings. (Hume, 1739: *A Treatise of Human Nature*, Book I, Part IV, Section II, p. 478).

Norman Kemp Smith (1941: 502-503) holds that Hume's doctrine of real substance differs from traditional substance-philosophy by its substituting *belief* in substance for the older *evidence* for substance.

Now of all forms of Indirect Realism the fideist form alone is logically coherent. For it is not logically incoherent to hold that we are naturally forced to believe in reality of bodies although reason cannot justify that belief. In the terminology of this essay, all objects of experience reduce to mind-dependent objective being; nevertheless natural belief can project us into the unknown beyond mind-dependent objects.

But the other forms of Indirect Realism claim evidence for their view where no evidence is available according to their position. As Realism their position claims to know what exists independently of the mind. But all data for indirect Realism are mind-dependent. How can it come to know mind-independent reality from data that are entirely mind-dependent? Whatever else it comes to know can be nothing more than the mind-dependent outcome of its mind-dependent data. Its mind-dependent data are a blindfold that hides any evidence for mind-independent reality.

Common sense Direct Realists hold that common sense is right: we directly perceive things and events outside us, e.g., people's faces (Ryle, 1954: 100-101, 109; Addis and Lewis, 1965: 63; Hirst, 1967c: 78-80). Gilbert Ryle is an outstanding common sense Direct Realist. Ryle holds that physiology and psychology have nothing to say about *what* seeing and hearing *are*, though they can give valuable information about how we digest food and what happens inside us when we drink alcohol (Ryle, 1954: 100). Secondly, the assumption that we see Phis inside us makes for an infinite regress. In order to see the zigzag lines on an encephalogram, the physiologist would need another physiologist to examine his brain on an encephalogram; and this second physiologist would have the same need, and so on to infinity (Ryle, 1954: pp. 100-101). Thirdly, physiologists have not even an idea of how to set up an experiment that traces events from Phis through Psis; the alleged process is inaccessible to observation and experimentation (Ryle, 1954: 101). Fourthly, it is contrary to linguistic usage to identify seeing and hearing with Psis like pain and tickle or with Phis like inflammation and knee jerk.

Fifthly, getting to what perception is, seeing and hearing are scoring an investigational success. They are like winning a race or scoring a goal. As Aristotle said (c. 348-330BC, *Metaphysics*, IV; VI, chs. 7-10), seeing is not a process of change. Like winning a race, seeing does not take place in time as a process of change does. Once I see, I have seen, just as once the runner wins, he has won; running a race takes time, winning is only at the finish of the race, and that is not in time. Hence seeing and hearing cannot be physiological or psychological processes of change, since change is in time (Ryle, 1954: 102-103). But seeing and hearing differ from winning a race inasmuch as the latter is behavior learned from others, whereas seeing and hearing are not. Moreover, seeing and hearing are best judged accurate by the individual, whereas winning a race is not (Ryle, 1954: 106-109).

I agree with all five of Ryle's arguments. But these arguments prove only public objects, not mind-independent public objects. Now we have seen that public objects need not be real. Admission of public objects does not convince a Heidegger or a Quine of the truth of Realism. The further question must be raised: granted that people's faces are public objects, what aspects of people's faces are mind-independent objects, irreducible to objective being? How can people's faces as public objects seen by us be mind-independent public objects? Do their faces exist only while seen in public? I suggest that only as present to us by real relations are their faces directly experienced as mind-independent objects. But Ryle is a common sense direct Realist: he thinks that he can dispense with this kind of subtle distinction between things in their intrinsic character and their real relation to us. As a common sense direct Realist he holds that a philosopher should stick to what "we ordinarily suppose," to our "unscheduled but well-disciplined conduct in ratiocination" about and "our untechnical generalities about seeing and hearing" (Ryle, 1954: 109-110). But, alas, this method does not lead him to distinguish between public objects and mind-independent real objects. Yet that distinction is fundamental to settling the claims of Realism.

According to Van Riet, many false problems arose for neo-Thomistic epistemologists because of the falsely "self-evident principle that the intellect is the faculty of the universal and that it is radically distinct from sensibility, the faculty of the singular" (Van Riet, 1946: II, 287). No doubt the chief false problem was: how to have an epistemology committed to evidence only (thus rejecting Hume's fideist indirect Realism) and yet have indirect Realism. Almost all of them were indirect Realists. As Thomists they held the doctrine that the intellect alone can know mind-independent reality as such. Now they separated the intelligible from the sensible in experience, as Van Riet reports. So they held that all directly intelligible objects were universal only: namely, universal necessary principles, or being as possible being, or possible essences. Hence the sole faculty capable of knowing mind-independent reality had as direct objects only what reduced entirely to mere objective being. For universal necessary principles, or being as possible being, or possible essences cannot exist except as objects of cognition. So the radical separation of the intelligible from the sensible in experience forced them into indirect Realism. Yet Aquinas had held, as cited earlier (1266-1274d), that the distinction of the intelligible from the sensible is not discernible in experience (*Summa Theologiae*, I, q. 87, art. 1). In contemporary philosophy, the distinction of the intellect from the senses as a distinct faculty is almost an unknown hypothesis, let alone an accepted fact of experience. History seems to have borne Aquinas out.

Our essay concerns direct experiential data only. Hence the distinction of the intelligible from the sensible does not concern us. In the direct data of experience, we find things that the traditional distinction between intellect and sense would allot to one or the other. What is directly experienced is psycho-socio-cultural objects; e.g., angrily shouting delegates at a national party convention seen on TV.

Different approaches have led us to admit direct experience of public objects. Kant (1787: 83-84) held that: "the universal communicability of our knowledge—is presupposed in every logic and every principle of knowledge that is not one of scepticism."[8] But communication is about public objects. Heidegger's philosophy of historically determined experience (though perhaps exaggerated in claiming complete determinism), at least proves public objects, since philosophical experience can only be historically determined by public objects. Ryle's arguments convincingly proved public objects. Then I have myself argued that one could not lead one's own private life without immediate experience of public objects as defined by public language; e.g., without recognizing chairs as something to sit on, beds as something to sleep in, stairs as something to climb, automobiles as something to drive. Hence, we do not approach the critical epistemological question with the ego-centric data of Bertrand Russell, but with public objects directly experienced.

Section 8. The results of our epistemological survey.

So we can cull the results of this survey. Common sense Direct Realism is not a valid critical epistemological position. Neither is Indirect Realism except in its fideist variety. Idealism and Phenomenalism have not been criticized. But it can be said in their favor that we directly experience a great abundance of mind-dependent objects that entirely reduce to objective being. Of the realist doctrines that seem plausible, I find only the doctrine allowing direct experience of real relations alone. This is the hypothesis here to be examined. Indirect fideist Realism seems hardly plausible even though it is not a logically incoherent position. To say that *I believe that* I have hands and feet seems to remove knowledge from the most evident of all things. It would therefore remove all valid knowledge claims. Such a position is hardly plausible, even if it cannot be excluded altogether. Now in view of the disparate epistemologies just enumerated as plausible, we must admit that Heidegger may be right after all. If such disparate philosophies of direct experience are philosophically plausible, perhaps the conviction of their respective partisans is due to their philosophical experience being completely historically determined. But we have seen that the doctrine of direct experience of public objects constitutes a revolution in epistemology. Perhaps the new situation permits the critical problem to be solved in favor of direct Realism through experience of real relations alone.

But public objects need not be mind-independent objects. Hence it is fallacious to orient the epistemological question around the problem of error. Orientation of the question around error assumes that by contrast to a normal situation of knowing mind-independent reality some few errors occur. The initial reading of the epistemological question is quite different; namely, in a historical "Western World" as background to public objects, which background entirely reduces to mere objective being, *do any of these objects not reduce entirely to objective being*? Hence the true question is: is error possible, i.e., is non-conformity to mind-independent reality possible, since it is uncertain whether we can know mind-independent reality? The initial outlook of epistemology can distinguish claims about orthodoxy or heresy, ingroup opinion or outgroup opinion, group opinion or individual opinion. But it cannot initially distinguish between mind-independent and mind-dependent objects. And hence it cannot have a problem of error as non-conformity to mind-independent objects.

The question arises: if what we directly experience is things in a historical world, how can perception be localized in the brain? This question asks about the *intrinsic nature* of experience; namely, about its property of being localized in the brain. Hence the answer to this question does not fall under direct experience, as shown above. So the question does not pertain to this essay. But no *right answer* could ever be given that destroys a fact of direct experience; namely, that we directly experience things in a historical world. Moreover, an explanation implying any form of indirect realism, except the fideistic form, is a false form of realism as shown above. For example, Herbert Feigl's hypothesis of identity between experience and brain states is indirect realism based on "logical analysis"; it is not fideistic. Now the sole reality with which experience is identified in this identity hypothesis can never be directly experienced. As Feigl admits for his form of realism, "there could not be any . . . conceivable empirical evidence" (Feigl, 1958a: 464). That is false realism, because from mere "objective" being it claims to conclude logically to reality. See below for a more complete answer to Feigl.

Feigl's identity hypothesis to explain objects of direct experience derives from the total separation in experience of elements traditionally classified as sensible and intelligible. The neo-Thomist epistemologists usually committed the same error. They separated the intelligible from the sensible in direct experience, and built on the intelligible alone. So their epistemology was built on universal necessary principles, or possible being, or possible essences. The identity hypothesis makes the same discrimination of sensible and intelligible elements in direct experience: but it chooses to build all experience out of "raw feels": love, hatred, tune as heard, etc. (Feigl, 1958a: 456). But the fact is that the distinction of the sensible and of the intelligible is a theoretical construct, as Aquinas long ago pointed out. It is not directly experienced: it is a philosophical conclusion. A conclusion is an honorable position in Aristotelian philosophy. It is a position that God also occupies.

And so I can conclude this chapter with the following right position of the problem of Realism. Does one directly experience the real in public objects? And the "real" means what does not totally reduce to objective being.

Chapter III

EXPERIENCE OF REAL RELATIONS

Section 1. Do I have direct private experience of real relations between public objects?

Our study has yielded five characteristics of direct private experience. 1. It is of public objects. 2. It does not directly experience the intrinsic natures and properties of things. 3. It does not discern the sensible from the intelligible. 4. Public objects are experienced against the background of a World (e.g., the Western World) that entirely reduces to objective being. 5. One's self and other selves are experienced as terms of the psycho-social-cultural unreal relations that characterize our historical world. As such, self and selves are mere mind-dependent terms of unreal relations.

In order to discover real relations we need a nominal description of what one is. A real relation can be described by contrasting it with familiarly experienced public objects such as Santa Claus. Santa Claus is experienced as a public object that entirely reduces to objective being. Such a public object as Santa Claus is something related to my experience. It is a public object that entirely reduces to mere objective being, since Santa is merely an unreal object in our historical world. (I take the broad sense of "objective being" as object of psychic life including actual and habitual, cognitive and appetitive, conscious and unconscious life). The relation of my experience to Santa Claus is therefore likewise a relation that entirely reduces to objective being, since Santa cannot exist except as object of psychic life. Now if I experience any public object that does not entirely reduce to mere objective being, it too will be an object related to my experience. But, by hypothesis, this object does not entirely reduce to mere objective being. Hence the relation of my experience to such an object will itself be irreducible to mere objective being. Such a relation will rightly be called a *real relation*.

In our Western World, it is customary to distinguish between natural objects and mind-dependent objects. Among mind-dependent objects psychological objects are distinguished from social objects like the mixed economy and from cultural objects like literature. Some public objects are the concern of the "natural" sciences of biology, physics and chemistry. Some public objects are the concern of psychology, sociology and cultural anthropology. "Natural" things are public objects believed to be mind-independent. Because of this belief the question whether one experiences mind-independent reality appears idle and silly to people not trained in philosophy. The difference between real public objects such as horses or stones and mind-dependent public objects such as movies or Santa Claus is believed to be a matter of daily experience.

This difference between public objects such as Santa Claus and public objects such as stones is not merely a matter of public belief. Stones, rivers, flowers and trees are rightly called "natural" because they manifest among themselves a constant order that does not reciprocate to our psycho-social-cultural relations to them. Cats, dogs, and horses are public objects that somewhat reciprocate our psycho-social-cultural relations to them. For they share in feelings of pleasure, displeasure or anger without the social and cultural relations that are characteristically human: marriage, religion and politics. To the extent of their sharing, they are part of our mind-dependent world. Small children likewise share in a limited way the mind-dependent world. But Santa Claus does not reciprocate at all to our relations to him because he totally reduces to objective being, since he is nothing but the term of psychic or social or cultural relations or some combination of these. Stones, rivers, flowers and trees are public objects similar to Santa Claus inasmuch as they do not at all reciprocate to our psychic, social, or cultural relations to them. But they are unlike Santa Claus inasmuch as they manifest among themselves a nameless constant order. This constant order of "natural" public objects among themselves is experienced as irreducible to psychic, or social, or cultural relations which entirely reduce to objective being. It is difficult to say what this constant order may be. But I directly experience this nameless constant order as irreducible to mere objective being. That irreducibility is directly experienced and not merely imagined.

It is only formation in the philosophical tradition that enables one to determine more accurately what one directly experiences that is irreducible to objective being. It is some public object. It is not the intrinsic natures or properties of things. It is experienced as having conjointly the characteristics of the sensible and of the intelligible. It is experienced as within a mind-dependent historical world as background. It is experienced as an object for a public of mind-dependent psycho-social-cultural selves that terminate that world's mind-dependent relations.

Since the constant order of "natural" public objects is not their intrinsic natures or properties, it is something extrinsic and relative. Now our bodies are among the "natural" public objects. Some relations are directly experienced in presence of our bodies. Errors may occur. But frequently, what is directly experienced as irreducible to objective being is relations between present "natural" public objects. Relations between the burning fire, the cold room and my body are frequently experienced as *real* relations. But the intrinsic character of these terms of relations is not directly experienced. For we do not directly experience the intrinsic nature or properties of burning fire, cold room or my body, as I have previously shown.

On the other hand, certain relations that entirely reduce to mere objective being have been shown by psychology to characterize perception. Such are the relations of figure to ground; and for enduring perceiving, the constancy of objects relating to changing backgrounds: the apparent motion of objects resulting from adjacent stimuli, e.g., points on a TV screen (Hirst, 1967a: 85).

It is precisely *because we distinguish these unreal relations from relations between natural bodies that we perceive what we do.* Because I perceive apparent motions and apparent object-constancy of figures on changing backgrounds of the TV screen, and see these *as apparent*, I perceive my head's stationary *real* relation to the TV set. I am tranquilly absorbed in the stirring events in the TV movie because I perceive these as unreal by contrast to my tranquil real relation to the TV set.

It is because I perceive figure and ground as unreal relations that I immediately perceive that my pointing finger is smaller than the distant skyscraper. But if I take pains to attend, the *appearance* is that my finger is not smaller than the skyscraper. The skyscraper hanging in the background of the blocks where I am walking seems to get larger and larger. As I get nearer, its color seems to change from blue-gray to whitish. But I am not perturbed by this apparent behavior of the skyscraper, as if it were trying to frighten me. I distinguish these apparent relations to the changing backgrounds from its real relation to me. *I directly experience my real relation to it and its to me by the very perceiving of these apparent relations as unreal.* I perceive the real relation by contrast with relations that entirely reduce to objective being.

Directly experienced real relations do not reveal the intrinsic natures or properties of their terms. We do not directly experience dogs and cats as *real* dogs and *real* cats. We experience directly real relations between public objects that are dogs and cats. And thus *extrinsically* we experience the reality of dogs and cats through the real relations of which they are the real terms. Their intrinsic natures and properties remain unexperienced except as real Xs. Direct experience does not settle the question whether dogs and cats have continuous extension: it may be that a living body is mostly empty space as the atomic constitution of matter is sometimes stated. Direct experience can neither support nor disqualify such positions. For it does not directly attain the intrinsic properties of things. For such questions reasoning must take over where direct experience leaves off.

Real relations give us only an extrinsic experience of their real terms. But that extrinsic experience is not general and abstract. Extrinsic and intrinsic do not differ in concreteness, but only in understanding of their objects. Hence experience of real relations between public objects justifies speaking of real trees, real dogs and real people quite as concretely as if we understood their intrinsic natures and properties.

Kant and Russell manifested the existence of real relations in private experience. But they did not take private experience as directly concerned with public objects. Thus they diminished the content of private experience and so made the manifestation of real relations less evident. Their method is good only *ad hominem* for people who do not grant direct experience of public objects.

In a certain way, our Western World is unreal. It exists only as a cultural network of historic institutions and institutionally defined roles of individuals and groups. In this way our Western World is a complex of unreal relations. Now we have shown that our bodies and those of other people are terms of real relations, for they are "natural" public objects whose relations are irreducible to objective being. So we can rightly speak of private experience of "real people" just as we speak of private experience of "real stones" and "real trees".

However, one's private experience of other people as other selves reveals more than relations to other public "natural" bodies. Direct private experience reveals other subjectivities that do not reduce to objective being for me. I experience other people as a constant source of surprise and incalculable novelty. I experience the subjectivity of another person as an object that cannot be reduced to mere objective being for me: *otherwise our duality would disappear*. So I experience a novel kind of real relation to other people because their subjectivity cannot entirely reduce to objective being for me.

This novel kind of real relation is experienced as contrasted with unreal cultural relations of our historical world. For example, in our Western World, the culture defines certain behavior as expected between an adult man and another man's wife. Even when freely jesting with married women this unreal cultural relation is the unreal ingredient in my experience that gives the genuine interpretation to the real relations involved in jesting. The real relations involved in free jesting are unprogrammed and unforeseeable, and so cannot be reduced to objective being. The expected unreal cultural relation in question is capable of being stated in clear negative terms and some positive ones: it can be reduced to mere objective being.

In the IInd Meditation Descartes says the hats and coats passing beneath his window might belong to robots (Descartes, 1641a: 32, p. 155 of English text). Today, we have marvelous robots such as the airman I saw in the Aerospace Museum in Washington D.C. He gives a talk, moves around in his seat, sweats and gesticulates. It is very difficult to distinguish that robot from a living person. Might not all other people besides me be mere robots? According to Herbert Feigl (1958a: 423):

> If by "thinking" one means a kind of performance which, starting with "input" premises yields "output" conclusions of deductive or inductive inference, and consists (at least) in certain observable relations between *input* and *output*, then there is no doubt that certain types of robots or computers do think. (Author's emphasis).

Once again the question arises: might not all other people besides me be robots?

In reply, I need only remark that robots, however sophisticated, have no self. Having no self, they do not share in our historical Western World. If the airman-robot were moved to a Marxist capital city, it would function just as it does in our own historical world. For the robot is never in a historical world as a subject, only as a "natural" public object. For the robot, public objects do not exist. Hence, for it, no historical world exists, since a historical world consists entirely of public historical objects. While in the Museum, I had a real relation to the robot as to a "natural" public object typical of Western technological skill. The robot was also for me a bizarre public object at which I marveled along with other tourists to the National Capital. In that amazing public object so expressive of our Western World I shared with the other tourists. In sharing their amazement at our technology, I experienced their subjectivities not only as irreducible to mere objective being for me; but I also felt their sharing in my historical world. For their subjectivity irreducible to objective being for me was precisely their amazement at this symbol of our historical world. So I experienced those tourists as objects quite different from the robot. I experienced real relations to them as subjectivities who shared my historical world. In other words, I experienced real human relations to them as persons.

I also enjoy unique real relations to higher animals, especially with the family dog. In the dog I also experience a subjectivity that does not entirely reduce to objective being for me. However, my real relations with the dog differ from those with persons because the dog does not share in my historical Western World.

Section 2. Objections against the existence of real relations.

William of Ockham (d. 1349) did not deny the existence of real relations (c.1320-1328: 120):

> Opposition in terms of relatives obtains among names which cannot be affirmed of the same thing with respect to the same thing. This holds true whether things outside the soul are opposed as relatives or not. It is not, however, because I deny that relations are things outside the mind that I speak of names as relatives. One could use the name apropos of things as well as the names of things.[1]

However, Ockham denied real relations were a *distinct category of reality*. He denied that real relations were distinct from things related (*ibid.*, 168):

> The distinction of being into absolute and relative is not a distinction of being qua being, but a distinction between terms. It is like the distinctions between abstract and concrete terms, proper and appelative terms, and nouns and adjectives. For on what basis could a thing be called absolute? . . . Because it does not require or depend on something else? In that case no accident would be an absolute thing, nor would substantial form, nor any created thing; for each of these requires something else and depends upon something else for its existence.[2]

Hence Ockham's position is not opposed to what I am defending as real relations. For I am not propounding real relations as distinct in some determinate way from their terms. I am saying that real relations as experienced do not reveal the intrinsic nature of their terms. Hence the distinction of real relations from the intrinsic nature of their terms is not experienced, in my view. If Ockham were right that real relations and their terms have the same nature, my position would still stand unaffected.

Locke (1690: 430) denied the existence of real relations:

> Relation [is] . . . not contained in the real existence of things, but [is] something extraneous and superinduced.

The reason why Locke denied real relations is because relations cease from existence without any alteration in the thing that was related (*ibid.*, pp. 428-429, par. 5):

> Caius, whom I consider today as a father, ceases to be so tomorrow, only by the death of his son, without any alteration made in himself. Nay, barely by the mind's changing the object to which it compares anything, the same thing is capable of having contrary denominations at the same time: v.g. Caius, compared to several persons, may truly be said to be older and younger, stronger and weaker, etc.

To Locke's objection, I reply thus. Relations indirectly manifest the mysterious intrinsic natures of things and mysterious changes in intrinsic natures. But mysteriousness of intrinsic natures and their mysterious changes do not disprove realities that we directly experience. Attraction, repulsion and vital movements of living matter are mysterious. But these changing relations are real facts despite the mystery. Caius being stronger than some and weaker than others is an example of a mysterious fact.

Moreover the argument does not hold against observed mutually related changes: for example, experience of a choir of singers or of a chorus of dancers. Here observable changes in some are coordinated with observable changes in the others.

Locke's argument does show that many alleged real relations may not be real. For example, what is the evidence that all white things in the universe are really related? Such a relation reeks of the mind's universalizing activity. It seems more likely to be a mind-dependent relation.

By contrast, because we observe the white petals of a morning glory opening together, we find them really related white things. Because we find the white furs of polar bears aid in species identification, we find these white things to be really related.

Finally, despite explicit denial of real relations, Locke has passages that seem to admit real relations. James Gibson (1960: 195) points out that for Locke: "Things agree or disagree as they really are." In particular, I find a doctrine of real relations in his account of 'ideas.'

Locke (1690: 170 par. 9) calls certain of our ideas, "ideas of primary qualities of body," namely those of "solidity, extension, figure, or mobility." By contrast our ideas of colors, sounds, and tastes are called "secondary qualities". Now the ideas of primary qualities of bodies are "resemblances" of the real qualities of bodies, and "their patterns do really exist in the bodies themselves." But the ideas of secondary qualities have no resemblance to the real patterns existing in bodies (*ibid.*, Par. 15):

> The ideas of primary qualities of bodies are resemblances of them, and their patterns do really exist in the bodies themselves, but the ideas produced in us by these secondary qualities have no resemblance of them at all.

Now the real patterns existing in bodies produce in us our ideas of primary qualities (*ibid.*, Par. 9):

> Primary qualities of body . . . I think we may observe to produce simple ideas in us, viz. solidity, extension, figure, motion or rest . . .

Furthermore, according to Locke, "ideas of primary qualities are all data of external sense" (*ibid.*, p. 151f. and p. 158, Par. 1). Hence these "primary qualities of bodies" are objects of present experience in the presence of bodies. So our "ideas of primary qualities" resemble the real patterns existing in bodies present to us. Furthermore, these existing patterns produce our "ideas of primary qualities." Such is Locke's position.

Our present experience, produced in us by patterns really existing in bodies, resemble those real patterns. So such ideas and those real patterns are really coordinated. Hence they are really related.

It is frequently objected that our mental images cannot resemble what exists outside the mind. For it seems mental images and extra-mental things are too diverse to allow of resemblance. Hence Locke would be wrong in admitting this resemblance. Consequently, the argument I draw from his admission of this resemblance would be fallacious. Now Aquinas already encountered this objection that ideas cannot be similar to their extramental objects. He countered the objection by observing (Aquinas, 1256-1259):

> Although in the mind there are only immaterial forms, these can be like-nesses of material things. For it is not necessary that the likeness and that of which it is the likeness have the same manner of existence, but only that they agree in intelligible character, just as the form of man in a golden statue need not have the same kind of existence as the form of man in bones and flesh. (*De Veritate*, q. 10, art. 4 ad 4).[3]

In Chapter II I presented Feigl's doctrine of hypothetical identity of brain states and "raw feels", i.e., sensations of color, sound, fear, etc. There, not yet having manifested direct experience of real relations, I could only reply to his position what can in general be said against Indirect Realism: namely, that one cannot argue logically from mere objective being to reality independent of objective being. Now I can thus answer Feigl. What we directly experience are real relations from eyes, ears, and feet to extrabodily things of unknown nature. These real temporal relations are directly experienced as distinct from unreal relations of our historical world: e.g., that we are climbing the steps of the Capitol in Washington on which presidents take their oath of office. It is not the *terms* of these relations that are directly experienced (e.g., color, sound, awe, eyes, ears, feet, Capitol steps). Philosophy has long understood that color, sound, awe, are terms whose intrinsic natures are not given in direct experience. Modern science has now shown the apparent bodily terms of these relations (eyes, ears, feet) are but *penultimate terms* extending the brain. But the real temporal relations directly experienced *remain irreducible* despite our changed understanding of their *intrabodily and extrabodily terms*. For these terms were never experienced *as real* except through the real relations between them; and they were never experienced in their intrinsic nature. These relations are real because they do not totally reduce either to our historical political world or to simultaneous space-time biologically determined by the brain.

When unaware of philosophy and science, I experience real relations of my eyes, ears, and feet to the Capitol stairs I ascend. When philosophy and science penetrate my perception, I directly experience *the same real relations* between eyes, ears and feet (*as penultimate terms*) to the color, sound and resistance of the steps (as realities of unknown nature). Of course, the term "brain" does not declare its "intrinsic nature" in the philosophic sense. Science does not claim to know the intrinsic nature of matter. Science and philosophy have taught me that the historical world without me and the biologically determined projections of the brain within me color my perception of real relations. But I distinguish the unreal "coloration" from the real temporal relations with which the "colors" are perceptually identified.

Leibniz (1704: 148) unequivocally denied the existence of real relations:

> This division of the objects of our thought into substances, modes, and relations is sufficiently to my taste. I believe that qualities are only modifications of substances, and that the understanding adds thereto the relations. (Book II, ch. XII, par. 5.)[4]

At first sight, this denial of real relations does not seem to shake his solidly grounded Realism. His Realism seems very well rooted in his doctrine of Monads. For Monads are substances. Moreover, they are "simple" substances without parts (Leibniz, 1714a: 1044 par. 1-3):

> 1. The *monad* which we are to discuss here is nothing but a simple substance which enters into compounds. *Simple* means without parts (*Theodicy*, Sec. 10).
> 2. There must be simple substances, since there are compounds, for the compounded is but a collection or an *aggregate* of simples.
> 3. But where there are no parts, it is impossible to have either extension, or figure, or divisibility. The monads are the true atoms of nature; in a word, they are the elements of things.[5]

Since the monads have neither extension, figure nor divisibility, they are "incorporeal" (*ibid.*, par. 18). Hence his denial of real relations does not seem to undermine his epistemological Realism, grounded in incorporeal substances.

However, Leibniz' Realism is merely apparent. For the so-called "substance" in which it is grounded entirely reduces to objective being. This is clear from two facts. 1. The simple-monad-substance has no qualities except *perceptions*. 2. The so-called "substance" does not differ from its activity (i.e., from its perception). As to the first point (Leibniz, 1714b: 1035):

> 1. There must of necessity be simple substances everywhere, for without simple substances there would be no compounds. As a result, the whole of nature is full of life.

2. *Monads*, having no parts, can neither be formed nor unmade. They can neither begin nor end naturally, and therefore they last as long as the universe, which will change but will not be destroyed. They cannot have shapes, for then they would have parts. It follows that one monad by itself and at a single moment cannot be distinguished from another except by its internal qualities and actions, and these can only be its *perceptions*—that is to say, the representations of the compound, or of that which is without, in the simple—and its *appetitions*—that is to say, its tendencies from one perception to another—which are the principles of change.[6]

As to the second point, that its activity (of perceiving) does not differ from its substance:

The concept of *forces* or *powers*, which the Germans call *Kraft* and the French *la force*, and for whose explanation I have set up a distinct science of *dynamics*, brings the strongest light to bear upon our understanding of the true concept of *substance*. Active force differs from the mere power familiar to the Schools, for the active power or faculty of the Scholastics is nothing but a close [propinqua] possibility of acting, which needs an external excitation or a stimulus, as it were, to be transferred into action. Active force, in contrast, contains a certain action or entelechy and is thus midway between the faculty of acting and the action itself and needs no help but only the removal of an impediment. This can be illustrated by the example of a heavy hanging body which strains at the rope which holds it or by a bent bow. (Leibniz, 1694: 709).[7]

But it may be objected, Leibniz' "substance" is not therefore totally reduced to mere objective being. For perception is a psychic *reality*. Perception is a mind-independent reality: "it does not totally reduce to mere objective being."

However, this objection does not hold in the philosophy of Leibniz. According to him, the perceptions of an individual depend on the logical nexus of possible events best for the individual. Thus the perceptions as mind-dependent events depend on the contingent logical nexus of best possibilities. But that contingent logical nexus is mere objective being. Hence mind-dependent perceptions depend on mere objective being. Leibniz writes (Leibniz, 1686: 477-478) that one might

show that the future dictatorship of Caesar is based in his concept or nature and that there is a reason in that concept why he resolved to cross the Rubicon . . . These proofs are not demonstrations of necessity, since these reasons are based only on the principle of the contingency or of the existence of things, that is to say, on what is or appears to be the best among several equally possible things. (*Discourse on Metaphysics*, par. 13).[8]

Leibniz equates "existence" with the "best" possible. But the best possible is mere objective being. Consequently, Leibniz defines the nature of an individual substance as what has the complete concept whence flow all that can be attributed to it (Leibniz, 1686: 472):

> It is the nature of an individual substance or complete being to have a concept so complete that it is sufficient to make us understand and deduce from it all the predicates of the subject to which the concept is attributed. (*Ibid.*, par. 8).[9]

But a concept is mere objective being. Since the nature of the individual is this complete concept, its mind-dependent perceptions reduce to the mere objective being from which they flow. Therefore the "substance"-monad entirely reduces to mere objective being.

Moreover, the world a monad experiences reduces entirely to objective being. It experiences a "world within". As experienced, this world within is a private object for that monad. It is not known as a public object except through knowledge of God:

> But we have already said, and it follows from what we have just said, that each substance is as a world apart, independent of everything outside of itself except God. Thus all our phenomena, that is to say, all the things that can ever happen to us, are only the results of our own being. And, since these phenomena maintain a certain order which conforms to our nature or so to speak, to the world which is within us, so that we are able to make observations that are useful for controlling our own conduct and justified by the success of future phenomena, with the result that we can often judge the future by the past without deceiving ourselves, this would be sufficient to enable us to say that these phenomena are true, without being put to the task of inquiring whether they are outside of us and whether others perceive them also . . . It is only God (from whom all individuals emanate continually and who sees the universe not only as they see it but also entirely differently from all of them), who is the cause of this correspondence between their phenomena and who makes public to all that which is peculiar to one; otherwise, there would be no interconnection. (Leibniz, 1686: 479 par. 14).[10]

Moreover, the private world within is not experienced as a *reality*:

> So only God constitutes the link or communication between the substances, and it is through him that the phenomena of the one meet with and agree with those of the others and that consequently there is reality in our perceptions. (*Ibid.*, pp. 499-500 par. 32).[11]

However, God's existence is not experienced, but needs demonstration, which Leibniz attempts to provide by several proofs (Leibniz, 1714a: par. 36-41). Hence, the world as experienced reveals nothing but private objects that totally reduce to objective being.

Leibniz believed that he could prove the existence of God and then through God establish the reality of our perceptions, so that each monad's private world would connect with the world of other monads. But the antecedent of his argument is mere mind-dependent objects that totally reduce to objective being. Hence the consequent can be no more: i.e., the mere idea of God that totally reduces to objective being. Hence, Solipsism is the final as well as the initial state of Leibniz' philosophy.

Leibniz reduces one's whole experiential world to mere objective being. Even one's perceptions reduce to the concept of one's individual substance. By reducing all experiential objects to objective being Leibniz cuts off all possible contact with reality whether by experience or reasoning. Now the contrary opposite of his position is experience of some objects that do not entirely reduce to mere objective being. Such objects are, for example, other people, since they are not entirely reducible to mere objective being for me. But other people are objects relative to my experience. Since other people do not entirely reduce to objective being, my relation to them is a real relation. Indeed, "an experiential object that does not entirely reduce to objective being" and a "real relation" are but *two expressions for the same fact*. For an experiential object is relative to my experience. So such an object irreducible to my experience names my relation to others as irreducible to my experience: i.e., it names my relation to them as a real relation. By experience of real relations to other people I escape both Solipsism and the prison of mere objective being. I experience mind-independent reality in my relations to other people.

Therefore experience of real relations is the contrary opposite of experiencing only objects that totally reduce to mere objective being. Hence philosophers of experience have wisely built their epistemological Realism on experience of real relations. *It is not possible to do otherwise.*

Thus I conclude the investigation of private experience. Private experience of real relations is a fact. It yields only indirect experience of the intrinsic nature of things: one experiences the reality of things extrinsically through real relations to them. Among real relations I experience, real human relations are a unique kind. For through real human relations I experience indirectly real persons who share my historical Western World. The question still remains whether I have indirect experience of the public as real. To this question I now turn.

Section 3. Do I have immediate experience of the public as real?

Direct experience and immediate experience are not the same. I directly experience real relations. But I only indirectly experience their real terms, since I experience them only extrinsically as terms of real relations. However, I nevertheless *immediately experience their real terms. For no inference is needed to prove the existence of the real term of a real relation.* As I experience my real relation of speaking to you, I need no proof you are being spoken to. The real relation itself *immediately* manifests its real term. Hence, I indirectly but immediately experience the real terms of real relations. By contrast, mediately experienced real objects are known only by inference. They are not experienced objects at all, since they are not manifested in experience as real.

Immediate experience of public objects signified in public language is a common thesis since Wittgenstein's attack on private language (Wittgenstein, 1936-1949, n. 256 ff.; Castañeda, 1967: 458). However, authors who accept immediate experience of public objects still maintain that the public itself is not immediately experienced, but only inferred (Feigl, 1958b: 986-987; Malcolm, 1958: 969, Castañeda, 1962: 533). For according to the classical English language philosophy, it is impossible to have immediate experience of other minds.

Now it is impossible to hold for immediate experience of public objects and not to hold for immediate experience of the public. For a public object is the proper correlative of the public for which it is an object. Either objects are immediately experienced as public and so the public as their correlative is immediately though indirectly experienced; or all objects immediately experienced are private, and the public is mediately inferred from private objects. But in this second thesis no immediate experience of public language can be admitted. Now this consequence has not been acceptable since Wittgenstein's attack on private language.

Now the question about immediate experience of public objects and the question about immediate experience of *real* public objects are distinct questions. I immediately experience public language and the objects signified by public language. But the terms so signified are merely the terms of unreal linguistic relations. I have direct immediate experience of systems of unreal social relations (political and economic systems) and of systems of unreal cultural relations (science and literature). The fact that I have immediately and indirectly experienced these terms as terms of unreal relations does not prove that they entirely reduce to objective being. But these terms are *at least immediately but indirectly experienced as objective being*.

But it has now been shown that my direct private experience reveals real relations between public objects. These real relations justify speaking of real dogs, real cats, and real people. But they are indirectly though immediately experienced as real only inasmuch as they are extrinsically experienced terms of real relations. Their intrinsic real natures and properties are not directly experienced. In the case of other persons I experience a unique type of real relation. Towards them I immediately and indirectly experience real relations to subjectivities sharing my historical world.

So my private experience of the public concerns not merely unreal selves in an unreal historical world, but also real persons. While I indirectly and immediately experience them as unreal selves terminating unreal relations, I also indirectly and immediately experience them as persons in real human relations. Moreover I identify and distinguish these two kinds of relations in some cases. The real person to whom I really relate by slapping him on the back is the very one to whom I am relating by unreal linguistic signs describing his many unreal (i.e., culturally determined) relations as citizen, husband, property holder, etc. I distinguish and identify these two kinds of relations. I identify them as relating materially to the same person; I distinguish them as real relations to a real person as against unreal relations to a mere public object, an unreal term of those relations. Yet the real relations and the unreal relations so identified and so distinguished as directly experienced have the same individual referent: that particular individual whom I am greeting. In ordinary perception I distinguish real relations to things from the unreal psychological relations of figure to background and object-constancy to changing background; so here I distinguish real relations to this person from unreal ones though both kinds have the same individual referent.

So I have immediate but indirect private experience of the public as made up of real persons. In so doing I *privately* experience the public as real. In immediately experiencing the public as real I privately identify and distinguish real and unreal relations. But can I immediately experience that the real members of the public do the same towards one another and towards me? In other words: *can I immediately experience the public as publicly relating to one another?*

This question can be reframed in the light of what has just been said. Public objects and the public are correlatives. Correlatives immediately mutually manifest each other without inference being needed. *If I immediately experience public objects in which real and unreal relations are identified and distinguished, then I immediately but indirectly experience the public that does so.* No inference is needed because the correlatives immediately manifest each other. So the question can be reframed thus: *Do I immediately experience public objects in which real and unreal relations are distinguished and identified?*

Section 4. Do I immediately experience public objects in which real and unreal relations are distinguished and identified?

I immediately experience as public objects the political and social conflict among the people with whom I live. People around me hold sharply differing views about real relations in our society: namely about relations of management and labor, of rich and poor, and of the well educated and the poorly educated. The reality of these relations is manifest in the interrelated behavior of the people concerned. Workers' behavior is really related to management's behavior; the schooling of the children of the rich is really related to the schooling of the children of the poor by a process of withdrawal from inferior schools of the poor children. Now some people have a loyalist view towards these real relations. For them, these real relations, sanctioned by our legal system, are seen as inequalities inevitably resulting from the functioning of a free society, and as normal in American life. They believe that where inequalities are too great, the normal functioning of a free society will gradually eliminate them. Others I know have a deviationist view of these real relations. They contest the loyalist *acceptance* of these relations without denying their *reality*. Deviationists charge that at least a good part of the real relations till now sanctioned by American law and taken for granted in American life should no longer be tolerated. Real relations long identified with legal order they now declare to be devoid of true legality. The legality of the existing system of real relations is seen as spurious and unreal legality. Yet they explicitly *identify* the present "unreal" legal order with the existing real relations. They explicitly also *distinguish* this "unreal" legal order from the existing real relations as manifesting an unreal interpretation of freedom.

The deviationist view of these real relations *makes the identification and distinction of these real and unreal relations into public objects that I directly experience*. In these public objects I immediately but indirectly experience deviationist members of my circle for whom the identification and distinction of these real and unreal relations are public objects. *Hence I immediately but indirectly experience the experience of deviationists thanks to the public objects to which they relate*. Similarly, I immediately but indirectly experience the loyalist interpretation of the deviationist interpretation of these real relations. So, in fine, I immediately but indirectly experience the real relations between these groups as experienced by each. *Thus, I immediately but indirectly experience the public as a publicly experienced reality*. The public as a publicly experienced reality is the real relations between people as public objects of mutually shared experience. This statement manifests common experience as manifest in common speech.[12]

The public as a publicly experienced reality is the origin of all science and philosophy. For it is the first publicly experienced reality. *Nothing else can count as science or philosophy unless it is derived from a reality publicly experienced by a real public*.

The breaking up of a family by divorce is also an immediate experience that manifests the identification and distinction of real and unreal relations as public objects. The gap between unreal expectations of loving relations and real experienced relations becomes an immediately experienced public object for the family involved as well as for a whole network of friends and professional people. Once again, immediately but indirectly, people experience one another's mutually experienced relations. And so they immediately experience themselves as a real public.

Thus it seems that real relations are those realities that all direct experience concerns as such: for it is real relations of things present to us that are directly experienced as real. And the first real relations to be publicly experienced are *the real human relations that constitute the public* as an immediately experienced reality. That experienced reality is the origin of all science and philosophy. Hence all science and philosophy are reducible to directly experienced real relations and the public as an immediately experienced reality.

By setting forth this claim I have attempted what Quine says Carnap failed to do: namely to reduce all science to directly experienced elements. For Carnap, according to Quine (1953: 116), the directly experienced elements were sense data:

> Radical reductionism, conceived now with statements as units, set itself the task of specifying a sense-datum language and showing how to translate the rest of significant discourse, statement by statement, into it. Carnap embarked on this project in the *Aufbau*.[13]

Quine grants that Carnap's *basic formula* was what science actually does: namely, reduce everything to the statement "quality q is at the [four dimensional space-time] point-instant xyzt." But Carnap was not able to translate this statement into sense data and logic (Quine, 1953: 117):

> Carnap did not seem to recognize, however, that his treatment of physical objects fell short of reduction not merely through sketchiness, but in principle. Statements of the form 'Quality q is at point-instant x,y,z,t' were, according to his canons, to be apportioned truth values in such a way as to maximize and minimize certain over-all features, and with growth of experience the truth values were to be progressively revised in the same spirit. I think this is a good schematization (deliberately oversimplified, to be sure) of what science really does; but it provides no indication, not even the sketchiest, of how a statement of the form 'Quality q is at x,y,z,t' could ever be translated into Carnap's initial language of sense data and logic. The connective 'is at' remains an added undefined connective; the canons counsel us in its use but not in its elimination.

It is not my concern whether Quine has correctly analyzed the failure of Carnap. But I do believe that the reduction of all data of science to experienced identification and distinction of real and unreal relations can translate the typical scientific statement: "quality q is at x,y,z,t." I translate the scientific formula thus. Quality q is at x,y,z,t means in the given direct experience: quality q of unknown nature is related by a real relation identified with and distinguished from the unreal relations of measure (x.y,z,t) to some "x" of unknown nature. The "is at" which Carnap is said to be incapable of handling appears to fit spontaneously into our proposed system.

Section 5. Transition from the epistemological problem to the problem of freely chosen realities.

We have concluded that real relations experienced among the public are the origin of all science and philosophy. Such real relations are human social relations. Now human social relations experienced among the public include social relations between husband and wife, those between workers and management, and those between political candidates and electors. Such directly experienced human relations are usually considered to constitute a free society. Moreover, people claim that they at certain times experience freely choosing these relations: e.g., when they get married and when they elect to political office. We saw in the Introduction that some political scientists claim to discern from experiential data alone between freely electing and unfree balloting. The question therefore arises whether, on the basis of experiential data alone, philosophy can discern freely chosen real relations from non-free real relations. That is the problem of discerning freely chosen realities.

Chapter IV

FREELY CHOSEN REALITY

Introduction

Real human relations have now been shown to be the origin of all science and philosophy. Hence we can now answer affirmatively the question posed at the beginning of the Introduction, namely: can philosophy think reality at the level of real relations, as political scientists do? It now remains to see how political scientists treat free choice as publicly manifest in terms of real relations exclusively. Finally, I shall attempt philosophical understanding of free choice publicly manifest in real and unreal relations exclusively.

Section 1. Political scientists on real relations.

Among political scientists some are behavioralists and others are anti-behavioralists. The behavioralists have made extensive statistical studies correlating politicians' performance with voters' behavior. Their basic question is: how much does voters' behavior really relate to politicians' performance? Their general finding is that the correlation is not very high. For politicians have a peculiar professional idiom that most voters do not understand. The behaviorist seeks to determine what percent of voters actually do relate to the politicians' performance by understanding the political idiom.

Philip E. Converse shows the vast difference in voting behavior between people who understand the politicians' idiom and those who do not. He claims that this finding has been made repeatedly, over several decades. It manifests that voting behavior really relates to politicians' behavior only to the degree that voters understand the politicians' idiom (Converse, 1964: 214, and 231-234). Converse praises two studies focusing on the behavior of politicians in response to voting behavior. Using sampling techniques, these studies measure the congruence between politicians' behavior and behavior of voters. Converse (1975: 149-151) calls this relation the Mass-elite linkage. Converse estimates that in ordinary times about 10% to 15% of voters really relate to politicians' behavior. But in exciting times heightened popular interest brings from 25% to 30% or 40% of voters to really relate to politicians' performance (Converse: 1975: 156-157).

V.O. Key, Jr. studied voting behavior in presidential elections between 1936-1960. He likened voters' behavior to the echo in an echo chamber. Voters' behavior bears an "inevitable and invariable relation" to politicians' input into the echo chamber. When politicians' input is reasonable, voting behavior is reasonable; when politicians' input is foolish, voting behavior is foolish (Key, 1966: 2-3). Responsible voters are those who appraise the actions of government and vote accordingly (*ibid.*, pp. 58-59). But perhaps many more than the majority of voters do not vote responsibly in most elections because they are confused by political propaganda (*ibid.*, pp. 113-114). Like Converse (1964: 248-249), Key finds that voting behavior really relates to government's actions to the degree that voters are not confused by political propaganda.

David RePass (1971: 394-397) studies voting behavior by measuring voters' perception of political reality. Correct perception of political reality is to see the opposing performance of rival parties and rival candidates on issues. Perception is "correct" when voters perceive the opposing ways in which parties and candidates "do something" or "stay out of something" on issues. Correct perception requires perceiving the opposing behavior of parties and candidates as consonant or not with one's own opinion. Especially, correct perception requires perceiving the behavior of the rival party as consonant with one's own and that one's own opinion is dissonant with the performance of one's preferred party (RePass, 1971: 399-400). Those with correct perception are the responsible voters of Key and Converse. RePass finds (p. 400) that the weight of the factors leading to correct perception is .23: the weight of factors leading to incorrect perception stands at .27 for party identification and .37 for candidate personality.

Bernard Crick, of the London School of Economics, holds (1964: 190-191) that the behaviorists have almost destroyed political science. Following Aristotle's basic doctrine, Crick holds that politics consists of the political relation between historic groups of incompatible interests (Crick, 1964: 18, 25, 33, 47, 141, 174-176, and 186). Politics involves genuine relationships between people who are irreducibly different (*ibid.*, p. 124). Political rule is only one form of government: the government with a minimum of violence (*ibid.*, pp. 18, 33, 141). The political relation is a public relation between men who have the status of freemen (*ibid.*, pp. 186, 199). No individual political interest exists; only public group political interests exist (p. 127). But loyalty among individuals against group interests is found only in a free political society (pp. 47 and 61). Crick's political relation between groups irreducibly different is manifestly a real relation. This real relation is also a public relation, so it is a public object. It is a relation between free men.

These political scientists, both behavioralists and anti-behavioralists, explain political freedom exclusively in terms of real relations.

Section 2. Philosophical understanding of freely chosen reality publicly manifest in real and unreal relations.

The origin of science and philosophy is identifying and distinguishing real and unreal relations among members of the public. The public experiencing its own reality has a priority of certitude over all other experience, and all reality experienced by the public has greater certitude than a privately experienced reality. But neither public nor private experience is errorless. Yet in the public experiencing its own reality the real and unreal relations involved are *publicly manifest*.

Social relations among men contain both the real relations between persons and the unreal cultural relations. For example, in Atlantic Democratic civilization industry is organized not only by the real relations between persons and machines but also by the unreal cultural relations that determine the cultural meaning of the real relations: i.e., who is "owner," who is "employee," who is "management" and who is "labor."

I propose to find experience of freedom in these publicly experienced facts of identity and distinction of real and unreal relations. This proposal may seem hopeless to persons who consider freedom to be either purely private, or purely subjective and unreal, or purely intellectual and not perceptual. Nevertheless, I propose that these aforementioned perceived public objects may be experienced as freely chosen.

Now interestingly enough, recent commentators on the *Nicomachean Ethics* believe they find a similar "hopeless" doctrine in Aristotle: namely the "impossible combination" of a doctrine of free choice with a doctrine of objects of free choice as *perceptual*.

For Aristotle (335-334BC: *Ethics*, Book III, ch. 4, p. 143), the good man is "measure and canon" of all moral truth. Right judgment of moral things in fact consists in conformity to right appetite (*ibid.*, Book 6, ch. 2, p. 329). So truthful moral judgment concerns what is and what is not conformed to right appetite. Affirmation and denial in moral judgment express pursuit of moral good and flight from moral evil (*ibid.*):

Pursuit and avoidance in the sphere of desire correspond to affirmation and denial in the sphere of intellect.

Now things to be pursued and avoided are experienced by intelligent perception (*ibid.*, ch. 11, p. 363): Practical intelligence

> apprehends the ultimate and contingent fact, and the minor premise, since these are the first principles from which the end is inferred, as general rules are based on particular cases; hence we must have perception of particulars, and this immediate perception is Intelligence.

Commenting on this passage, Gauthier and Jolif (1959: 538-539) explain this intelligent perception as "moral sense": e.g., perception of a concrete fact as morally evil, as "this is a lie". So, for Aristotle, moral principles emerge from perceived concrete moral facts; perception of moral facts precedes grasp of moral principles. Grasp of moral principles is not the origin of moral experience. Intelligent perception of moral facts is the origin of moral experience; *the intellectual and the sensory factors are not separated in the origin of moral experience*, according to the Stagirite. For Aristotle, the concrete good man and his concrete intelligent perception of moral facts is the origin of truth about what is and what is not a morally good thing. These moral facts perceived by the good man are *open to public experience*, since what he perceives is the "measure and canon" of what the public should perceive, because "the good man judges everything correctly" (Aristotle, *Ethics*, Book III, ch. 4, p. 143).

For a moment, let us assume on the authority of Aristotle that it is not foolish to look for moral freedom in publicly experienced facts such as real relations. Next, the question arises: what about a real relation could manifest it as a freely chosen reality? I answer: *that it could not exist independently of intelligent experience* would do so. By intelligent experience I understand *a perception of the difference between a real relation and an unreal one*. If the real relation cannot exist outside of the intelligent experience of the difference between its reality and the unreal one, then such a real relation is dependent on intelligent perception of their difference. For only within intelligent experience can perception of the difference occur.

Section 3. Examining a proposed nominal description of "freely chosen reality".

"Freely chosen reality" requires nominal description before any proof could identify it as a reality. "Intelligent perception" of real relations can yield this needed description.

First of all, we have found in some cases that the distinction of real and unreal relations is a publicly experienced object: e.g., in the disputes between loyalists and deviationists in American politics. In these cases perceptual objects are appropriately called "intelligent perception." For the distinction of the real and unreal is traditionally called "intelligent."

Moreover, as we have seen, experience of the reality of the public itself consists in just this distinction becoming a public object. Indeed, all social relations are public objects: e.g., those between husband and wife, between management and labor, etc. As we have seen, social relations contain both real and unreal relations. In fact, the real relational component of social relations *cannot be social* except as identified with an unreal cultural relation that provides its public meaning. For example, the unreal cultural relation "adultery" gives public meaning to certain real relations with another man's wife.

Now I hypothesize, under certain conditions, that the *real relational component* of social relations could not exist except within intelligent perception. If that were true, then intelligent perception would be at least *the necessary condition* of the existence of such a real relation. Since this reality (the real relation) would be dependent on intelligent perception, it should rightly be called a "freely chosen reality." Now a reality that could not exist except as necessarily conditioned by existence as object within intelligent perception is rightly called a "freely chosen reality." For this real social relation would be a *reality* that cannot exist *except so long as it is an intelligently perceived object*. So it would be a *real practical effect of intelligent perception*. Such a real practical effect is rightly called a "freely chosen reality." So my nominal definition of "freely chosen reality" is: *a real relation that cannot exist except as object of intelligent perception of unknown nature*.

Freely chosen reality so described can be a matter of experience. In fact, as we shall see, experience of freely chosen reality involves no more than what we have already found in experience of the public as a reality. Freely chosen reality as a matter of experience fits common sense. For common sense is convinced it experiences real things freely chosen.

Moreover my nominal description seems to fit the common element in what philosophers have discussed under the name of "freedom." Mortimer Adler, thanks to a remarkable dialectic, has reduced all philosophers' descriptions of a free man to one formula (Adler, 1958: 616): A man

> is free in the sense that he has in himself the ability or power whereby he can make what he does his own action and what he achieves his property.

Adler intends his formula to undercut the differing conceptions of freedom held by philosophers. His formula of concord not only leaves undetermined points disputed; it also intends to be determinable by their opposing opinions. So his proposal leaves undetermined: a) whether freedom belongs to an individual self (1958: 167-170), or whether it belongs to a collectivity (*ibid.*, pp. 370-399); b) whether freedom permits an individual to do as one pleases (*ibid.*, 171-201), or whether it enables people to do as everyone ought (*ibid.*, 400-422 and 87-90); c) whether it is an external circumstance of an individual, an acquired characteristic, or a natural characteristic of everyone (*ibid.*, 161-166); d) whether it is a voluntary act or scientific understanding (*ibid.*, 370-399); e) whether freedom changes the self or does not (*ibid.*, 400-422).

Adler finds these differing concepts combined into three overall views of freedom, one of which contains two distinctive positions. So four overall views sum up the history of the philosophy of freedom. All four views hold in common for some indeterminate ability or power. This indeterminate ability Adler expresses by the words "can" and "is able." He states this indeterminate ability as the common subject of his four descriptions, using the phrase: "A man [is free] who is able . . ."

The first view is as follows:

> A man [is free] who is able (A) under favorable circumstances, to act as he wishes for his own individual good as he sees it. (Adler, 1958: 608).

This view combines the following concepts listed above. What has freedom (a) is an *individual self*, characterized (b) by doing what is only subjectively pleasing to the individual. And (c) that freedom is only circumstantial inasmuch as it is had *if only* no external circumstance impedes whatever one subjectively believes to be good for oneself. For these philosophers, the good is not a reality; it is whatever merely subjective object one desires. In my terms, the good entirely reduces to objective being (p. 184).

The second view contains two distinctive views:

> A man [is free] who is able (B) through acquired virtue or wisdom, to will or live as he ought in conformity to the moral law or an ideal befitting human nature. (*Ibid.*, 608).

With the phrase "or an ideal befitting human nature," Adler describes the position of Marxists and others for whom freedom is not *ethical freedom.* For them, freedom consists in conforming

> to scientific formulations of how things *do* behave, rather than theologically, morally, or juridically declared rules of how men *should* behave . . . Such laws are inviolable and, therefore, can either be put to beneficial use or not, but never disobeyed, in contrast to ethical prescriptions, which are violable and may or may not be voluntarily obeyed. (Adler, 1958: 389-390).

Hence, this second phrase introduces a new and very distinctive view of freedom as *non-ethical.* It constitutes in fact a fourth view. I shall call it

(B) [2], indicating by the square brackets that I am interpreting Adler's text.

The overall view (B) [1] is as follows.

A man [is free] who is able (B) [1] through acquired virtue or wisdom to will or live as he ought in conformity to the moral law.

This view (B) [1] combines the following concepts listed above. What has freedom is (a) the individual self, (b) respecting a real good existing independently of subjective belief. This freedom is (c) possessed only thanks to an acquired characteristic of virtue or wisdom. Virtue and wisdom are acquired through reason, according to the philosophers (pp. 277-278). According to Christian theologians it cannot be had without God's redeeming grace (p. 279). This freedom (d) is exercised by a voluntary act (pp. 276-278).

The overall view (B) [2] is as follows (p. 608):

A man [is free] who is able (B) [2] to live in conformity to an ideal befitting human nature.

This view (B) [2] combines the following concepts listed above. What has freedom (a) is the collective self, respecting the common ideal of progressive humanity; acquired thanks to scientific understanding of the laws of nature and society, rather than by voluntary acts (pp. 385-390).

The third overall view is as follows (*ibid.*, p. 608).

A man [is free] who is able (C) by a power inherent in human nature, to change his own character creatively by deciding for himself what he shall do or shall become.

This third view combines the following concepts listed above. What has freedom (a) is an individual self, respecting (b) real goods existing independently of subjective desire. This freedom (c) is natural to all human beings. It enables one (d) by voluntary acts (e) to change one's self (pp. 420-422).

Now my nominal description of freely chosen reality fits what Adler's dialectic found common to the four opinions of philosophers concerning freedom. Adler's formula of concord is (p. 608): A free man

has in himself the ability or power whereby he can make what he does his own action and what he achieves his property.

My nominal description of freely chosen reality runs as follows: a real relation that cannot exist except as object of intelligent perception of unknown nature. My nominal description agrees with Adler's formula.

His formula contains two points. The first point is: "A free man has in himself the ability or power whereby he can make what he does his own action." Adler's ability or power leaves indeterminate whether it be rational volition, subjective desire, or scientific understanding. So likewise, my "intelligent perception" is of unknown nature. The two agree. Adler's formula leaves indeterminate whether "the good" be real goods existing independently of subjective desire, or merely subjectively desirable to the individual, or ideals of progressive humanity. My description leaves indeterminate whether the real terms of these real relations are desirable independently of subjective belief. The two statements agree also in this respect.

Still respecting Adler's first point, his formula leaves indeterminate whether freedom belongs to this ability or power thanks to external circumstances, or by acquisition, or by nature. Likewise my description leaves these things indeterminate respecting intelligent perception. For intelligent perception is of unknown nature. So we cannot know how it stands respecting freely chosen reality. So the two statements agree.

Finally, Adler's formula leaves the first point indeterminate as to whether freedom belongs to an individual self or a collective self. Likewise my description leaves this indeterminate respecting intelligent perception. Since the intrinsic nature of intelligent perception remains unknown, it remains open to both interpretations. The two statements therefore agree as regards Adler's first point.

His second point is this: freedom makes what one achieves one's property. My nominal definition can easily be applied to the question of property. But property is both individual property and collective property. Now real relations that cannot exist except as objects of intelligent perception somehow "humanize" their real terms in the natural environment. In every culture the natural environment becomes part of the human historical world: it is our "fatherland", our "native land." Moreover, in every culture we find both individual and collective property. Thus a people's real relations to natural environment have become identified with these unreal cultural and historical relations. When a people comes also to see the distinction as well as the identity of these real and unreal relations, then they have become objects of intelligent perception. At that point I claim their identity and distinction cannot exist except as objects of intelligent perception. And that is my nominal definition of freely chosen reality. Hence my nominal definition agrees with Adler's second point.

So our nominal description is a good one. It fits what is common in the philosophers' discussion of freedom.

Now confusion of the real and unreal relations composing social relations is common even among social scientists. Adam Smith believed that capitalist industrial organization consisted of inalterable natural relations, according to Leslie Stephen (Stephen, 1900: II, p. 206):

Left to itself the industrial organism generates those economic harmonies upon which the optimist delighted to dwell. 'Natural' seems to take the sense of 'providential.' The 'economic harmonies' are, like the harmonies perceived by Paley or the Bridgewater Treatise writers in external nature, so many proofs of the divine benevolence; any attempt to interfere with them could only lead to disaster.

For Schumpeter, ideological confusion of the real and unreal affects the primitive vision underlying all social science. However, social science has rules and phenomena that correct this ideological confusion (Schumpeter, 1954: 42-43):

Analytic work begins with material provided by our vision of things, and this vision is ideological almost by definition. It embodies the picture of things as we see them, and wherever there is any possible motive for wishing to see them in a given rather than another light, the way in which we see things can hardly be distinguished from the way in which we wish to see them. The more honest and naive our vision is, the more dangerous is it to the eventual emergence of anything for which general validity can be claimed. The inference for the social sciences is obvious, and it is not even true that he who hates a social system will form an objectively more correct vision of it than he who loves it. For love distorts indeed, but hate distorts still more. Our only comfort is in the fact that there is a large number of phenomena that fail to affect our emotions one way or the other, and that therefore look to one man very much as they do to another. But we also observe that the Rules of procedure that we apply in our analytic work are almost as much exempt from ideological influence as vision is subject to it. Passionate allegiance and passionate hatred may indeed tamper with these rules. In themselves these rules, many of which, moreover, are imposed upon us by the scientific practice in fields that are little or not at all affected by ideology, are pretty effective in showing up misuse.

The confusion of the real and unreal in social relations is also common in public life. The political scientists cited above indicate that the majority of voters only apparently participate in democracy. Such voters confuse the real relation of government to society with its unrealistic description in political propaganda. Similarly, in the world of economics, Adam Smith's inalterable capitalistic natural harmonies are still believed in by conservative business circles. These business people likewise illustrate the confusion of social relations, which always have an unreal relational component besides a real relation, with natural relations in the physical world that never do.

The only real relations I propose to prove freely chosen are the real relations involved in perception itself. Such real perceptual relations may be social relations between people or an individual's perceptual relation to natural environment. Among adults, linguistic and other unreal cultural relations enter into both these sorts of real perceptual relations. Whenever the real and unreal components of perceptual relations are confused, the unreal relation has failed to be perceived as a public object distinct from and identified with the real perceptual relation. In such cases real perceptual relations, whether of other people or of natural environment, are not freely chosen realities.

One might satirically object to my proposal as follows. This is a marvelous system. Consider the real gravitational relation of your body to the earth. Now intelligently perceive your real gravitational relation as identified with and distinguished from the unreal public object, the cultural relation called the "law of gravity." Then your real gravitational relation becomes a freely chosen reality; and you are free to levitate as you please. I reply that the playful objector has misunderstood the proposed system. The real relation to be identified with and distinguished from unreal relations is my real perceptual relation to real objects, e.g., other people or natural environment. It is only this real perceptual relation that may become freely chosen thanks to intelligent perception. My real gravitational relation to environment remains a necessary real relation.

Section 4. Proof of freely chosen reality.

My proof is as follows. A real relation dependent on intelligent experience of the difference between it and an unreal relation is *a freely chosen reality*. First, in such an experience, the unreal relation is experienced as *contingent*: since it is experienced as the unreal meaning of the real one. For example, let the unreal relation be that of workers to management in an industrial plant within a capitalistic economic system. The unreal capitalist relation of "workers" to "management" is the meaning of the workers' activity being really related to the activity of management. Suppose now that this unreal capitalist relation has recently come to be experienced as an *unreal* relation whereas it was hitherto believed to be real because of social enculturation. For example, social enculturation had formed people to perceive these unreal cultural relations as like real relations of attraction and repulsion in matter. Since capitalist cultural relations were perceived as real, the terms of capitalist relations were perceived as public "natural" bodies. So capitalist property and wage labor were perceived as public "natural" bodies like dogs and cats.

But, in my supposition, people have recently come to see capitalist meaning-giving relations as unreal cultural relations. Capitalist cultural relations are now seen as one unreal system of economic organization among the innumerable systems found in the history of the nations. Since the capitalist meaning-giving relations are now seen as *unreal*, they are also perceived as *contingent*.

Due to the enculturation process, the capitalist economic relations had been perceived as not only real but also as *necessary* just because of that spurious reality. For thanks to their spurious reality they were assimilated to attraction and repulsion in matter, which are indeed necessary. Now that they are perceived as unreal, they lose that spurious necessity *and are perceived* as *contingent*.

Then in this situation the *real* relation between workers and management will also be experienced *as contingent*. For the real relation cannot function as social relation between the two groups without its meaning, since the real relation cannot be a social relation *unless it be identified as a meaningful public object*. Hence in this situation the real relation between workers and management is experienced as contingent, thanks to its identification with and its distinction from its unreal contingent meaning. Therefore *both the real and the unreal relations* will be experienced as *contingent*. Moreover, their contingency depends on the intelligent experience outside of which their distinction and identity cannot exist. Hence the real relation will be contingent on intelligent experience outside of which it could not exist. *But a contingent reality here and now dependent for its existence on intelligent experience is a freely chosen reality*. This dependent real relation is a *real practical effect chosen* against its discontinuance as a social relation.

In this situation, the capitalist social relations are already manifest as freely chosen reality, without first discussing the psychological and interior acts that may be involved in choosing. I mean, it is not necessary to determine previously even whether persons choosing *have voluntary acts or not*. For already without this further discussion, the capitalist social relations are perceived as *alternative real relations*. For the *unreal* capitalist meaning relations are now experienced as publicly obtaining only so long as they, rather than some alternative meaning relations, are identified with their real industrial relations. Hence their present capitalist relations, conflated of real and unreal relations, exist only as an alternative conflation contingent on intelligent perception. Hence their present capitalist relations have become freely chosen reality. This is already true whether or not there be psychological or interior acts involved in choice by members of the public.

Whenever the distinction and identification of real and unreal relations is made, the real relation involved cannot exist apart from intelligent experience. Moreover, that experience is a *liberating intelligent experience*. It is an experience that breaks the psychological determinisms of figure and ground and of object constancy by distinguishing these psychologically determined relations from biologically determined real relations of the perceiver's body to the objects involved. It breaks socio-cultural determinisms to traditional objects when traditional relations are first perceived as unreal public relations distinct from real relations between people. This perception occurred in Western nations when monarchy was seen not to be the inevitable political relation, a tradition that had existed for centuries. It happens when people perceive national frontiers as unreal public relations distinct from real relations between neighboring peoples. It happens when people perceive property relations as unreal legal systems distinct from real relations between people.

In private experience, one likewise experiences freely chosen realities. Our nominal definition of freely chosen reality is: "a real relation that cannot exist except as object of intelligent perception of unknown nature." Now in discussing private experience of real relations, we found many real relations experienced in their distinction from unreal relations. Examples were as follows. Apparent motion and object constancy on the TV screen are experienced as unreal relations by contrast with one's real relation to the TV set. The skyscraper's apparent changes were experienced as distinct from one's own changing relation to it. I experience other people's feelings and attitudes as irreducibly different from my own: i.e., I experience a relation to them irreducibly different from my relation to them as mere objects for me.

In all these cases, one privately experiences a real relation that cannot exist except in intelligent perception. For these real relations cannot exist except as distinguished from unreal ones. The person watching the TV gun fight does not flee the room, because one distinguishes real relation to the TV from the unreal relations of apparent motion and object constancy on the TV screen. One's stationary relation to the TV cannot exist except because of the intelligent perception of the difference between that real relation and those unreal ones.

In talking with someone else I must experience the other's feelings and opinions as irreducibly other than mere objects for me; otherwise I would never experience conversation with others. One's mind is apt to wander while listening to a public speaker. Only by turning attention back does one listen. Then one's real relation of listener to speaker cannot exist except as perceived to be different from one's daydreaming (that totally reduces to objective being). Sometimes, in conversation with others, one must deliberately pay attention rather than slip into daydreaming.

Hence these real relations are the practical effect of intelligent perception. One chooses not to flee the TV room because the violence is "only on TV." One chooses to really relate to the public speaker rather than "turn him off." These are typical cases of freely chosen reality in private experience.

Now it is to the real public and to natural things in their intrinsic reality that one relates, although one experiences them only extrinsically. The public experiencing itself and any other reality publicly experienced has a priority of certitude over any privately experienced reality to which one relates. The relation whereby one relates to these intrinsic realities cannot exist except within intelligent experience at least somewhat liberated from psychological and socio-cultural determinisms. So, to the extent of this liberation, these relations are *freely chosen realities*. For they are realities inseparable from intelligent experience whereby one relates to the intrinsic reality of the public and to other realities publicly or privately experienced.

The foregoing proof of the existence of freely chosen relations seems to be confirmed by R. M. Hare's analysis of moral thinking. Here is an analytic philosopher well known for his work in ethics. Like other members of his school, he confines himself to experiential data only. So he treats the "essence of man" as "philosophical mystification" (Hare, 1963: 222). His data for ethics are collected according to the maxim, "There but for my good fortune go I" (*ibid.*, p. 222). Hare leaves unsolved the problem of reconciling free choice with predictability based on scientific laws (*ibid.*, pp. 212-3). He admits it possible that human behavior may yet become as predictable as any contingent events, thanks to advances in neurology (*ibid.*, p. 62). He is content to claim that, despite scientific predictability, we could still raise moral questions. However, his analysis of moral thinking (*ibid.*, p. 199) uses the same data that I have used to prove freely chosen reality. The coincidence of his data for moral thinking with the data for my more difficult problem is a guarantee against the "philosophical mystification" of non-experiential data. Thus Hare confirms my argument as regards data used.

That Hare's data are the same as mine is shown as follows. He rejects the so-called *naturalist understanding of moral good*. "The naturalist seeks to tie certain moral judgments analytically to certain moral *content*" (*ibid.*, p. 195; Hare's emphasis). In his view, on the contrary, absolutely no content of moral judgment is ruled out. For Hare, "what circumscribes moral prescriptions . . . is the desires and inclinations of the human race" (*ibid.*, p. 195). But the desires of others are not merely taken as *facts* to which one conforms. That would be "a form of naturalism akin to that form often called 'old fashioned subjectivism' " (*ibid.*, p. 199). According to him, good moral judgment "tailors" one's desire "to fit the particular volitions which other people have, and which, therefore, are treated as if they were one's own" (*ibid.*, p. 199). Now first of all, "tailoring" one's desires "to fit the particular volitions of others'' is just what I have shown to imply real relations. Secondly, treating other people's particular volitions as if they were one's own implies an unreal relation whereby one imagines that other people's volitions proceed from one's self. Thirdly, ''treating other people's volitions as if they were one's own'' is to identify these unreal imaginary relations with one's own real relations tailoring to other people's desires. Hence, Hare describes good moral judgment as identifying and distinguishing real and unreal relations. Therefore the data for his description of good moral judgment coincides with those for my argument for freely chosen reality. So the methods that rate his data as experiential confirm my data as experiential.

Furthermore, Hare uses his data just as I do. For he identifies and distinguishes real and unreal relations in order to describe good moral judgment. Therefore he confirms the use that I have made of these experiential data, even though his purpose is different from mine. My claim about identifying and distinguishing real and unreal relations could seem odd. But Hare uses the same method to contrast his doctrine of good moral judgment with the naturalist doctrine, old-fashioned subjectivism. Thus he confirms my argument as regards the use of these experiential data.

Do animal societies distinguish real and unreal components in their social relations? C. F. Hockett's concept of linguistic ''duality'' may provide an answer. According to Hockett (1958: 574), ''duality'' is the double structure of a human language:
1. the structure of elementary speech sounds language speakers are trained to contrast.
2. the meaningful elements they are trained to discern.
Elements of sound distinguished constitute the phonological structure; meaningful elements constitute the elements of grammar.

This is what we mean by ''duality'': a language has a phonological system and also a grammatical system.

Now the relation between a grammatical element and what it signifies is (Hockett, 1977: 170) ''independent of any physical or geometrical resemblance.''

It seems the phonological system of contrasted sounds constitutes experience of what does not *totally* reduce to objective being: so it yields experience of objects to which one is really related. The other system, the grammatical system, affords experience of unreal relations since such a relation is ''independent of any physical or geometrical resemblance.'' Hence ''duality'' is constituted by distinguishing real and unreal relations. This ''duality'' of real and unreal relations distinguished from each other has not been verified in any animal society, according to Hockett (Hockett, 1977: 155).

Now the intrinsic nature of intelligent experience is not itself experienced, just as no other intrinsic natures are directly experienced. But intelligent experience is a reality, whatever its intrinsic nature may be. For what is really related to other realities must itself be real. Our intelligent experience has been shown to be really related to realities of unknown nature, namely, to natural environment and to other people. So a freely chosen real relation depends on *a real* intelligent perception whose intrinsic nature is unknown.

So we have direct experience of real and free causality; i.e., the experience of freely chosen real relations dependent on real intelligent experience. Hence, contrary to Hume's doctrine, we have *direct experience of real causality*. I need not again refute Hume's indirect realism, since it has already been shown to be false. But it must be added that the real causality here defended is no more than a real necessary condition. Since the intrinsic nature of real intelligent experience is as yet unknown in this enquiry, the intrinsic nature of its causality likewise remains unknown. But real intelligent perception has been shown to be the necessary real condition of freely chosen real relations, since such free real relations cannot exist outside intelligent experience. Hence intelligent perception has been shown to be *at least* the real *per accidens* cause (necessary condition) of that real and free relation. The freely chosen real relations we directly experience. The mode of the real causality of perception respecting these real relations remains obscure to direct experience.

Section 5. Objections against this argument.

C. D. Broad has contributed importantly to stating the problem of moral responsibility versus determinism (Broad, 1952: 195-217). His contribution is his statement of the problem in terms of the minimal conditions under which we could believe in moral responsibility. Since Broad argues against that very concept of moral responsibility which C. A. Campbell is defending, Campbell highly praises him for his almost perfect statement of the problem (Campbell, 1967: 51-52).

First of all, Broad states the need of posing the claim to moral responsibility in intelligible terms, independently of truth claims (Broad, 1952: 210). He does not think that defenders of moral responsibility ever do this, otherwise they would see the impossibility of their claim (*ibid.*, p. 214).

Secondly, he defines a completely determined event and a not-completely determined event. A completely determined event is one that ''has a zero range of indetermination for every determinable characteristic of which it is a manifestation.'' A non-completely determined event is one that ''a finite range of indetermination for at least one dimension of at least one characteristic of which it is a manifestation" (*ibid.*, p. 210). Three terms in these definitions need clarification. Broad distinguishes diverse *characteristics* of an *event* from the different *dimensions* of that characteristic, and again distinguishes the *range* of variability of the dimensions from the dimensions. He uses as an example a flash of light. The *color* of the flash is a *characteristic* of the flash-*event*. The shade, saturation and intensity of the color are its *dimensions*. The extent of possible variation of these dimensions is their *range* of variation.

Thirdly, he defines Determinism as the doctrine that every event is completely determined. He defines Indeterminism as the doctrine that some events, and it may be all, are not completely determined (*ibid.*, p. 210).

Fourthly, he gives the conditions under which Determinism and Indeterminism would be true (*ibid.*, p. 211). Determinism would be true if no first cause exists in a given series of causes. Indeterminism would be true if a first cause does exist in some series of causes. For an example of a first cause he gives Adam as a possible first cause in the series of mankind. He defines a first cause as a cause in a series of causes which is itself not a completely determined cause. He gives the name "causal progenitor" to such a supposed first cause.

Fifthly, he states a negative and a positive condition for the existence of moral responsibility. The negative condition is that some causal progenitor exists. The positive condition is that some substantial self exists that stands above the series of temporal events (*ibid.*, pp. 214-215). Such a substantial self would be a causal progenitor (p. 215).

Finally, he frames the question: What *might* be the *sufficient* condition for a causal progenitor? Broad's answer can be schematized as follows (*ibid.*, pp. 214-215): *Major*: For moral responsibility of a causal progenitor, it *might be a sufficient condition*:
1. To be one single negative indeterminate condition among many conditions of an event, or
2. To be the positive condition, a substantial self standing outside the temporal series of causes.

Minor: But 1: A negative indeterminate condition of an event *probably* is *not* a sufficient condition for moral responsibility. For the event would occur by chance as a *mere accident* respecting such a causal progenitor. But 2: A substantial self standing above the causal series is impossible. For such a substance or continuant standing above the events cannot enter into the events, since it lacks any temporal determination to the date of events.

Conclusion: Therefore, moral responsibility of a causal progenitor is probably an illusion (*ibid.*, p. 217).

To this argument I reply as follows:

Ad majorem: A third possibility must be included along with, on the one hand, the negative indeterminate condition, and on the other, the positive condition, a substantial self. This third possibility is a certain *determinate* condition *sine qua non* of the event among other conditions of the event. This determinate condition is the intelligent perception of a real temporal relation identified and distinguished from an unreal relation. Such intelligent perception is a *necessary* condition *sine qua non* of that real relation. For if a single indeterminate condition of an event might be a sufficient condition for moral responsibility, then *a fortiori* a single determinate condition *sine qua non* might be a sufficient condition.

Ad minorem:

1. I concede that a negative indeterminate condition would only refer to the event by chance and accidentally.

2. I concede that a substantial self is not an object of experience. Hence its existence is irrelevant to discussion restricted to experiential data only. The nature of intelligent perception is admittedly unknown to direct experience. Hence it is not claimed to be a substantial self or a substantial nature or continuant.

3. Such a real temporal relation is directly perceived, whereas events are only indirectly perceived as terms of real temporal relations. Thus Broad has not set up his problem in terms of critical epistemology.

4. Intelligent perception of identity and distinction of the real and unreal relations is in some cases a *necessary* condition *sine qua non* of the real relation. Hence it is not referred to this relation of events by chance or accidentally. Therefore Broad's reason for rejecting the sufficiency of other conditions for moral responsibility does not hold here. (He rejected the sufficiency of negative indeterminate conditions in part 1 of the Minor.)

5. In ordinary language, reflecting common experience, *less* is required for a sufficient condition of moral responsibility than for a sufficient condition of the total physical effect. Moral responsibility is usually attributed to those who place necessary conditions *sine qua non* of an event. Thus a man who deliberately knocks a pole from under a weight is held responsible for the damage caused by the fall of the weight. But he is only a necessary condition *sine qua non* of the falling body. Gravity is the sufficient physical cause of the falling body.

6. Intelligent perception of the identity and distinction of the real and unreal relations is a necessary condition *sine qua non* of the real relations, as has been shown. Hence the intelligent perception of the identity and distinction of these relations is a *sufficient* condition for moral responsibility for that real relation.

Another, the Determinist John Hospers (1967: 339-340), argues thus against everyone's *seeming* experience of the fact of free choice. The seeming experience of free choice is as follows. It is a fact of experience that "I often experience that I could have done otherwise." This fact is incompatible with Determinism. For Determinism holds that we could *not* have done otherwise had the set of conditions preceding our action been exactly the same. Therefore, Determinism is false.

To this claim Hospers replies (1967: 340): I deny the alleged experiential fact. "Since we never have the same exact set of conditions twice in human behavior, how can we know that 'we would have acted differently' is a fact?"

I reply thus to Hospers' rejection of this alleged experience. We do not need to go outside of ordinary present experience to find "what I could have done otherwise." His talk of "the same set of conditions twice in human behavior" is not drawn from ordinary experience but from the determinist's philosophical concepts. This talk can be easily dispensed with in formulating our question.

The direct experience of identifying and distinguishing real and unreal relations often contains indirect experience of *rejecting the alternative* of failing to distinguish them. For example, when you hear shots in the next room and rush in to find a Western shootout on TV, you directly experience distinguishing your real relation to the TV set from imaginary relation to a shootout. But, indirectly, you experience the frightful confusion from which you are emerging. You freely choose *the alternative* of freely distinguishing *over against the dreadful unfree* confusing of the relations.

We frequently have the indirect experience of emerging from confused unfreedom as *a rejected alternative*. It happens when we awake from a dream; it happens whenever we return out of a daydream to awareness of our surroundings.

In some experiences, emerging from confusion is a rejected alternative *directly* experienced. This happens as we walk toward a skyscraper that seems to grow taller as we approach block after block. We reject the illusion of a growing building by subjecting illusion to the discipline of reality in preference to leaving illusion its autonomy. By identifying while distinguishing the imaginary growing building with our real relation to the building, this imaginary relation is deprived of its autonomy as it is subjected to the discipline of reality. *In all our waking experience* at least *some* such discipline of illusory psychological relations occurs. The illusory psychological relations of figure and ground are constantly being identified with and distinguished from real relations to our surroundings. Therefore we constantly experience rejection of imaginary relations as autonomous from real relations. Thus we constantly experience free relation to environment as rejection of the unfree alternative relation to it. Hence I do not need to go outside present experience to find "what I could do otherwise."

Certain philosophers who reject direct realism consequently deny that reality as such is freely chosen.

For Heidegger, epistemological realism is a variant of correspondence truth. For him, correspondence truth has had two basic forms. In Greek and medieval philosophy, it was conformity of our ideas to real things. In modern philosophy, it has been conformity of things to our ideas (Heidegger, 1947a: 21-22). The late Heidegger tirelessly repeats that the whole history of metaphysics from its beginning in Plato till its consummation in Nietzsche is the history of correspondence truth (1947a: 269-270):

> Plato's thinking follows the change of the essence of truth, which change becomes the story of metaphysics and which has begun its unconditional fulfillment in Nietzsche's thinking. Plato's doctrine of "truth" is therefore not something of the past . . . The story told in the allegory of the cave gives the aspect of what is now and always will be what really happens in the history of the humanity molded in the West: man thinks in terms of the fact that the essence of truth is the correctness of the representing of all beings according to "ideas" and esteems everything real according to "values." The decisive point is not which ideas and which values are set, but that the real is expounded according to "ideas" at all, that the "world" is weighed according to "values" at all.[1]

Now Heidegger's *Being* of beings is non-being by contrast with the "beings": yet this Being of beings is inseparable from the presence of "beings" (Heidegger, 1956: 94-96):

> Within the horizon of scientific conception, which only knows being, that which is not being (namely Being) in any way at all can, on the other hand, present itself only as nothingness . . . "Man is the seat-holder for nothingness." This sentence means that man is holding the place open for the complete other of being, so that in its openness there can be such a thing as being present (Being). This nothingness which is not being but is just the same, is nothing negative. It belongs to being present.[2]

Heidegger opposes Humanism and all systems of conformity truth. The "objectivity" of conformity truth forgets that the non-being of Being determines how beings appear in any metaphysical system. The illusory correspondence truth of metaphysical systems consists in forgetting that the "beings" they so differently construe are inseparable from the non-being of Being they forget.

> Humanism is opposed because it does not set the humanitas of man high enough. However, the essential dignity of man does not lie in the fact that he is as the "subject" of beings, their substance, so that as the

despot of Being he may let the character of beings dissolve into an "objectivity" that is much too loudly praised. Man is rather "cast" by Being itself into the truth of Being, in order that he, ex-sisting thus, may guard the truth of Being; in order that in the light of Being, beings as beings may appear as what it is. Whether and how it appears, whether and how God and the gods, history and nature, enter, presenting and absenting themselves in the clearing of Being, is not determined by man. The advent of beings rests in the destiny of Being. (Heidegger, 1947b: 281).[3]

Hence the clue to the hopelessly incompatible claims of metaphysical systems lies in their forgetting the non-being of Being that determines their divergent conceptions of the "beings."

"Being" as non-being is the concealed lighting on the "beings" that explains the hopeless contradictions between metaphysical systems. "Being" as non-being is the truth as *Alaetheia* dominating the conformity truth of metaphysical systems. Metaphysical systems seek man's freedom by dominance over beings. But their quest of freedom by dominance over beings constitutes their unfreedom fatefully subjected to the "Being" they forget. So when Heidegger speaks of man's freedom he does not mean man's freedom from *Sein* as its *Da* (1943: 308-309):

Man does not "possess" freedom as a property, it is the contrary that is true: freedom, or ex-sistent, revelatory Da-sein possesses man and moreover in so original a manner that it alone confers upon him that relationship with what-is-in-totality which is the basis and distinctive characteristic of his history. Only existent man is historical. "Nature" has no history.[4]

The destining power of "Being" over men comes from their forgetting "Being." That forgotten "Being" is the non-being unsegregated from their understanding of the "beings." Hence, man's fateful unfreedom against "Being" is due to his incapacity to distinguish the real from the unreal: such is the implication of Heidegger's doctrine. The late Heidegger's "step back" out of metaphysics even abandons all effort to distinguish "Being" from the "beings" (1957: 71):

That which bears such a name directs our thinking to the realm which the key words of metaphysics—Being and beings, the ground and what is grounded—are no longer adequate to utter. For what these words name, what the manner of thinking that is guided by them represents, originates as that which differs by virtue of the difference. The origin of the difference can no longer be thought of within the scope of metaphysics.[5]

Therefore Heidegger denies men's freedom against "Being" because they cannot distinguish the real from the unreal. According to him, men cannot choose the *real as such* since they cannot distinguish the real from what is not real. Heidegger's denial illumines our argument that men are free because they distinguish real and unreal relations.

Louis Althusser is an orthodox Marxist. According to him, strict Marxist theory is anti-humanist. For Marxism denies the two basic postulates of humanism (Althusser, 1965: 234):

1. A universal human essence exists.
2. This essence is the attribute of individuals taken in isolation: they are its real subjects.[6]

The reason for rejecting these two postulates is (continuing the same passage):

> In order for these empirical individuals to exist, it is necessary that each of them carry the whole human essence, if not in fact at least by right. But that implies idealism of the essence.

What is usually attributed to liberty is due to ideological confusion of the real and unreal (*ibid.*, pp. 239-240):

> Ideology is indeed a system of representations. But these representations most of the time have nothing to do with consciousness. Most of the time they are images, sometimes concepts. But above all as structures they are imposed upon the vast majority of men without ever becoming conscious. They are perceived—accepted—undergone cultural objects that act functionally on men by a process that escapes them . . . Yet what is meant by saying ideology concerns men's consciousness? It means first that ideology is distinct from other social processes. But also it means: men *live* their actions. Actions that classical tradition assigns to liberty and conscience are lived in ideology and through ideology. In short, the lived relation of men to the world and to History (political action or inaction) passes through ideology or rather is ideology itself.[7]

Ideology is a complex relation comprising a real and an unreal relation. Ideology (*ibid.*, p. 240):

> supposes both a real relation and a 'lived' imaginary relation. Thus ideology is the expression of men to their world. It is, in other words, the 'overdetermined' unity of the real and unreal relations to their real conditions of existence.[8]

Since this confusion of real and unreal relations is unconscious, it precludes liberty, according to Althusser. Thus strict Marxist analysis confirms a good part of what I have said in this essay. But I add: when this confusion is replaced by identifying and distinguishing the real and unreal relations in social relations, *then freedom obtains*.

Hume considered free-will to be contradictory because it confused *cause* and *chance* (Hume, 1739: 188):

> According to my definitions, necessity makes an essential part of causation; and consequently liberty, by removing necessity, removes also causes, and is the very same thing with chance. As chance is commonly thought to imply a contradiction, and is at least directly contrary to experience, there are always the same arguments against liberty or freewill. (*A Treatise of Human Nature*, Book II, Part III, Sect. 1).

But, for Hume, cause itself was mere custom. It belonged more to the sentient than to the cogitative part of our nature:

> Nature, by an absolute and uncontrollable necessity has determin'd us to judge as well as to breathe and feel; nor can we any more forbear viewing certain objects in a stronger and fuller light, upon account of their customary connexion with a present impression, than we can hinder ourselves from thinking as long as we are awake, or seeing the surrounding bodies, when we turn our eyes towards them in broad sunshine . . . My intention then in displaying so carefully the arguments of that fantastic sect, is only to make the reader sensible of the truth of my hypothesis, that all our reasonings concerning causes and effects are deriv'd from nothing but custom; and that belief is more properly an act of the sensitive, than of the cogitative part of our natures. (*Ibid.*, Book I, Part IV, Sect. 1, against the "sect" of sceptics.)

So free will was explained by causality. But causality itself was mere subjective custom. Hence Hume's denial of free will is due to his interpreting it in terms of *blind belief in causality*.[9] Blind belief cannot distinguish the real and unreal. That blindness grounded his denial of free choice.

According to Kant, practical freedom is proved through experience of reason as *a* cause in determining our will. But freedom as independence of phenomenal causes seemed contrary to all possible experience (Kant, 1787: 634; for German text, see Chapter I, note 42):

> While we thus through experience know practical freedom to be one of the causes in nature, namely, to be a causality of reason in the determination of the will, transcendental freedom demands the independence of this reason—in respect of its causality, in beginning a series of appearances—from all determining causes of the sensible world. Transcendental freedom is thus, as it would seem, contrary to the law of nature, and therefore to all possible experience; and so remains a problem.

My argument for freely chosen reality meets Kant's demands for transcendental freedom. For the reality proved dependent on intelligent perception is itself independent of phenomenal causes, by reason of its very reality. Reality certainly does not depend on phenomena, but vice versa. So also is intelligent perception independent of phenomenal causes because it too was shown to be a reality of unknown nature. Kant's denial of transcendental freedom results from not analysing freedom in terms of experienced distinction of the real and unreal. Yet my argument demands no experience of reality, save of real relations. Kant admitted experience of real relations.

Skinner gives us a "domino" argument. Freedom is constantly being expelled from more and more objects formerly attributed to its domain; and so we can foresee that science will ultimately expel freedom from all its possessions (Skinner, 1971: 21). But Skinner's target is the isolated individual, and the interior life that he attacks is that of the isolated individual. The true origin of freely chosen reality is the public itself experiencing itself, and science and philosophy that are objects of public experience. These Skinner does not attack. Skinner attacks and destroys a mythical entity: the isolated individual.

I foresee a Thomist would make four objections against my position.

1. A necessary condition is not a *per se* cause of freely chosen reality. But, in my position, intelligent perception is a necessary condition of the real relation that constitutes the freely chosen reality.
Therefore intelligent perception is not a *per se* cause of freely chosen reality.

I reply thus. I deny the major: "A necessary condition is not a *per se* cause of freely chosen reality." For a *per se* cause is always at least a necessary condition. Hence *some* necessary conditions are *per se* causes. However every *per se* cause is a substance, according to the axiom: "actions belong to supposit." Hence, before we have the distinction of substance and accidents we cannot discern the *per se* efficient cause. Now the other genera of causality are reciprocal to the efficient cause: the final cause as attracting it, the material and formal causes as composing it. Hence prior to discovering the distinction of substance and accidents, no genus of *per se* cause can be discerned from a necessary condition. Hence at this experiential level of enquiry the conclusion of the objection is false: "Therefore intelligent perception is not a *per se* cause of freely chosen reality." For if a human being were shown to be a substance, intelligent perception might well prove to be a *per se* cause of freely chosen reality, according to the axiom, "actions belong to supposits."

The objector presupposes the distinction of substance and accidents is evident in experience. For he supposes that one could manifest in experience that something were a *per se* cause; whereas I fall short by only showing a necessary condition. But the distinction of substance and accidents is not manifest in experience, according to what we have seen in Aquinas. However, once that distinction were manifested, it seems no new data would be needed to make intelligent perception a *per se* cause of freely chosen reality, according to the cited axiom, "actions belong to supposits." My argument goes as far as experiential data can take it. It does not *fail to reach per se* causality, as the objector supposes. For *per se* causality cannot be reached in experiential data, according to Aquinas.

Preliminary explanation: We have seen that thanks to real relations we immediately but extrinsically experience their real terms. Hence the freely chosen realities in my argument include not only the real relations but also their immediate but extrinsically experienced real terms. Now a Thomist would object against the real terms supposedly freely chosen, using the following argument.

> 2. Freely chosen realities are *bonum in rebus*, i.e., *real goods*, according to Aquinas. But terms of these real relations are not real goods because they are not objects of rational appetite. They are not objects of rational appetite because my nominal definition limits what my argument proves. But my nominal definition admitted both the irrational freedom of individual-do-as-one-pleases, and the non-ethical Marxist 'scientific understanding' doctrine of freedom. Both doctrines preclude objects of rational appetite. Therefore the terms of these real relations are not freely chosen realities, according to Aquinas.

I reply thus. I concede the terms of these real relations are not the proper object of rational appetite. The reason is that faculties of the soul cannot be distinguished at the experiential level. But nevertheless I deny real terms of real relations are never desirable realities; e.g., food and other people. Moreover the real relations chosen are always identified with cultural relations that express the historic experience of a people. Hence in choosing desirable food and desirable people, one avails oneself of the experience of one's people showing these real relations have real terms that are desirable.

What is said about my conclusion being limited by my nominal definition is irrelevant. My argument demands no more than experience of the public as real. Both the individualist who wants protection from the public and the Marxist concede the reality of the public. My argument asks no more of them. That much is enough to yield my nominal definition. Experience of the public as real is had by experiencing identification and distinction of real and unreal relations as a public object. My nominal definition of freely chosen reality merely states that intelligent perception is the necessary condition of just that public object. Admittedly, my conclusion goes beyond what individualist do-as-you-please freedom and Marxism would grant. But that is not because I did not stick to the agreed nominal definition.

> 3. The objects of science and philosophy are public objects of intelligent perception. But the objects of science and philosophy are not freely chosen realities. Therefore freely chosen realities are not public objects of intelligent perception.

I reply by distinguishing the minor: "the objects of science and philosophy are not freely chosen realities." Some public objects of science and philosophy are freely chosen realities. For no work in science or philosophy can dispense with experiential objects and an account of them to colleagues. When accounting is made, the scholar must show he has distinguished real and unreal relations in experience. Thereby he will be rendering public his freely chosen real relations to extrinsically experienced realities.

I am not saying that no objects of science or philosophy are necessary. Real relations between physico-chemical and biological processes within and without the human body are not free. But these processes are also public objects defined by cultural relations in science and philosophy. Our intelligent experience of distinguishing and identifying our perceptual real relations and cultural relations to these processes relates us freely to them. Scientific and philosophic procedure freely relates us to reality precisely because, unless it breaks loose from biologically, psychologically, and culturally determined relations to its objects, it does not discern the real from the unreal. Unless it does that, it is not scientific or philosophic procedure. Accordingly Aquinas (1266-1267) wrote in the *De Malo*, q. 6: *Intelligo enim quia volo*, i.e., I understand because I so will.

> 4. All objects of experience are inevitably experienced, since experience belongs to the sensory order. But no freely chosen reality is inevitably experienced. Therefore, no freely chosen reality is an object of experience.

I reply as follows. I deny the major is a Thomistic position. Namely, I reject as Thomistic the statement: "All objects of experience are inevitably experienced, since experience belongs to the sensory order."

According to Aquinas (1266-1274), experience is the act of the cogitative and feeds the memory. But the cogitative and memory in man concern relations, according to his already cited doctrine: real relations for the cogitative and unreal ones for the memory. Experience and memory are concerned with these relations because of their "connection with abstract reason, by a kind of overflow" (*Summa Theologiae*, I, q. 78, art. 4 ad 5). Hence experience and memory of these real and unreal relations are *not* merely of the sensory order. They *are intellectualized experience and memory*, in Aquinas' doctrine.

Moreover, such intellectualized experience and memory are the matter of prudential judgment concerning contingent things (*Summa Theologiae*, I-II, q. 14, art. 6 ad 2). In these prudential matters, "rights are often entangled with wrongs and wrongs wear the air of good" (*ibid.*, q. 49, art. 8).[10] Hence for prudence one needs circumspection concerning present circumstances (*ibid.*, art. 7), and memory concerning the past (art. 1). One needs docility to elders and others (art. 3). One needs easy and rapid conjecture concerning practical things, e.g., "A man divining that the friendship of two people sprang from a common enmity" (art. 4, ad 1). Now all these together at least require the relations experienced by the cogitative and retained by the memory.

Hence identifying real relations in intellectualized experience with unreal relations retained in intellectualized memory is manifest in prudential judgment. Such prudential judgment is *free judgment: choice, liberum arbitrium*, the very core of Thomas' concept of human freedom. Thus the choice is a kind of judgment, which is why it is called in Latin "free judgment."[11] Indeed, "free judgment" is an act of will, according to Aquinas (*ibid.*, I, q. 83, art. 4). But the fact remains, the objects of this free judgment, which are intellectualized experience and memory, are *free*. Hence not all objects of experience are inevitably experienced, according to Aquinas.

It is from *such objects* of intellectualized experience that any doctrine of *acts* of choice must be derived. For in Thomistic method, acts are distinguished through their objects (*Summa*, I, q. 77, art. 3).

Chapter V

THE REPUBLIC OF THE FREE

Real and unreal relations identified and distinguished as public objects are the cornerstones of science, philosophy and freedom. That sums up our findings. Science and philosophy are at home among free men. For free choice derives from the distinction and identification of real and unreal relations in public objects just as do science and philosophy. If the "inner man" is understood as the free one, we must refuse to say with B. F. Skinner "good riddance" to the inner man. Yet to the inner man as the man of isolated individual conscience whose freedom is supposed to be purely subjective, no contemporary writer needed to say good riddance. His supposedly subjective freedom was devised two centuries ago just in order to rid the world of that freedom *as a public reality*. For that purpose, Kant had already withdrawn freedom from the public world and confined it to the subjective experience of practical reason. Contrary to that tradition, we have now concluded that the free man is the man whose freedom achieves freely chosen reality of public objects.

Heidegger's complete historical determinism of experience has now come to be seen as a partial phenomenon. Thorough-going historically determined experience exists only so long as the real and unreal relations involved in that experience are not distinguished. Once unreal cultural relations and real relations are distinguished and identified, unreal historical relations provide the public objects in which the real itself becomes a public object by identity.

Our conclusion seems to open up a triple perspective on philosophy.

First of all, it should be possible to build an ethics and politics concerned with real human goods. Aristotle built his ethics and politics on perceived free objects open to the public. Our conclusion has led us to real social relations as experiential objects. It seems an ethics and politics concerned with *bonum humanum in rebus* could replace the current fashion in ethics concerned only with the logic of ethical decision.

This supposition may seem unfounded. Can real social relations be the *bonum humanum in rebus* of an ethical and political doctrine? Do not real social relations seem too superficial a basis in reality to be the *bonum humanum in rebus?* This objection forgets that relations have the same reality content as the unknown natures and properties of the things related. The whole reality content of the real social relations and of the real people related is the same. So *bonum humanum in rebus* is already denoted by real social relations as the foundation of freedom, science, and philosophy, although further (and never final) research is required to discover this reality content.

In fact, we have already treated an ethical problem in this way. In Chapter IV we have seen how R.M. Hare's ethics uses the same experiential data as I use and uses them in the same way. Now a strange paradox appears. My doctrine of freely chosen realities makes the moral good a physical part of nature. But Hare has been hunted like a hare by a redoubtable feminine philosopher, Phillipa Foot, because he denies moral goods are real existing things. Mrs. Foot argues that one need not know the reason why one chooses to be or to have a good parent, daughter or friend. Hence these existing "beings" are called "good" independently of our choice (Foot, 1959: 227: Hare answers her in Hare, 1969: 252-257). Whereas my doctrine appears to be identical to Hare's on this point, he is attacked by Foot for denying the very thing that I am affirming. Moreover this question on which Hare is attacked is said to be "the central problem in moral philosophy."[1] Hence the doctrine of freely chosen reality seems to wedge its way between the warring parties on the central problem of moral philosophy.

Meantime, John Leslie Mackie has written his *Ethics: Inventing Right and Wrong* (1977), in which he rejects moral good as existing in physical nature. Mackie has abandoned the method of linguistic analysis on this question. For belief in the real existence of the moral good in nature, he concedes, is ingrained in common sense thought and in the meanings of the ordinary language of men. Hence Mackie (1977: 35) advocates an "error theory" to expel the ingrained habits of mankind about the real existence of moral goods. However I believe mankind may be proven right after all against Mackie, if freely chosen relations can wedge their way between the warring parties to this dispute. So it is reasonable to hold that totally experiential ethics can be constructed on the basis of such real relations only, as I will attempt to do in a sequel to the present volume.

The Nobel prize-winning French biologist, Jacques Monod (1970), agrees with Mackie that people take human values as part of nature. Monod, however, attributes this belief to the very structure of the human brain. For the human need of cohesion within the clan over ages of evolutionary time has resulted through natural selection in structuring the human brain to think in accordance with innate categories. Although men may infringe tribal law, because of these innate brain patterns it is not likely that any man could ever escape thinking in moral categories (Monod, 1970: 166-167). Indeed, the same evolutionary pressure for group survival produced another innate need in the brain: the need to assign man a necessary place in nature's scheme (*ibid.*, pp. 167, 169, 177). So if Monod is right, belief in the moral good as part of physical nature is an inevitable perception of mankind. Neither Mackie's method nor any other seems likely to change perceptions imposed on man by the structure of his brain. "Justice" and "red" would be on the same footing despite the best efforts of linguistic analysts: both would be perceptions inevitably resulting from the structure of the brain in the presence of appropriate stimuli. This unsuccessful effort to remove belief about moral values as part of nature recalls a line of Horace often quoted in the 17th century: *Naturam expelles furca, tamen usque recurret.* That's rendered by the poet Robert Grove in "Marigolds":

> With a fork drive nature out,
> She will ever yet return (Bartlett, 1882: 972b).

Secondly, real relations may be the experiential door into the intrinsic properties and natures of things. Was Locke not right that (1690: 321) "freedom can be attributed to nothing else" but human substance? Man is dissolved into the unfree environment, unless he is an existing individual unit (i.e., a substance in the Aristotelian sense). May not, likewise, the vast variety of real relations in the physical world be the experiential door into distinguishing the intrinsic properties and natures of things?

Thirdly, if freely chosen reality is an experiential fact, the antecedent of the theological argument for God's existence seems to be provided. For real relations do not differ in reality content from the things related. So freely chosen real relations do not differ in reality content from the things related. But freely chosen real relations are plainly purposeful. Therefore the realities of which they are the real relations are purposeful. With freedom replaced in reality as a part of the furniture of the real world, the antecedent of the theological argument for God's existence seems well founded.

According to the anthropologist Clifford Geertz (1968: 97), the typical religious perspective is:

> conviction that the values one holds are grounded in the inherent structure of reality, that between the way one ought to live and the way things really are there is an unbreakable inner connection.

Now real purposeful relations are values found "in the inherent structure of reality." Hence our manifesting real, purposeful relations in experience coincides with typical religious experience, according to Geertz.

Philosophers have taken that experience of real purposes for antecedent in proving God's existence.

According to the philosopher Sartre (1946: 33), "if God does not exist":

> it is nowhere written that "the good" exists, that one must be honest or must not lie, since we are now upon a plane where there are only men.[2]

Now one form of the hypothetical syllogism runs as follows: "If NON-A, NON-B, But B exists, therefore A exists" (Gredt, 1899-1901: I, 78 par. 73). So we argue, taking Sartre's statement as major premise:

> If God does not exist, the good does not exist. But the good exists, since freely chosen realities are existing goods. Therefore God exists.

Cornelio Fabro (1961: 1062) shows how modern atheism springs from "immanentism." Immanentism is the absorption of the real into human thought:

> *An immanenetist stand on being* can only involve a denial of *that transcendence in the epistemological dimension wherein consists the first step of theism rightly and radically understood* (author's emphasis).

Manifesting real relations as the origin of philosophy thus removes that immanentism from which atheism springs, according to Fabro.

Thus our conclusion opens a new perspective on many philosophical questions. That fruitfulness in hypotheses suggests that real relations may be in fact the origin of philosophy.

NOTES

Notes to General Introduction

1. Kant, 1790: Par. 21, p. 239 (I place in square brackets the part of the text not cited by me): "[Da sich nun diese Stimmung selbst muss allgemein mittheilen lassen, mithin auch das Gefühl derselben (bei einer gegebenen Vorstellung); die allgemeine Mittheilbarkeit eines Gefühls aber einen Gemeinsinn voraussetzt: so wird dieser mit Grunde angenommen werden können, und zwar ohne sich desfalls auf psychologische Beobachtungen zu fussen, sondern als] die nothwendige Bedingung der allgemeinen Mittheilbarkeit unserer Erkenntniss, welche in jeder Logik and jedem Princip der Erkenntnisse, das nicht skeptisch ist, vorausgesetzt werden muss."

English trans., p. 84: "Since, now, this disposition itself must admit of being universally communicated, and hence also the feeling of it (in the case of a given representation), while again, the universal communicability of a feeling presupposes a common sense: it follows that our assumption of it is well founded. And here, too, we do not have to take our stand on psychological observations, but we assume a common sense as the necessary condition of the universal communicability of our knowledge, which is presupposed in every logic and every principle of knowledge that is not one of scepticism."

2. "Πάντα δὲ τὰ πρός τι πρὸς ἀντιστρέφοντα λέγεται, οἷον ὁ δοῦλος δεσπότου δοῦλος λέγεται καὶ ὁ δεσπότης δούλου δεσπότης."

3. "Freedom, consisting in the in-sistent ex-sistence of *Da-sein*, is the essence of truth (in the sense of propositional rightness) only because freedom itself springs from the original essence of truth, from the reign of mystery in error."

German text (1949: 23): "Die Freiheit, aus der in-sistenten Eksistenz des Da-seins begriffen, ist das Wesen der Wahrheit (im Sinne der Richtigkeit des Vorstellens) nur deshalb, weil die Freiheit selbst dem anfänglichen Wesen der Wahrheit, dem Walten des Geheimnisses in der Irre, entstammt.

4. "In whatever manner beings are interpreted—whether as spirit, after the fashion of spiritualism; or as matter and force, after the fashion of materialism; or as becoming and life, or idea, will, substance, subject, or *energeia*; or as the eternal recurrence of the same events—every time, beings as beings appear in the light of Being. Wherever metaphysics represents beings, Being has entered into the light. Being has arrived in a state of unconcealedness (Ἀλήθεια). But whether and how Being itself involves such unconcealedness, whether and how it manifests itself in, and as, metaphysics, remains obscure. Being in its revelatory essence, i.e. in its truth, is not recalled. Nevertheless, when metaphysics gives answers to its question concerning beings as such, metaphysics speaks out of the unnoticed revealedness of Being. The truth of Being may thus be called the ground in which metaphysics, as the root of the tree of philosophy, is kept and from which it is nourished."

German text (1949: 7-8): "Wie auch immer das Seiende ausgelegt werden mag, ob als Geist im Sinne des Spiritualismus, ob als Stoff und Kraft im Sinne des Materialismus, ob als Werden und Leben, ob als Vorstellung, ob als Wille, ob als Substanz, ob als Subjekt, ob als Energeia, ob als ewige Wiederkehr des Gleichen, jedesmal erscheint das Seiende als Seiendes im Lichte des Seins. Überall hat sich, wenn die Metaphysik das Seiende vorstellt, Sein gelichtet. Sein ist in einer Unverborgenheit (Ἀλήθεια) angekommen. Ob und wie Sein solche

Unverborgenheit mit sich bringt, ob und wie gar Es selbst sich in der Metaphysik und als diese anbringt, bleibt verhüllt. Das Sein wird in seinem entbergenden Wesen, d. h. in seiner Wahrheit nicht gedacht. Gleichwohl spricht die Metaphysik in ihren Antworten auf ihre Frage nach dem Seienden als solchem aus der unbeachteten Offenbarkeit des Seins. Die Wahrheit des Seins kann deshalb der Grund heissen, in dem die Metaphysik als die Wurzel des Baumes der Philosophie gehalten, aus dem sie genährt wird."

5. Heidegger, 1957: 134: "Unendlich unmöglicher bleibt es, 'das Sein' als das Allgemeine zum jeweilig Seienden vorzustellen. Es gibt Sein nur je und je in dieser und jener geschicklichen Prägung: Φύσις, Λόγος, Ἕν, Ἰδέα, Ἐνέργεια, Substanzialität, Objektivität, Subjektivität, Wille, Wille zur Macht, Wille zum Willen. Aber dies Geschickliche gibt es nicht aufgereiht wie Äpfel, Birnen, Pfirsiche, aufgereiht auf dem Ladentisch des historischen Vorstellens."

English trans., p. 66: "It is still infinitely more impossible to represent "Being" as the general characteristic of particular beings. There is Being only in this or that particular historic character: Φύσις, Λόγος, Ἕν, Ἰδέα, Ἐνέργεια, Substantiality, Objectivity, Subjectivity, the Will, the Will to Power, the Will to Will. But these historic forms cannot be found in rows, like apples, pears, peaches, lined up on the counter of historical representational thinking."

6. Heidegger, 1961: I, 469: "Weil Nietzsches metaphysische Grundstellung in dem gekennzeichneten Sinne das Ende der Metaphysik ist, deshalb vollzieht sich in ihr die grösste und tiefste Sammlung, d.h. Vollendung aller wesentlichen Grundstellungen der abendländischen Philosophie seit Platon und im Licht des Platonismus, in einer von daher bestimmten, aber selbst schöpferischen Grundstellung. Sie bleibt jedoch nur dann eine wirklich wirkende metaphysische Grundstellung, wenn sie ihrerseits in allen ihren wesentlichen Kräften und Herrschaftsbereichen zur *Gegenstellung* entfaltet wird."

Magnus, 1970: XI, comments: "Heidegger's own interpretation of Nietzsche raises obvious additional difficulties. It is guided by no conventional standards of critical scholarship. For example, Heidegger views the doctrine of eternal recurrence as the last metaphysical thought in the Western tradition, the culmination and completion of metaphysics, a thought which is fated to appear when it does as Nietzsche's response to the claim of the Being (*Sein*) of beings (*Seienden*). Clearly we are dealing here with no ordinary interpretation. Heidegger's interpretation is propelled by an inner necessity of his own thinking which pursues the meaning of Being."

7. Heidegger, 1943: 17: "die seltenen und einfachen Entscheidungen der Geschichte."

8. Heidegger, 1950: 336: "*Die Seinsvergessenheit ist die Vergessenheit des Unterschiedes des Seins zum Seienden.*" (Heidegger's emphasis).

Notes to Chapter I

1. Aristotle, 335-322BCa: p. 22: "ὥστε τὰ ἄλλα πάντα ἤτοι καθ᾽ ὑποκειμένων λέγεται τῶν πρώτων οὐσιῶν ἢ ἐν ὑποκειμέναις αὐταῖς ἐστίν. μὴ οὐσῶν οὖν τῶν πρώτων οὐσιῶν ἀδύνατον τῶν ἄλλων τι εἶναι."

2. Ross comments: "Parmenides is ignorant of the distinctiveness of the categories of being and of the difference between potential and actual being .... Parmenides' two assumptions were: (1) 'being' has but one meaning, and (2) there is nothing besides being. From this he argued that reality is one and indivisible. Aristotle refutes the argument by making parallel suppositions about 'white', viz. that (a) 'white' has but one meaning, and (2) there is nothing but what is white (a26, cf. 29-30), and by showing that these are compatible with there being many white things" (Ross, 1936, p. 473). Thus Aristotle substitutes the *one experiential object white* for the non-empirical object *being*. Then he shows that the one experiential object *white* contains the non-empirical plurality of subject and accident. This non-empirical plurality of subject and accident is what Ross calls "the difference between potential and actual being." But Parmenides had not yet come to see this non-empirical difference between subject and accident.

3. Aristotle, 335-322BCb: 186a 25-32: "ψευδὴς μὲν ἢ ἁπλῶς λαμβάνει τὸ ὂν λέγεσθαι, λεγομένου πολλαχῶς, ἀσυμπέραντοσ δὲ ὅτι, εἰ μόνα τὰ λευκὰ ληφθείη, σημαίνοντος ἕν τοῦ λευκοῦ, οὐθὲν ἧττον πολλὰ τὰ λευκὰ καὶ οὐχ ἕν. οὔτε γὰρ τῇ συνεχείᾳ ἕν ἔσται τὸ λευκὸν οὔτε τω λόγῳ· ἄλλο γὰρ ἔσται τὸ εἶναι λευκῷ καὶ τὸ δεδεγμένῳ, καὶ οὐκ ἔσται παρὰ τὸ λεψκὸν οὐθὲν χωριστόν· οὐ γὰρ ἢ χωριστὸν ἀλλὰ τῶ εἶναι ἕτερον τὸ λευκὸν καὶ ῷ ὑπάρχει. ἀλλὰ τοῦτο Παρμενίδης οὔπω ἑώρα."

4. Aquinas, 1269-1270: lib. I, lect. 6, no. 40: "Sed hoc nondum erat consideratum tempore Parmenidis, scilicet quod aliquid esset unum subiecto et multa ratione: et ideo credidit quod si nihil sit extra aliquod subiectum, quod sequatur id esse unum. Sed hoc falsum est tum propter multitudinem partium, tum propter diversam rationem subiecti et accidentis."

In his commentary on Book I of the Physics, Aquinas repeats this argument from the non-empirical difference of subject and accidents (*lectio* 7, #48 of the Marietti edition). But only in this text of *lectio* 6 does he say that in Parmenides' days *the distinction was unknown (Nondum consideratum)*. As Ernan McMullin points out (1963: 203), Positivists, analytic philosophers, and logical empiricists of our day refuse to make this distinction.

5. "Φύσις μὲν οὖν ἐστι τὸ ῥηθέν· φύσιν δὲ ἔχει ὅσα τοιαύτην ἔχει ἀρχήν. καὶ ἔστι πάντα ταῦτα οὐσία· ὑποκείμενον γάρ τι, καὶ ἐν ὑποκειμένῳ ἐστὶν ἡ φύσις ἀεί."

6. "Posset autem aliquis credere quod quia materia dicitur natura et etiam forma, quod compositum possit dici natura; quia substantia dicitur de forma et materia et de composito.

Sed hoc excludit dicens quod compositum ex materia et forma, ut homo, non est ipsa natura, sed est aliquid *a natura*."

7. "Μεταβολὴ δ' οὐκ ἔστιν οὐδεμία ἄπειρος. ἅπασα γὰρ ἦν ἔκ τινος εἴς τι καὶ ἡ ἐν ἀντιφάσει καὶ ἡ ἐν ἐναντίοις· ὥστε τῶν μὲν κατ' ἀντίφασιν ἡ φάσισ καὶ ἡ ἀπόφασις πέρας, οἷον γενέσεως μὲν τὸ ὄν φθορᾶς δὲ τὸ μὴ ὄν, τῶν δὲ ἐν τοῖς ἐναντίοις τὰ ἐναντία (ταῦτα γὰρ ἄκρα τῆς μεταβολῆς), ὥστε καὶ ἀλλοιώσεως πάσησ·[1] ἐξ ἐναντίων γάρ τινων ἡ ἀλλοίωσις. ὁμοίως δὲ καὶ αὐξήσεως καὶ φθίσεως·"

[1][I have punctuated so as to indicate that ἀλλοιώσεωσ ἁάσης is governed by πέρας ἐστὶ τὰ ἐναντία (not ἄκρα) understood.—C.]

8. ''879. [Postquam Philosophus ostendit quod impartibile non movetur,] *hic intendit ostendere quod nulla mutatio est infinita;* quod est contra Heraclitum, [qui posuit omnia moveri semper.

''Et circa hoc duo facit:]
primo ostendit quod nulla mutatio est infinita secundum propriam speciem; [secundo ostendit quomodo possit esse infinita tempore, ibi: *Sed si sic contingit* etc.

''Circa primum duo facit:
primo ostendit quod mutatio non est infinita secundum speciem in aliis mutationibus praeter motum localem;
secundo ostendit idem in motu locali, ibi: *Loci autem mutatio* etc.]
''880. Prima ratio talis est. Supra dictum est quod omnis mutatio est ex quodam in quiddam. Et in quibusdam quidem mutationibus, quae scilicet sunt inter contradictorie opposita, ut generatio et corruptio, vel inter contraria, ut alteratio, et augmentum et decrementum, manifestum est quod habent praefixos terminos. Unde in his mutationibus quae sunt inter contradictorie opposita, terminus est vel affirmatio vel negatio, sicut terminus generationis est *esse,* corruptionis vero *non esse.*

''Similiter illarum mutationum quae sunt inter contraria, ipsa contraria sunt termini ad quos, sicut ad quaedam ultima, mutationes huiusmodi terminantur.''

9. ''οὕτως οὐδὲ περὶ τοῦ νῦν ῥηθέντος πρὸς τὸν φνσικόν· ὑπόθεσις γὰρ ὅτι ἡ θύσις ἀρχὴ τῆς κινήσεω.

Σχεδὸν δέ τι καὶ το ἀναι πάντα κινεῖσθαι ψεῦδος μέν, ἧττον δὲ τούτου παρὰ τὴν μέθοδον· ἐτέθη μὲν γὰρ ἡ φύσις ἐν τοῖς Φυσικοῖς ἀρχή, καθάπερ κινήσεως, καὶ ἠρεμίασ, ὅμως δὲ φυσικὸν (μαλλον) ἡ κίνησις.''

10. ''Et primo comparat hanc opinionem praecedenti opinioni, quae ponebat omnia semper quiescere: et dicit quod dicere omnia moveri semper, ut Heraclitus dixit, est quidem falsum et contra principia scientiae naturalis; sed tamen minus repugnat arti haec positio quam prima.

''Et quod quidem repugnet arti manifestum est: quia tollit suppositionem scientiae naturalis, in qua ponitur quod natura non solum est principium motus, sed etiam quietis; et sic patet quod similiter naturale est quies, sicut et motus.''

11. ''Dicebat enim Plato quod accidens est non ens . . . Licet enim diceret accidens esse non ens, non tamen dicebat accidens esse nihil, sed aliquid.''

12. ''Ad quartum dicendum quod accidentia hujusmodi, manente substantia panis et vini, non habebant ipsa esse nec alia accidentia; sed substantia eorum habebat hujusmodi esse per ea, sicut nix est alba per albedinem. Sed post consecrationem ipsa accidentia quae remanent, habent esse. Unde sunt composita ex *esse* et *quod est,* sicut in Prima Parte de angelis dictum est.''

13. ''Si igitur potentia non inest alicui nisi quando agit, sequitur quod nihil est calidum vel frigidum, dulce vel amarum, et huiusmodi, nisi quando sentitur immutans sensum. Hoc autem patet esse falsum. Nam si hoc esset verum, sequeretur quod opinio *Protagorae* esset vera, quae dicebat omnes proprietates et

naturas rerum consistere solum in sentiri et opinari. Ex quo consequebatur contradictoria simul esse vera.''

14. ''601.—Quod autem praedicta huic principio conveniant, sic ostendit. Impossibile enim est quemcumque 'suscipere', sive opinari, quod idem sit simul et non sit: quamvis quidam arbitrentur *Heraclitum* hoc opinatum fuisse. — Verum est autem, quod Heraclitus hoc dixit, non tamen hoc potuit opinari. Non enim necessarium est, quod quicquid aliquis dicit, haec mente suscipiat vel opinetur.''

15. ''[Manifestum est ergo quod certissimum principium sive firmissimum, tale debet esse,] ut circa id non possit errari, et quod non sit suppositum et quod adveniat naturaliter.''

16. ''Hujus autem ratio est, quia potentia cognoscitiva proportionatur cognoscibili. Unde intellectus angelici, qui est totaliter a corpore separatus, objectum proprium est substantia intelligibilis a corpore separata; et per hujusmodi intelligibilia materialia cognoscit. Intellectus autem humani, qui est conjunctus corpori, proprium objectum est quidditas sive natura in materia corporali existens; et per hujusmodi naturas visibilium rerum etiam in invisibilium rerum aliqualem cognitionem ascendit. De ratione autem hujus naturae est, quod in aliquo individuo existat, quod non est absque materia corporali: sicut de ratione naturae lapidis est quod sit in hoc lapide, et de ratione naturae equi quod sit in hoc equo, et sic de aliis. Unde natura lapidis, vel cujuscumque materialis rei, cognosci non potest complete et vere, nisi secundum quod cognoscitur ut in particulari existens. Particulare autem apprehendimus per sensum et imaginationem. Et ideo necesse est ad hoc quod intellectus actu intelligat suum objectum proprium, quod convertat se ad phantasmata, ut speculetur naturam universalem in particulari existentem.''

17. ''RESPONSIO: Dicendum quod singulare in rebus materialibus intellectus noster directe et primo cognoscere non potest. Cujus ratio est, quia principium singularitatis in rebus materialibus est materia individualis: intellectus autem noster, sicut supra dictum est, intelligit abstrahendo speciem intelligibilem ab hujusmodi materia. Quod autem a materia individuali abstrahitur est universale. Unde intellectus noster directe non est cognoscitivus nisi universalium.
''Indirecte autem, et quasi per quandam reflexionem, potest cognoscere singulare: quia, sicut supra dictum est, etiam postquam species intelligibiles abstraxit, non potest secundum eas actu intelligere nisi convertendo se ad phantasmata, in quibus species intelligibiles intelligit, ut dicitur.
''Sic igitur ipsum universale per speciem intelligibilem directe intelligit; indirecte autem singularia, quorum sunt phantasmata. Et hoc modo format hanc propositionem, *Socrates est homo.*''

18. ''594 [13]. Deinde cum dicit [438]: *Quod autem dictum est* etc., manifestat quod dictum est in praecedenti solutione, quantum ad hoc quod ex experimento singularium accipitur universale; et dicit quod illud quod supra dictum est, et non plane, quomodo scilicet ex experimento singularium fiat universale in anima, iterum oportet dicere, ut planius manifestetur. Si enim accipiantur multa singu-

laria, quae sunt indifferentia quantum ad aliquid unum in eis existens, illud unum secundum quod non differunt, in anima acceptum, est primum universale, quidquid sit illud, sive scilicet pertineat ad essentiam singularium, sive non. Quia enim invenimus Socratem et Platonem et multos alios esse indifferentes quantum ad albedinem, accipimus hoc unum, scilicet album, quasi universale quod est accidens. Et similiter quia invenimus Socratem et Platonem et alios esse indifferentes quantum ad rationalitatem, hoc unum in quo non differunt, scilicet rationale, accipimus quasi universale quod est differentia.

''595 [14]. Qualiter autem hoc unum accipi possit, manifestat consequenter. Manifestum est enim quod singulare sentitur *proprie* et *per se*, sed tamen sensus est quodammodo etiam ipsius universalis. Cognoscit enim Calliam non solum in quantum est Callias, sed etiam in quantum est hic homo, et similiter Socratem in quantum est hic homo. Et exinde est quod tali acceptione sensus praeexistente, anima intellectiva potest considerare hominem in utroque. Si autem ita esset quod sensus apprehenderet solum id quod est particularitatis, et nullo modo cum hoc apprehenderet universalem naturam in particulari, non esset possibile quod ex apprehensione sensus causaretur in nobis cognitio universalis.''

19. ''[Experitur enim unusquisque seipsum esse qui intelligit. Attribuitur autem aliqua actio alicui tripliciter, ut patet per Philosophum. Dicitur enim movere aliquid aut agere vel secundum se totum, sicut medicus sanat, aut secundum partem, sicut homo videt per oculum, aut per accidens, sicut dicitur quod album aedificat, quia accidit aedificatori esse album. Cum igitur dicimus Socratem aut Platonem intelligere, manifestum est quod non attribuitur ei per accidens; attribuitur enim ei inquantum est homo quod essentialiter praedicatur de ipso. Aut ergo oportet dicere quod Socrates intelligit secundum se totum, sicut Plato posuit, dicens hominem esse animam intellectivam, aut oportet dicere quod intellectus est aliquid pars Socratis. Et primum quidem stare non potest, ut supra ostensum est, propter hoc quod] ipse idem homo est qui percipit se et intelligere et sentire; [sentire autem non est sine corpore, unde oportet corpus aliquam esse hominis partem.].''

20. ''Quaedam enim sunt quae secundum esse totum completum sunt extra animam; et hujusmodi sunt entia completa, sicut homo et lapis. [Quaedam autem sunt quae nihil habent extra animam, sicut somnia et imaginatio chimerae. Quaedam autem sunt quae habent fundamentum in re extra animam, sed complementum rationis eorum quantum ad id quod est formale, est per operationem animae, ut patet in universali. Humanitas enim est aliquid in re, non tamen ibi habet rationem universalis, cum non sit extra animam aliqua humanitas multis communis; sed secundum quod accipitur in intellectu, adjungitur ei per operationem intellectus intentio, secundum quam dicitur species: et similiter est de tempore, quod habet fundamentum in motu, scilicet prius et posterius ipsius motus; sed quantum ad id quod est formale in tempore, scilicet numeratio, completur per operationem intellectus numerantis. Similiter dico de veritate, quod habet fundamentum in re, sed ratio ejus completur per actionem intellectus, quando scilicet apprehenditur eo modo quo est. Unde dicit Philosophus (6 Metaph., text. 8), quod verum et falsum sunt in anima; sed bonum et malum in rebus. Cum autem in re sit quidditas ejus et suum esse, veritas fundatur in esse rei magis quam in quidditate, sicut et] nomen entis ab esse imponitur.''

21. ''Et inde est quod, sicut dicit Boëtius, *quaedam sunt dignitates vel propositiones per se notae communiter omnibus*; et hujusmodi sunt illae propositiones
quarum termini sunt omnibus noti, ut 'Omne totum est majus sua parte' et 'Quae
uni et eidem sunt aequalia sibi invicem sunt aequalia'.''

22. ''[Et ideo secundum doctrinam Aristotilis via media inter has duas tenen-
da est in omnibus praedictis: formae enim naturales praeexistunt quidem in
materia, non in actu, ut alii dicebant, sed in potentia solum de qua in actum
reducuntur per agens extrinsecum proximum, non solum per agens primum, ut
alia opinio ponebat; similiter etiam secundum ipsius sententiam in VI Ethicorum
virtutum habitus ante earum consummationem praeexistunt in nobis in quibusdam naturalibus inclinationibus quae sunt quaedam virtutum inchoationes, sed
postea per exercitium operum adducuntur in debitam consummationem;] similiter etiam dicendum est de scientiae acquisitione quod praeexistunt in nobis quaedam scientiarum semina, scilicet primae conceptiones intellectus quae statim
lumine intellectus agentis cognoscuntur per species a sensibilibus abstractas, sive
sint complexa sicut dignitates, sive incomplexa sicut ratio entis et unius et huiusmodi quae statim intellectus apprehendit; in istis autem principiis universalibus
omnia sequentia includuntur sicut in quibusdam rationibus seminalibus: quando
ergo ex istis universalibus cognitionibus mens educitur ut actu cognoscat particu-
laria quae prius in universali et quasi in potentia cognoscebantur, tunc aliquis
dicitur scientiam acquirere.''

23. ''Alia est divisio formalis quae fit per oppositas vel diversas formas; et
hanc divisionem sequitur multitudo quae non est in aliquo genere sed est de
transcendentibus, secundum quod ens dividitur per unum et multa.''

24. ''Tertio modo dicitur aliquid addere super alterum secundum rationem
tantum, quando scilicet aliquid est de ratione unius quod non est de ratione
alterius, quod tamen nihil est in rerum natura sed in ratione tantum, sive per illud contrahatur id cui dicitur addi sive non: caecum enim addit aliquid super
hominem, scilicet caecitatem, quae non est aliquid ens in natura, sed rationis tantum ens est comprehendentis privationes; et per hoc homo contrahitur, non enim
omnis homo caecus est; sed cum dicimus talpam caecam non fit per hoc addi-
tum aliqua contractio . . .
''Id autem quod est rationis tantum non potest esse nisi duplex, scilicet negatio et aliqua relatio. Omnis enim positio absoluta aliquid in rerum natura existens
significat. Sic ergo supra ens, quod est prima conceptio intellectus, unum addit
id quod est rationis tantum, scilicet negationem: dicitur enim unum quasi ens
indivisum; sed verum et bonum positive dicuntur unde non possunt addere nisi
relationem quae sit rationis tantum.''

25. ''[Non autem potest esse quod super ens universale aliquid addat aliquid
primo modo, quamvis illo modo possit fieri additio super aliquod ens particulare; nulla enim res naturae est quae sit extra essentiam entis universalis quamvis aliqua res sit extra essentiam huius entis.] Secundo autem modo inveniuntur aliqua addere super ens quia ens contrahitur per decem genera, quorum
unumquodque addit aliquid super ens, non quidem aliquod accidens vel aliquam
differentiam quae sit extra essentiam entis sed determinatum modum essendi
qui fundatur in ipsa existentia rei. [Sic autem bonum non addit aliquid super ens,
cum bonum dividatur aequaliter in decem genera ut ens, patet in I Ethicorum.]''

26. "387 [*Secunda* ratio ponitur ibi [272]: *Sed neque communium principiorum* etc., quae sumitur ex principiis communibus; et dicit quod] non possunt esse aliqua principia communia, ex quibus solum omnia syllogizentur, sicut hoc est principium commune. *De quolibet est affirmatio vel negatio;* quod quidem communiter est verum in omni genere; non tamen est possibile, quod ex solis aliquibus taliter communibus possint omnia syllogizari: quia genera entium sunt diversa, et diversa sunt principia quae sunt solum quantitatum principia, ab his quae solum sunt principia qualitatum; quae oportet coassumere principiis communibus ad concludendum in qualibet materia. Puta si in quantitatibus oporteat ex dicto principio communi syllogizare, oportet accipere quod, cum haec sit falsa, *punctus est linea,* oportet hanc esse veram, *punctus non est linea.* Et similiter in qualitatibus oportet coassumere aliquid proprium qualitati. Unde relinquitur quod impossibile sit esse eadem principia omnium syllogismorum."

27. "In his autem quae in apprehensione hominum cadunt quidam ordo invenitur. Nam illud quod primo cadit sub apprehensione est ens, cujus intellectus includitur in omnibus quaecumque quis apprehendit. Et ideo primum principium indemonstrabile est quod non est simul affirmare et negare, quod fundatur supra rationem entis et non entis; et super hoc principio omnia alia fundantur, ut dicit Philosophus in IV *Meta.*"

28. "Sed multitudo etiam secundum rationem consequenter se habet ad unum, quia divisa non intelligimus habere rationem multitudinis nisi per hoc quod utrique divisorum attribuimus unitatem. Unde unum ponitur in definitione multitudinis, non autem multitudo in definitione unius. Sed divisio cadit in intellectu ex ipsa negatione entis. Ita quod primo cadit in intellectu ens, secundo quod hoc ens non est illud ens et sic apprehendimus divisionem, tertio unum, quarto multitudinem."

29. "Insunt enim nobis naturaliter quaedam principia prima complexa omnibus nota, ex quibus ratio procedit ad cognoscendum in actu conclusiones quae in praedictis principiis potentialiter continentur, [sive per inventionem propriam, sive per doctrinam alienam, sive per revelationem divinam; in quibus omnibus modis cognoscendis homo iuvatur ex principiis naturaliter cognitis: *vel* ita quod ipsa principia cognita ad cognitionem acquirendam sufficiant adminiculantibus sensu et imaginatione, sicut cum aliquam cognitionem acquirimus per inventionem vel doctrinam; *vel* ita quod principia praedicta ad cognitionem acquirendam non sufficiant; nihilominus tamen in huiusmodi cognoscendis principia dirigunt, in quantum inveniuntur non repugnare principiis naturaliter cognitis: quod si esset, intellectus nullo modo eis assentiret, sicut non potest dissentire principiis.]
"Et similiter in intellectu insunt nobis etiam naturaliter quaedam conceptiones omnibus notae, ut entis, unius, boni, et huiusmodi, a quibus eodem modo procedit intellectus ad cognoscendum quidditatem uniuscuiusque rei, per quem procedit a principiis per se notis ad cognoscendas conclusiones; et hoc *vel* per ea quae quis sensu percipit, sicut cum per sensibiles proprietates alicuius rei concipio illius rei quidditatem; *vel* per ea quae ab aliis quis audit, [ut cum laicus qui nescit quid sit musica, cum audit aliquam artem esse per quam discit canere vel psallere, concipit quidditatem musicae, cum ipse praesciat quid sit ars, et quid sit canere; *aut etiam* per ea quae ex revelatione habentur, ut est in his quae fidei sunt.]

["Ipsa autem conceptio caritatis, quam intellectus format modo praedicto, non est solum similitudo caritatis sicut species rerum in sensu vel imaginatione: quia] sensus et imaginatio nunquam pertingunt ad cognoscendum naturam rei, sed solummodo accidentia, quae circumstant rem; et ideo species quae sunt in sensu vel imaginatione, non repraesentant naturam rei, sed accidentia eius tantum, sicut sensus repraesentat hominem quantum ad accidentalia, sed intellectus cognoscit ipsam naturam et substantiam rei. Unde species intelligibilis est similitudo ipsius essentiae rei, et est quodammodo ipsa quidditas et natura rei secundum esse intelligibile, non secundum esse naturale, prout est in rebus. Et ideo omnia quae non cadunt sub sensu et imaginatione, sed sub solo intellectu, cognoscuntur per hoc quod essentiae vel quidditates eorum sunt aliquo modo in intellectu."

30. "His praeintellectis, primo ponam ordinem originis in cognitione actuali eorum quae concipiuntur confuse, — et quoad hoc dico quod primum actualiter cognitum confuse, est species specialissima, cuius singulare efficacius et fortius primo movet sensum, et hoc, supposito quod sit in debita proportione praesens sensui."

31. "Secundam rationem pertracto sic: sicut argutum est etiam quod Deus non est cognoscibilis a nobis naturaliter nisi ens sit univocum creato et increato, ita potest argui de substantia et accidente. Si enim substantia non immutat immediate intellectum nostrum ad aliquam intellectionem sui, sed tantum accidens sensibile, sequitur quod nullum conceptum quiditativum poterimus habere de illa nisi aliquis talis possit abstrahi a conceptu accidentis; sed nullus talis quiditativus abstrahibilis a conceptu accidentis est, nisi conceptus entis.

"Quod autem est suppositum de substantia, quod non immutat intellectum nostrum immediate ad actum circa se, hoc probatur, quia quidquid praesens immutat intellectum, illius absentia potest naturaliter cognosci ab intellectu quando non immutatur, sicut apparet II *De anima*, quod visus est tenebrae perceptivus, quando scilicet lux non est praesens, et ideo tunc visus non immutatur. Igitur si intellectus naturaliter immutatur a substantia immediate, ad actum circa ipsam, sequeretur quod quando substantia non esset praesens, posset naturaliter cognosci non esse praesens, — et ita naturaliter posset cognosci in hostia altaris consecrata non esse substantiam panis, quod est manifeste falsum."

32. Vol. 26, p. 504: "12. *Accidens in concreto primo cognitum non concipitur sub ratione inhaerentis.*—Atque hinc infero, quod, licet res primo ac per se cognita, revera sit accidens, tamen ab intellectu ex vi illius conceptus non cognoscitur formaliter sub ratione accidentis, id est, sub ratione inhaerentis alicui, sed solum sub ratione hujus sensibilis et materialis entis. Imo neque ex vi illius conceptus discernitur, an illud objectum sit compositum ex forma et subjecto, vel quid simplex, sed tantum praecise et abstracte id concipitur per modum unins. Quod satis nobis ostendit mysterium Eucharistiae; non enim magis concipimus substantiam ubi est sub accidentibus, quam ubi non est. Formalis ergo conceptio accidentis ut inhaerentis, et substantiae ut sustentantis, vel per se stantis, discursu postea acquiritur, et maxime ex rerum mutationibus; nam dum videmus accidentia mutari, mutari intelligimus. Unde si comparatio fiat inter hos conceptus expressos et formales accidentis, ut accidens est, et substantiae, ut est substantia, videtur sane non esse inter eos necessarius ordo prout in nobis sunt; quia in principio per

modum correlativorum substantiam et accidens videmur concipere, cum solum per illam mutuam habitudinem illa discernere incipiamus; postea vero indifferenter possumus excitari ad utrumque directe cognoscendum, et indirecte seu in obliquo semper cognitio unius terminatur aliquo modo ad alterum; quia, ut dixi, semper conceptio est connotativa seu respectiva; quamvis hoc in accidente proveniat ex imperfectione ejus; in substantia vero ex nostra. Sed de his latius in scientia de Anima.''

33. Vol. 26, p. 503: ''[Et probatur, quia, licet substantia secundum se sit perfectior et intelligibilior, tamen respectu nostri accidens habet majorem vim ad immutandum intellectum, quia] intellectus noster non immutatur, nisi mediis speciebus sensibus impressis; sensibus autem non imprimuntur species substantiae, sed accidentium tantum; ergo accidentia sunt, quae primo immutant intellectum; ergo prius concipiuntar ab intellectu quam substantia.

''*Hujus puncti resolutio cum aliquali opinionum concordia.*

''[9. Inter has opiniones haec posterior mihi videtur absolute vera;] est tamen intelligenda, ut non omnino excludatur substantia a primo conceptu intellectus. [Est igitur advertendum, cum dicitur accidens prius cognesci, non esse intelligendum de accidente in abstracto, sed in concreto, ut expresse declarat Hervaeus, et Soncinas etiam notavit, et experientia constat, et ex ratione facta cum proportione applicata. Nam objecta sensibilia, quae movent sensum, non sunt accidentia in abstracto, sed in concreto, prout in re sunt; non enim immutat visum albedo, sed album, ut Aristoteles notat, opusc. de Sensu et sensibus, quia actiones sunt singularium subsistentium. Sensus ergo exterior videt quidem accidens, non tamen abstracte, sed concrete, et ideo dicitur videre per se albedinem, per accidens autem substantiam, de Anim., cap. 6, quia videt album seu coloratum, in quo includitur aliquo modo substantia; ergo similiter] intellectus, licet primum mutetur ad cognitionem alicujus accidentis per se sensibilis, non tamen ut illud in abstracto concipiat, sed in concreto. Ex quo fit ut a primo illo conceptu non omnino excludatur substantia, quia in illo objectivo conceptu accidentis concreti necessario involvitur substantia, quasi tecta et involuta accidentibus. Unde dicere possumus, rem per se ac formaliter primo cognitam esse accidens; rem autem adaequate et quasi materialiter cognitam, esso substantiam seu compositum ex substantia et accidente, quod per modum unius subsistentis in tali forma accidentali concipitur.''

34. Poinsot, 1633: Q. 1, art. 3: ''DICES: Potest attingi ab intellectu quidditas singularitatis quoad an est, et non quoad quid est, et sic facilius cognoscetur ipsum an est singularitatis quam naturae.] Sed esto ita sit, quod intellectus incipiat cognoscere quidditatem sui obiecti non quidditative, sed quoad an est, ita quod neque de ipsa natura neque de ipsa singularitate attingat aliud praedicatum quam ipsum an est, tamen hoc ipso non cognoscitur singulare ut singulare est, sed sub confusione et ratione quadam communissima ipsius esse, ita quod de ipsa singularitate non cognoscit nisi quod sit ens. Hoc autem est cognoscere aliquid commune ipsi singulari et ipsi naturae; de utroque enim datur cognitio quoad an est, et sic ipsum esse seu an est ut concretum seu applicatum alicui singulari sensibili erit primum cognitum intellectus. Quare (quod valde advertendum est) quando intellectus cognoscit aliquid quoad an est, non praescindit a quod quid seu a quidditate, hoc enim est impossibile, cum sit formale eius obiectum et primo

et per se intelligibile, sed solum non cognoscit quidditative, id est penetrando constitutionem propriam quidditatis et causas essendi, sed in ipsa quidditate solum attingit praedicatum quoddam valde commune et confusum, quod est ipsum esse; et hoc est, quod tunc cognoscit ut quod quid."

"Et quia tanto aliquid est confusius, quanto pauciores rationes discernuntur, ita quod earum propriae differentiae seu praedicata non distinguantur, illud erit maxime confusum, in quo nec ipsi supremi gradus et communiora praedicata, v.g. substantia et accidens discernuntur. Et hoc vocamus ens concretum seu applicatum quidditati sensibili, id est in natura aliqua sensibili inventum, non ut subest statui abstractionis et universalitatis [secundum habitudinem et respectum ad inferiora, ad quae potentialiter se habet, sed ut actualiter intrat ipsam compositionem rei, et ut cognoscitur secundum se; siquidem modo loquimur de cognitione confusa totius actualis, non totius potentialis. Totum enim potentiale dicit ordinem ad inferiora et supponit praecessisse cognitionem totius actualis, quia hoc est subiectum et fundamentum illus universalitatis et ordinis ad inferiora, quae non statim in prima cognitione homo format, quia perfectiorem requirit cognitionem, id est collativam cum extremis. Dicitur tamen incipere intellectus ab universaliori, quia incipit ab eo praedicato, quod maiori universalitati substerni aptum est.]."

35. "Nam in ipsa intuitiva cognitione etiam dantur gradus, et quaedam est imperfectior alia, ut patet, cum videmus e longe aliquid, quod nullo modo discernimus in particulari, quid sit, ubi solum datur intuitiva cognitio quoad an est. Sic intellectus in sua prima cognitione id, quod ipsi proponitur, videt quasi a longe in genere intelligibili, licet praesens sit obiectum, et sic illa notitia intuitiva solum de obiecto attingit ipsum esse seu quoad an est, quod est esse intuitivam imperfecte et cum omnimoda confusione respectu quidditatis et discretionis praedicatorum."

36. "Ut autem sit sensibile per accidens absolute et respectu omnium sensuum requiritur, quod a nullo sensu percipiatur per se. Et hoc solum potest esse substantia seu subiectum ipsum, cui inest ratio obiectiva sensus. Sentitur enim, non quia per se constituat aut conducat ad rationem obiecti, sive tamquam specificans sive tamquam modificans, sed quia sustinet et recipit id, quod praebet rationem obiectivam visus vel alterius sensus, et sic percipitur ut coniunctum obiecto, non ut constituens obiectum vel conducens ad lineam obiecti, licet conducat ad sustentationem obiecti in suo esse. Cuius signum manifestum est, quia mutato subiecto vel etiam omnino remoto, ut si accidens separetur ab omni subiecto, eodem modo poterit movere sensum illud accidens separatum atque coniunctum, mutato subiecto vel non mutato, dummodo maneat sensibile illud proprium cum sensibilibus communibus, quae sunt modificationes per se requisitae ad exercendam sensationem."

37. Burgersdyk ("Burgerdijck," etc.) is characterized as follows in an unsigned *Encyclopaedia Brittanica* article of 1868: "BURGERSDYK, or Burgersdicius, Francis, a celebrated Dutch logician, was born at Lier, near Delft, in 1590, and died at Leyden in 1629, in the thirty-ninth year of his age. He studied at the university of Leyden, and after completing his academical career there with great distinction, travelled through Germany and France. On arriving at Saumur in the

latter country he began to study theology, and was so successful, that, while still a very young man, he was appointed professor of philosophy in that town. This office he held for five years, at the end of which period he returned to Leyden, where he accepted the chair of logic and moral philosophy, and afterwards that of natural philosophy. His *Logic* was at one time widely used, and is still a very valuable compendium. His treatise on ethics, entitled *Idea Philosophiae Moralis*, was published posthumously in 1644.''

Further notices can be found in Sassen, 1967, and Weisheipl, 1967: 1162.

38. ''Est autem differentia inter has duas cognitiones. Nam ad primam cognitionem de mente habendam, sufficit ipsa mentis praesentia, quae est principium actus ex quo mens percipit seipsam . . . .

''Sed ad secundam cognitionem de mente habendam, non sufficit ejus praesentia, sed] requiritur diligens et subtilis inquisitio. Unde et multi naturam animae ignorant, et multi etiam circa naturam animae erraverunt.''

39. Kant, 1790, German text, pp. 238-239: ''Erkenntnisse und Urtheile müssen sich sammt der Überzeugung, die sie begleitet allgemein mittheilen lassen; denn sonst käme ihnen keine Übereinstimmung mit dem Object zu: sie wären insgesammt ein bloss subjectives Spiel der Vorstellungskräfte, gerade so wie es der Skepticism verlangt. Sollen sich aber Erkenntnisse mittheilen lassen, so muss sich auch der Gemüthszustand, d.i. die Stimmung der Erkenntnisskräfte zu einer Erkenntniss überhaupt, und zwar diejenige Proportion, welche sich für eine Vorstellung (wodurch uns ein Gegenstand gegeben wird) gebührt, um daraus Erkenntniss zu machen, allgemein mittheilen lassen: weil ohne diese als subjective Bedingung des Erkennens das Erkenntniss als Wirkung nicht entspringen könnte. Dieses geschieht auch wirklich jederzeit, wenn ein gegebener Gegenstand vermittelst der Sinne die Einbildungskraft zur Zusammensetzung des Mannigfaltigen, diese aber den Verstand zur Einheit desselben in Begriffen in Thätigkeit bringt. [Aber diese Stimmung der Erkenntnisskräfte hat nach Verschiedenheit der Objecte, die gegeben werden, eine verschiedene Proportion. Gleichwohl aber muss es eine geben, in welcher dieses innere Verhältniss zur Belebung (einer durch die andere) die zuträglichste für beide Gemüthskräfte in Absicht auf Erkentniss (gegebener Gegenstände) überhaupt ist; und diese Stimmung kann nicht anders als durch das Gefühl (nicht nach Begriffen) bestimmt werden. Da sich nun diese Stimmung selbst muss allgemein mittheilen lassen, mithin auch das Gefühl derselben (bei einer gegebenen Vorstellung); die allgemeine Mittheilbarkeit eines Gefühls aber einen Gemeinsinn voraussetzt: so wird dieser mit Grunde angenommen werden können, und zwar ohne sich desfalls auf psychologische Beobachtungen zu fussen, sondern als die nothwendige Bedingung] der allgemeinen Mittheilbarkeit unserer Erkenntniss, welche in jeder Logik und jedem Princip der Erkenntnisse, das nicht skeptisch ist, vorausgesetzt werden muss.''

40. Kant, 1793, German text, p. 137: ''In allen Glaubensarten, die sich auf Religion beziehn, stösst das Nachforschen hinter ihre innere Beschaffenheit unvermeidlich auf ein Geheimniss, d.i. auf etwas Heiliges, war zwar von jedem Einzelnen gekannt, aber doch nicht öffentlich bekannt, d.i. allgemein mitgetheilt, werden kann.—Als etwas Heiliges muss es ein moralischer, mithin ein Gegenstand der Vernunft sein und innerlich für den praktischen Gebrauch hinreichend

erkannt werden können, aber als etwas Geheimes doch nicht für den theoretischen: weil es alsdann auch jedermann müsste mittheilbar sein und also auch äusserlich und öffentlich bekannt werden können.''

41. German text, p. 138: ''[So ist die Freiheit, eine Eigenschaft, die dem Menschen aus der Bestimmbarkeit seiner Willkür durch das unbedingt moralische Gesetz kund wird, kein Geheimniss,] weil ihr Erkenntniss jedermann mitgetheilt werden kann; der uns unerforschliche Grund dieser Eigenschaft aber ist ein Geheimniss, weil er uns zur Erkenntniss nicht gegeben ist.''

42. German text, pp. 521-522: ''Die praktische Freitheit kann durch Erfahrung bewiesen werden. Denn nicht bloss das, was reizt, d.i. die Sinne unmittelbar afficirt, bestimmt die menschliche Willkür, sondern wir haben ein Vermögen, durch Vorstellungen von dem, was selbst auf entferntere Art nützlich oder schädlich ist, die Eindrücke auf unser sinnliches Begehrungsvermögen zu überwinden; diese Überlegungen aber von dem, was in Ansehung unseres ganzen Zustandes begehrungswerth, d.i. gut und nützlich, ist, beruhen auf der Vernunft . . . Wir erkennen also die praktische Freiheit durch Erfahrung als eine von den Naturursachen, nämlich eine Causalität der Vernunft in Bestimmung des Willens, indessen dass die transcendentale Freiheit eine Unabhängigkeit dieser Vernunft selbst (in Ansehung ihrer Causalität, eine Reihe von Erscheinungen anzufangen) von allen bestimmenden Ursachen der Sinnenwelt fordert und so fern dem Naturgesetze, mithin aller möglichen Erfahrung zuwider zu sein scheint und also ein Problem bleibt.''

43. German text, pp. 49-50 note: ''Die, welche diese unerforschliche Eigenschaft als ganz begreiflich vorspiegeln, machen durch das Wort Determinismus (den Satz der Bestimmung der Willkür durch innere hinreichende Gründe) ein Blendwerk, gleich als ob die Schwierigkeit darin bestände, diesen mit der Freiheit zu vereinigen, woran doch niemand denkt; sondern: wie der Prädeterminism, nach welchem willkürliche Handlungen als Begebenheiten ihre bestimmende Gründe in der vorhergehenden Zeit haben (die mit dem, was sie in sich hält, nicht mehr in *unserer Gewalt* ist), mit der Freiheit, nach welcher die Handlung sowohl als ihr Gegentheil in dem Augenblicke des Geschehens in der Gewalt des Subjects sein muss, zusammen bestehen könne: das ists, was man einsehen will und nie einsehen wird.''

44. German text, p. 40: ''Von diesen Wissenschaften, da sie wirklich gegeben sind, lässt sich nun wohl geziemend fragen: wie sie möglich sind; denn dass sie möglich sein müssen, wird durch ihre Wirklichkeit bewiesen.''

45. German text, pp. 23-24 note: ''Allein ich bin mir meines Daseins in der Zeit (folglich auch der Bestimmbarkeit desselben in dieser) durch innere Erfahrung bewusst, und dieses ist mehr, als bloss mich meiner Vorstellung bewusst zu sein, doch aber einerlei mit dem empirischen Bewusstsein meines Daseins, welches nur durch Beziehung auf etwas, was mit meiner Existenz verbunden ausser mir ist, bestimmbar ist. Dieses Bewusstsein meines Daseins in der Zeit ist also mit dem Bewusstsein eines Verhältnisses zu etwas ausser mir identisch verbunden, und es ist also Erfahrung und nicht Erdichtung, Sinn und nicht Ein-

bildungskraft, welches das Äussere mit meinem inneren Sinn unzertrennlich ver-
knüpft . . . .
''[Nun aber jenes intellectuelle Bewusstsein zwar vorangeht, aber die innere
Anschauung, in der mein Dasein allein bestimmt werden kann, sinnlich und an
Zeitbedingung gebunden ist, diese Bestimmung aber, mithin die innere Erfahrung selbst, von etwas Beharrlichem, welches in mir nicht ist, folglich nur in etwas
ausser mir, wogegen ich mich in Relation betrachten muss, abhängt: so ist die
Realität des äusseren Sinnes mit der des innern zur Möglichkeit einer Erfahrung
überhaupt nothwendig verbunden: d.i.] ich bin mir eben so sicher bewusst, dass
es Dinge ausser mir gebe, die sich auf meinen Sinn beziehen, als ich mir bewusst
bin, dass ich selbst in der Zeit bestimmt existire.''

46. German text, pp. 191-192: ''Nun ist das Bewusstsein in der Zeit mit dem
Bewusstsein der Möglichkeit dieser Zeitbestimmung, nothwendig verbunden:
also ist es auch mit der Existenz der Dinge ausser mir, als Bedingung der Zeitbestimmung, nothwendig verbunden; d.i. das Bewusstsein meines eigenen Daseins ist zugleich ein unmittelbares Bewusstsein des Daseins anderer Dinge ausser
mir.''

47. German text, p. 122: ''Indem nun Wahrnehmung die Grundlage dessen,
was für Wahrheit gelte, bleiben soll, so erscheint die Allgemeinheit und Noth-
wendigkeit als etwas Unberechtigtes, [als eine subjektive Zufälligkeit, eine blosse
Gewohnheit, deren Inhalt so oder anders beschaffen seyn kann.]''

48. German text, p. 45: ''α) Das Allgemeine der Physik ist abstract, oder nur
formell; est hat seine Bestimmung nicht an ihm selbst, und geht nicht zur Besonderheit über. β) Der bestimmte Inhalt ist eben deswegen ausser dem Allgemeinen,
damit] zersplittert, zerstückelt, vereinzelt, abgesondert, ohne den nothwendigen
Zusammenhang in ihm selbst, eben darum nur als endlicher.''

49. German text, p. 38: ''Diess ist jedoch in Beziehung auf die Nothwendig-
keit des Inhalts kein Berufen auf die Erfahrung.''

50. German text, p. 44: ''Die Naturphilosophie nimmt den Stoff, den die
Physik ihr aus der Erfahrung bereitet, an dem Punkte auf, bis wohin ihn die
Physik gebracht hat, und bildet ihn wieder um, ohne die Erfahrung als die letzte
Bewährung zu Grunde zu legen; [die Physik muss so der Philosophie in die
Hände arbeiten, damit diese das ihr überlieferte verständige Allgemeine in den
Begriff übersetze, indem sie zeigt, wie es als ein in sich selbst nothwendiges
Ganze aus dem Begriff hervorgeht.]''

51. German text, pp. 23-24: ''Man wird gegen diesen Beweis vermuthlich
sagen: ich bin mir doch nur dessen, was in mir ist, d.i. meiner Vorstellung äus-
serer Dinge, unmittelbar bewusst; folglich bleibe es immer noch unausgemacht,
ob etwas ihr Correspondirendes ausser mir sei, oder nicht. Allein ich bin mir
meines Daseins in der Zeit (folglich auch der Bestimmbarkeit desselben in dieser)
durch innere Erfahrung bewusst, und dieses ist mehr, als bloss mich meiner
Vorstellung bewusst zu sein, doch aber einerlei mit dem empirischen Bewusstsein meines Daseins, welches nur durch Beziehung auf etwas, was mit meiner
Existenz verbunden ausser mir ist, bestimmbar ist. Dieses Bewusstsein meines

Daseins in der Zeit ist also mit dem Bewusstsein eines Verhältnisses zu etwas ausser mir identisch verbunden, und es ist also Erfahrung und nicht Erdichtung, Sinn und nicht Einbildungskraft, welches das Äussere mit meinem inneren Sinn unzertrennlich vernüpft; [denn der äussere Sinn ist schon an sich Beziehung der Anschauung auf etwas Wirkliches ausser mir, und die Realität desselben zum Unterschiede von der Einbildung beruht nur darauf, dass er mit der inneren Erfahrung selbst, als die Bedingung der Möglichkeit derselben, unzertrennlich verbunden werde, welches hier geschieht.] . . .

"[Nun aber jenes intellectuelle Bewusstsein zwar vorangeht, aber die innere Anschauung, in der mein Dasein allein bestimmt werden kann, sinnlich und an Zeitbedingung gebunden ist, diese Bestimmung aber, mithin die innere Erfahrung selbst, von etwas Beharrlichem, welches in mir nicht ist, folglich nur in etwas ausser mir, wogegen ich mich in Relation betrachten muss, abhängt: so ist die Realität des äusseren Sinnes mit der des innern zur Möglichkeit einer Erfahrung überhaupt nothwendig verbunden:] d.i. ich bin mir eben so sicher bewusst, dass es Dinge ausser mir gebe, die sich auf meinen Sinn beziehen, als ich mir bewusst bin, dass ich selbst in der Zeit bestimmt existire. [Welchen gegebenen Anschauungen nun aber wirklich Objecte ausser mir correspondiren, und die also zum äusseren Sinne gehören, welchem sie und nicht der Einbildungskraft zuzuschreiben sind, muss nach den Regeln, nach welchen Erfahrung überhaupt (selbst innere) von Einbildung unterschieden wird, in jedem besondern Falle ausgemacht werden, wobei der Satz, dass es wirklich äussere Erfahrung gebe, immer zum Grunde liegt. Man kann hiezu noch die Anmerkung fügen: die Vorstellung von etwas Beharrlichem im Dasein ist nicht einerlei mit der beharrlichen Vorstellung; denn diese kann sehr wandelbar und wechselnd sein, wie alle unsere und selbst die Vorstellungen der Materie und bezieht sich doch auf etwas Beharrliches] welches also ein von allen meinen Vorstellungen unterschiedenes und äusseres Ding sein muss, dessen Existenz in der Bestimmung meines eigenen Daseins nothwendig mit eingeschlossen wird und mit derselben nur eine einzige Erfahrung ausmacht, die nicht einmal innerlich stattfinden würde, wenn sie nicht (zum Theil) zugleich äusserlich wäre."

52. German text, p. 24, note: "[Man kann hiezu noch die Anmerkung fügen: die Vorstellung von etwas Beharrlichem im Dasein ist nicht einerlei mit der beharrlichen Vorstellung; denn diese kann sehr wandelbar und wechselnd sein, wie alle unsere und selbst die Vorstellungen der Materie und bezieht sich doch auf etwas Beharrliches, welches also ein von allen meinen Vorstellungen unterschiedenes und äusseres Ding sein muss,] dessen Existenz in der Bestimmung meines eigenen Daseins nothwendig mit eingeschlossen wird und mit derselben nur eine einzige Erfahrung ausmacht, [die nicht einmal innerlich stattfinden würde, wenn sie nicht (zum Theil) zugleich ausserlich wäre.]"

53. "Πάντα οὖν τὰ πρός τι, ἐάν πέρ οἰκείως ἀποδιδῶται, πρὸς ἀντιστρέφοντα λέγεται, [ἐπεὶ ἐάν γε πρὸς τὸ τυχὸν ἀποδιδῶται καὶ μὴ πρὸς αὐτὸ ὃ λέγεται, οὐκ ἀντιοτπέφει.]"

54. "[With the works of Mach, Kirchhoff, and Hertz the logical development of the process of eliminating the concept of force from mechanics was completed. This development in mathematical physics from the time of Newton onward was essentially an attempt to explain physical phenomena in terms of mass points

and their spatial relations. Since the time of Keill and Berkeley, it became increasingly clear that the concept of force, if divested of all its extrascientific connotations, reveals itself as an empty scheme, a pure relational or mathematical function. Mach's, Kirchhoff's, and Hertz's contribution was the final stage in stripping off all the artificial trappings and embroideries from the concept; it was a process of purification, of methodological clarification.] The concept of force in its metaphysical sense as causal transeunt activity had no place in the science of the empirically measurable. [Whether the notion of force was tenable in general was outside the jurisdiction of physics]."

55. Kant, 1787: 279: "2. *Agreement* and *Opposition*.—If reality is represented only by the pure understanding (*realitas noumenon*), no opposition can be conceived between the realities, i.e. no relation of such a kind that, when combined in the same subject, they cancel each other's consequences and take a form like $3-3=0$. On the other hand, the real in appearance (*realitas phaenomenon*) may certainly allow of opposition. When such realities are combined in the same subject, one may wholly or partially destroy the consequences of another, as in the case of two moving forces in the same straight line, in so far as they either attract or impel a point in opposite directions, or again in the case of a pleasure counterbalancing pain.

3. The *Inner* and the *Outer*.—In an object of the pure understanding that only is inward which has no relation whatsoever (so far as its existence is concerned) to anything different from itself. It is quite otherwise with a *substantia phaenomenon* in space; its inner determinations are nothing but relations, and it itself is entirely made up of mere relations. We are acquainted with substance in space only through forces which are active in this and that space, either bringing other objects to it (attraction), or preventing them penetrating into it (repulsion and impenetrability). We are not acquainted with any other properties constituting the concept of the substance which appears in space and which we call matter."

German text, pp. 217-218: "2. Einstimmung und Widerstreit. Wenn Realität nur durch den reinen Verstand vorgestellt wird (realitas noumenon), so lässt sich zwischen den Realitäten kein Widerstreit denken, d.i. ein solches Verhältniss, da sie, in einem Subject verbunden, einander ihre Folgen aufheben, und $3-3=0$ sei. Dagegen kann das Reale in der Erscheinung (realitas phaenomenon) unter einander allerdings im Widerstreit sein und, vereint in demselben Subject, eines die Folge des andern ganz oder zum Theil vernichten, wie zwei bewegende Kräfte in derselben geraden Linie, sofern sie einen Punkt in entgegensetzter Richtung entweder ziehen oder drücken, oder auch ein Vergnügen, was dem Schmerze die Wage hält.

"3. Das Innere und Äussere. An einem Gegenstande des reinen Verstandes ist nur dasjenige innerlich, welches gar keine Beziehung (dem Dasein nach) auf irgend etwas von ihm Verschiedenes hat. Dagegen sind die innern Bestimmungen einer substantia phaenomenon im Raume nichts als Verhältnisse und sie selbst gang und gar ein Inbegriff von lauter Relationen. Die Substanz im Raume kennen wir nur durch Kräfte, die in demselben wirksam sind, entweder andere dahin zu treiben (Anziehung), oder vom Eindringen in ihn abzuhalten (Zurückstossung und Undurchdringlichkeit); andere Eingenschaften kennen wir nicht, die den Begriff von der Substanz, die im Raum erscheint, und die wir Materie nennen, ausmachen."

56. Lachelier, 1905 annotation retained in Lalande 1962: 438-440, on *Idéalisme*: ''Je crois qu'on peut donner à ce terme une signification très precise . . . L'*idéalisme*, au sens philosophique, consiste, ce me semble, à croire que le monde,—tel du moins que je puis le connaître et en parler,—se compose exclusivement de représentation, et même de *mes* représentations, actuelles ou possibles, matérielles ou formelles. Par représentations *possibles*, j'entends par exemple celle du soleil lorsqu'il est au-dessous de l'horizon; par représentations *formelles*, j'entends celles du temps, de l'espace et de tout ce qu'on peut y construire *a priori*; j'entends aussi celles (pour lesquelles il faudrait peut-être un autre nom) des lois qui régissent *a priori* tous les phénomènes, comme celles de causalité ou de finalité.

''Mais n'existe-t-il que *mes* représentations?—Pour moi et dans mon monde, oui; mais il peut y avoir d'autres systèmes de représentations, d'autres mondes, en partie parallèles, en partie identiques au mien: parallèles dans tout ce qu'ils ont de sensible, les représentations des autres sujets sentant différant des miennes selon la différence des points de vue, comme le voulait Leibniz; identiques dans tout ce qu'ils ont d'intelligible, c'est-à-dire de mathématique ou de métaphysique, car la représentation du temps, de l'espace, de la causalité, de la finalité ne peut pas différer d'un sujet pensant à un autre.

''Il n'y a même de sujets pensants différants qu'en tant que leurs pensées s'incorporent à des représentations sensibles différentes,—ou plutôt il n'y a, à proprement parler que des sujets sentants, qui pensent d'une seule et même pensée. Rien n'empêche, dès lors, de considérer cette unique pensée comme la substance commune dont les différents sujets sentants ne sont que les accidents. Ainsi l'idéalisme, qui se présentait d'abord sous une forme psychologique, devient une doctrine métaphysique: *mon* monde devient *le* monde, dans la mesure où ma pensée devient la vérité, et à ce titre, la substance unique et universelle. Par là se réconcilient, ce me semble les deux sens que ce mot a, en effet, dans l'histoire de la philosophie.

''Je ne vois donc rien qui empêche d'admettre les définitions citées dans votre *Critique*, et en particulier celle de M. Bergson. Je ne ferais aux deux premières qu'une très légère correction: j'éliminerais l'idée de sujets, distincts de leurs représentations et qui seraient encore, à leur manière, des choses: je dirais que pour l'idéaliste, il n'existe absolument que des représentations, les unes sensibles et individuelles, les autres intellectuelles et impersonnelles.''

Lalande suggests it would be desirable but difficult to restrict the meaning of Idealism to Lachelier's definition, *ibid.*, p. 440:

''Ces observations de J. Lachelier définissent avec beaucoup de force et de clarté *une* doctrine philosophique à laquelle on ne saurait nier que le nom d'*idéalisme* s'applique très bien. Mais est-elle *la seule* que puisse être appelée de ce nom? Il est certain que, soit historiquement, soit dans l'usage contemporain, ce terme s'applique à beaucoup de théories qui ne présentent pas toutes les déterminations énoncées ci-dessus.—Doit-on, d'autre part, considérer cette définition comme s'appliquant non à l'usage actuel, mais à l'usage futur, et comme une proposition de restreindre dorénavant à cette signification précise le sens du terme *idéalisme*? Ce serait peut-être souhaitable, mais il paraît bien difficile d'obtenir cette limitation d'un terme si souvent employé, et dans des cas si divers. (A.L.)''

57. ''Sur les *Propositions de relation*.—Quand je dis 'Pierre est fils de Paul', je pense à Paul comme à un être réel, et réellement existant en dehors de Pierre.

Quand je dis 'tout homme est mortel' je ne pense pas du tout *mortel* comme une réalité quelconque existant au même titre que les hommes et en relation avec eux. Je pense seulement qu'il est, en vertu de leur nature, nécessaire qu'ils meurent. Il est vrai que, pour les logiciens, homme est une notion, et *mortel* une autre notion, en relation avec la première. Mais c'est là une *seconde intention*, une pensée sur ma pensée primitive et objective. Classe, genre, espèce, sujet, prédicat, compréhension, extension, tout cela n'a d'existence que *in mente*. Assimiler le rapport d'un sujet avec un prédicat à celui d'un homme avec un autre homme, c'est mettre des formalités logiques sur le même pied que des existences réelles; c'est véritablement 'comedere secundas intentiones' comme la chimère de Rabelais. (J. Lachelier.)''

58. German text, pp. 216-217: ''[Der ideale Urteilsgehalt steht demnach in der Übereinstimmungsbeziehung. Diese betrifft sonach einen Zusammenhang zwischen idealem Urteilsgehalt und dem realen Ding als dem, *worüber* geurteilt wird.] Ist das Übereinstimmen seiner Seinsart nach real oder ideal oder keines von beiden? [*Wie soll die Beziehung zwischen ideal Seiendem und real Vorhandenem ontologisch gefasst werden?* Sie besteht doch und besteht in faktischen Urteilen nicht nur zwischen Urteilsgehalt und realem Objekt, sondern zugleich zwischen idealem Gehalt und realem Urteilsvollzug; und hier offenbar noch inniger?

''Oder darf nach dem ontologischen Sinn der Beziehung zwischen Realem und Idealem (der μέθεξις) nicht gefragt werden? Die Beziehung soll doch *besteh-en*. Was besagt ontologisch Bestand?

''Was soll die Rechtmässigkeit dieser Frage verwehren? Ist es Zufall, dass dieses Problem seit mehr denn zwei Jahrtausenden nicht von der Stelle kommt? Liegt die Verkehrung der Frage schon im Ansatz, in der ontologisch ungeklärten Trennung des Realen und Idealen?''

59. German text, p. 37: ''[Von dem Verhältniss der Philosophie zum Empirischen ist in der allgemeinen Einleitung die Rede gewesen. Nicht nur muss] die Philosophie mit der Natur-Erfahrung übereinstimmend seyn, [sondern die Entstehung und Bildung der philosophischen Wissenschaft hat die empirische Physik zur Voraussetzung und Bedingung.]''

60. 1830b German text, p. 44: ''Die Naturphilosophie nimmt den Stoff, den die Physik ihr aus der Erfahrung bereitet, an dem Punkte auf, bis wohin ihn die Physik gebracht hat, und bildet ihn wieder um, ohne die Erfahrung als die letzte Bewährung zu Grunde zu legen; die Physik muss so der Philosophie in die Hände arbeiten, damit diese das ihr überlieferte verständige Allgemeine in den Begriff übersetze, indem sie zeigt, wie es als ein in sich selbst nothwendiges Ganze aus dem Begriff hervorgeht.''

61. ''[Das Ungenügende nun der physikalischen Denkbestimmungen lässt sich auf zwei Punkte zurückführen, die aufs engste zusammenhagen. α) Das Allgemeine der Physik ist abstract, oder nur formell; es hat seine Bestimmung nicht an ihm selbst, und geht nicht zur Besonderheit über. β) Der bestimmte Inhalt ist eben deswegen ausser dem Allgemeinen, damit] zersplittert, zerstückelt, vereinzelt, abgesondert, ohne den nothwendingen Zusammenhang in ihm selbst, eben darum nur als endlicher.''

62. Hegel, 1830b German text, Par. 286, p. 203, Zusatz ("Zusatz" means that this text was taken from students' notes on Hegel's lecture on the text, not from Hegel's text itself): "Was aber der Beobachtung nicht unterworfen ist, existiert in diesem Felde nicht; denn das Existiren ist eben das Seyn-für-Anderes, das Sich-Bemerklich-Machen: und diese Sphäre ist eben die der Existenz."

63. German text, p. 121: "[In dem Schlusse, welcher die Idee der Schwere enthält,—] sie selbst nämlich als den Begriff, der durch die Besonderheit der Körper in die äusserliche Realität sich ausschliesst, und zugleich in deren Idealität und Reflexion-in-sich, in der Bewegung sich mit sich selbst zusammenge-schlossen zeigt, —ist die vernünftige Identität und Untrennbarkeit der Momente enthalten, welche sonst als selbstständig vorgestellt werden. Die Bewegung als solche hat überhaupt schlechthin nur im Systeme mehrerer, und zwar nach verschiedener Bestimmung zu einander im Verhältniss stehender Körper Sinn und Existenz."

64. German text, p. 120: "[Die allgemeine Gravitation muss für sich als ein tiefer Gedanke anerkannt werden, wenn er schon Aufmerksamkeit und Zutrauen vornehmlich durch die damit verbundene quantitative Bestimmung auf sich gezogen, und seine Bewährung auf die vom Sonnensystem bis auf die Erschein-ung der Haarröhrchen herab verfolgte Erfahrung gestellt worden ist; so dass er, in der Sphäre der Reflexion gefasst, auch nur die Bedeutung der Abstraction überhaupt, und concreter nur die der Schwere in der Grössbestimmung des Falls,] nicht die Bedeutung der im §. angegebenen in ihrer Realität entwickelten Idee hat."

65. Aquinas, 1266-1274a: "Ita quod primo cadit in intellectu ens, secundo quod hoc ens non est illud ens et sic apprehendimus divisionem, tertio unum, quarto multitudinem.

66. "Hoc est ergo quod dicit, quod sicut ex memoria fit experimentum, ita etiam ex experimento, aut etiam ulterius *ex universali quiescente in anima* [(quod scilicet accipitur ac si in omnibus ita sit, sicut est experimentum in quibusdam - Quod quidem universale dicitur esse quiescens in anima; in quantum scilicet consideratur praeter singularia, in quibus est motus. Quod etiam dicit esse *unum praeter multa*, non quidem secundum esse, sed secundum considerationem in-tellectus, qui considerat naturam aliquam, puta hominis, non respiciendo ad Socratem et Platonem. Quod etsi secundum considerationem intellectus sit unum praeter multa, tamen secundum esse est in omnibus singularibus unum et idem, non quidem numero, quasi sit eadem humanitas numero omnium hominum, sed secundum rationem speciei. Sicut enim hoc album est simile illi albo in albedine, non quasi una numero albedine existente in utroque, ita etiam Socrates est similis Platoni in humanitate, non quasi una humanitate numero in utroque existente.)] - ex hoc igitur experimento, et ex tali universali per experimentum accepto, est in anima id quod est principium artis et scientiae."

67. "Manifestum est enim quod singulare sentitur *proprie* et *per se*, sed tamen sensus est quodammodo etiam ipsius universalis. Cognoscit enim Calliam non solum in quantum est Callias, sed etiam in quantum est hic homo, et similiter

Socratem in quantum est hic homo. Et exinde est quod tali acceptione sensus praeexistente, anima intellectiva potest considerare hominem in utroque. Si autem ita esset quod sensus apprehenderet solum id quod est particularitatis, et nullo modo cum hoc apprehenderet universalem naturam in particulari, non esset possibile quod ex apprehensione sensus causaretur in nobis cognitio universalis."

68. "Sed multitudo etiam secundum rationem consequenter se habet ad unum, quia divisa non intelligimus habere rationem multitudinis nisi per hoc quod utrique divisorum attribuimus unitatem. Unde unum ponitur in definitione multitudinis, non autem multitudo in definitione unius. Sed divisio cadit in intellectu ex ipsa negatione entis. Ita quod primo cadit in intellectu ens, secundo quod hoc ens non est illud ens et sic apprehendimus divisionem, tertio unum, quarto multitudinem."

69. "Experimentum enim est ex collatione plurium singularium in memoria receptorum. Huiusmodi autem collatio est homini propria, et pertinet ad vim cogitativam, quae ratio particularis dicitur: quae est collativa intentionum individualium, sicut ratio universalis intentionum universalium."

70. "Sed necessarium est animali ut quaerat aliqua vel fugiat, non solum quia sunt convenientia vel non convenientia ad sentiendum, sed etiam propter aliquas alias commoditates et utilitates, sive nocumenta. Sicut ovis videns lupum venientem fugit, non propter indecentiam coloris vel figurae, sed quasi inimicum naturae. Et similiter avis colligit paleam, non quia delectat sensum, sed quia est utilis ad nidificandum . . .
"Et ideo quae in aliis animalibus dicitur aestimativa naturalis in homine dicitur cogitativa, quae per collationem quandam hujusmodi intentiones adinvenit."

71. "Ad quintum dicendum quod illam eminentiam habet cogitativa et memorativa in homine, non per id quod est proprium sensitivae partis, sed per aliquam affinitatem et propinquitatem ad rationem universalem, secundum quandam refluentiam. Et ideo non sunt aliae vires, sed eaedem, perfectiores quam sint in aliis animalibus."

72. "SED CONTRA Christus habuit animam rationalem, ut supra habitum est. Propria autem operatio animae rationalis est conferre et discurrere ab uno ad aliud. Ergo in Christo fuit scientia discursiva vel collativa."

73. "594 [13]. Deinde cum dicit [438]: *Quod autem dictum est* etc., manifestat quod dictum est in praecedenti solutione, quantum ad hoc quod ex experimento singularium accipitur universale; et dicit quod illud quod supra dictum est, et non plane, quomodo scilicet ex experimento singularium fiat universale in anima, iterum oportet dicere, ut planius manifestetur . . .
"Cognoscit enim Calliam non solum in quantum est Callias, sed etiam in quantum est hic homo, et similiter Socratem in quantum est hic homo. Et exinde est quod tali acceptione sensus praeexistente, anima intellectiva potest considerare hominem in utroque."

74. "[Et tune est reminisci, scilicet cum aliquo modo resumimus priorem apprehensionem, non autem ita quod reminiscentia sit aliquid eorum quae dicta sunt, vel sensus, vel memoria, vel phantasia, vel scientia; sed per reminiscentiam accidit memorari, quia] reminiscentia est quidam motus ad memorandum. [Et sic memoria sequitur reminiscentiam, sicut terminus motum. Vel secundum aliam literam, reminiscentia sequitur memoriam, quia sicut inquisitio rationis est via ad aliquid cognoscendum, et tamen ex aliquo cognitio procedit, ita reminiscentia est via ad aliquid memorandum, et tamen ex aliquo memorato procedit, ut infra patebit.]"

75. "Similiter etiam quandoque reminiscitur aliquis incipiens ab aliqua re cujus memoratur, a qua procedit ad aliam, triplici ratione. Quandoque quidem ratione similitudinis; sicut quando aliquid aliquis memoratur de Socrate, et per hoc occurrit ei Plato, qui est similis ei in sapientia. Quandoque vero ratione contrarietatis, sicut si aliquis memoretur Hectoris, et per hoc occurrit ei Achilles. Quandoque vero ratione propinquitatis cujuscumque; sicut cum aliquis memor est patris, et per hoc occurrit ei filius. Et cadem ratio est de quacumque alia propinquitate, vel societatis, vel loci, vel temporis; et propter hoc fit reminiscentia . . ."

Notes to Chapter II

1. "Notitia intuitiva est 'notitia rei praesentis,' notitia vero abstractiva est 'notitia rei absentis.' Ubi praesentia et absentia non sumuntur intentionaliter pro ipsa praesentia seu unione obiecti cum potentia. Constat enim nulli notitiae posse deesse hanc praesentiam, siquidem sine obiecto unito et praesenti potentiae nulla potest oriri notitia in potentia. Igitur dicitur notitia rei praesentis et absentis, sumpta praesentia et absentia pro ea, quae convenit rei in se. Unde dicit D. Thomas in q. 3. de Veritate art. 3. ad 8., quod scientia visionis (quae est idem, quod notitia intuitiva) addit supra simplicem notitiam aliquid, quod est extra genus notitiae, scilicet existentiam rerum. Ergo addit existentiam realem, nam intentionalis et obiectiva non est extra genus notitiae. Et in 3. dist. 14. q. 1. art. 2. quaestiunc. 2. dicit, quod 'illud proprie videtur, quod habet esse extra videntem'. Ergo existentia, quam requirit notitia intuitiva, realis et physica esse debet."
For the most authoritative account of translating and interpreting Poinsot's texts concerning relation, see Deely, 1982, esp., concerning the notion of *relatio secundum dici*, note 15 to the "Second Preamble," and the "Editorial Afterword," Section III.C.2.(a) and (b), and III.D.1.

2. "Fundamentum est, quia relationes secundum dici habent esse absolutum et non totum sunt ad aliud; relationes rationis non sunt nisi in intellectu apprehendente, a quo habent esse obiectivum; sed in re nullo intellectu considerante inveniuntur aliqua non habentia aliud esse quam ad aliud. Ergo inveniuntur relationes reales, quae non sunt secundum dici et sic praedicamentum seorsum a rebus absolutis possunt constituere."

3. Jolivet (1929: 122) rightly contrasts Descartes with Kant regarding the thinking subject as a directly experienced reality: "On peut juger maintenant

combien la position cartésienne est contraire à celle que Kant adoptera plus tard. De l'une à l'autre, il y a toute la distance du réalisme à l'idéalisme. Descartes ne voulait pas admettre que le moi ne pût être atteint en lui-même, qu'il ne fût, selon la terminologie kantienne, qu'un noumène étranger au champ de l'expérience. Car, dans le jugement: *je pense*, le sujet pensant ne se perçoit pas identique à la pensée au point d'être tout entier constitué par elle, mais par le même acte et simultanément l'esprit atteint la pensée et le sujet pensant: dans le jugement *je suis pensant*, il y a, entre le prédicat et le sujet, non pas sans doute identité formelle, mais identité objective. Avec le *Cogito*, nous sommes en plein réalisme.''

Now Descartes (1641b: 254) denied real accidents as distinct from substance: ''Quod autem opinio, quae realia ponit accidentia, cum Theologicis rationibus non conveniat, puto hic satis peispicue ostendi; quodque Philosophicis plane adversetur, spero me in summa Philosophiae, quam jam habeo in manibus, clare esse demonstraturum; ibique quo pacto color, sapor, gravitas, & reliqua omnia quae sensus movent, a sola extima corporum superficie dependeant, ostendam.'' (Cf. Descartes, English text, 1641b: 120; Latin text, 1644: 322-323; English text, 1641a: 295-296). Jolivet (1929: 139) rightly claims denial of real distinction between substance and accidents made Descartes' doctrine of substance unintelligible. Consequently it is true Descartes directly experienced his own *reality*. But it is false he experienced his substantial being as Jolivet claims (1929: 128).

4. Latin text, vol. VII, p. 42: ''Atque haec omnia, quo diutius & curiosius examino, tanto clarius & distinctius vera esse cognosco. Sed quid tandem ex his concludam? Nempe si realitas objectiva alicujus ex meis ideis sit tanta ut certus sim eandem nec formaliter nec eminenter in me esse, nec proinde me ipsum ejus ideae causam esse posse, hinc necessario sequi, non me folum esse in mundo, sed aliquam aliam rem, quae istius ideae est causa, etiam existere. Si vero nulla talis in me idea reperiatur, nullum plane habebo argumentum quod me de alicujus rei a me diversae existentia certum reddat; omnia enim diligentissime circumspexi, & nullum aliud potue hactenus reperire.''

5. Cronin, 1966: 149: ''This objective concept of being in Suarez, is, as is Descartes' objective reality of ideas, of a real, non-actual essence as this is within knowledge on the side of the object known. That this is true, is manifest from the very description which Suarez gives of the objective concept.''

Cronin gives the tradition of the doctrine of *esse objectivum* from Suarez and Descartes back to Scotus and Avicenna (*loc. cit.*, Appendix II, pp. 167-199). In that tradition, *esse objectivum* adds some diminished but real being to the knowing subject. It adds the distinctive reality of a necessary nature as known. In this essay, I do *not* presuppose that objective being adds anything real to the knowing subject.

6. German text, p. 11: ''Das so und im strengen Sinne allein Offenbare wird frühzeitig im abendländischen Denken als 'das Anwesende' erfahren und seit langem 'das Seiende' genannt.''

7. ''Mais n'existe-t-il que *mes* représentations? —Pour moi et dans mon monde, oui; mais il peut y avoir d'autres systèmes de représentations, d'autres mondes, en partie parallèles, en partie identiques au mien: parallèles dans tout

ce qu'ils ont de sensible, les représentations des autres sujets sentant différant des miennes selon la différence des points de vue, comme le voulait Leibniz; identiques dans tout ce qu'ils ont d'intelligible, c'est-à-dire de mathématique ou de métaphysique, car la représentation du temps, de l'espace, de la causalité, de la finalité ne peut pas différer d'un sujet pensant à un autre.

"Il n'y a même de sujets pensants différents qu'en tant que leurs pensées s'incorporent à des représentations sensibles différentes,—ou plutôt il n'y a, à proprement parler que des sujets sentants, qui pensent d'une seule et même pensée. Rien n'empêche, dès lors, de considérer cette unique pensée comme la substance commune dont les différents sujets sentants ne sont que les accidents."

English trans. in Ballard, 1960: "Thinking subjects are not different, even, except insofar as their thoughts are incorporated in different sensible representations,—or rather, properly speaking, there exist only feeling subjects who think one and the same thought. From this point on nothing hinders our considering this unique thought as the common substance of which the different feeling subjects are the accidents. Thus at the start Idealism is presented in a psychological form, and then it becomes a metaphysical doctrine. *My* world becomes *the* world to the degree that my thought becomes true, and in this respect it becomes the unique and universal substance. In such a manner, it seems to me, the two meanings attributed to this word (Idealism) in the history of philosophy are reconciled."

8. German text, p. 239, par. 21: "[Da sich nun diese Stimmung selbst muss allgemein mittheilen lassen, mithin auch das Gefühl derselben (bei einer gegebenen Vorstellung); die allgemeine Mittheilbarkeit eines Gefühls aber einen Gemeinsinn voraussetzt: so wird dieser mit Grunde angenommen werden können, und zwar ohne sich desfalls auf psychologische Beobachtungen zu fussen, sondern als] die nothwendige Bedingung der allgemeinen Mittheilbarkeit unserer Erkenntniss, welche in jeder Logik und jedem Princip der Erkenntnisse, das nicht skeptisch ist, vorausgesetzt werden muss."

Notes to Chapter III

1. Latin text, I, cap. 36, p. 103: "Relative autem opponuntur nomina relativa quae non possunt de eodem respectu eiusdem verificari. Et hoc verum est sive res extra animam aliquae opponantur relative sive non. Nec propter hoc quod dico 'nomina relativa' nego relationem esse extra animam, quia 'relativum' potest dici tam de re quam de nomine rei. [Quod enim sint aliqua nomina relativa patet per grammaticos, qui nomen relativum ponunt esse unam speciem nominum.]"

2. Latin text, I, cap. 51, pp. 167-168: "Similiter distinctio entis per absolutum et respectivum non est entis in quantum ens sed terminorum, sicut distinctio per abstractum et concretum, per proprium et appellativum, per adiectivum et substantivum, cum nulla res proprie dicatur absoluta vel respectiva. Quare enim diceretur absoluta? [Aut quia distinguitur a quolibet alio: et tunc relatio, quam moderni ponunt extra, esset absoluta, cum ponant eam distingui realiter a quolibet alio.] Aut quia non coexigit aliquid aliud seu non dependet ad aliquid aliud: et sic nullum accidens esset absolutum, nec forma substantialis, nec aliqua creatura; horum enim quodlibet alio indiget et ab alio dependet ut sit."

3. Latin text: "Ad quartum dicendum quod, quamvis in mente non sint nisi immateriales formae, possunt tamen esse similitudines materialium rerum: non enim oportet quod eiusmodi esse habeat similitudo et id cuius est similitudo, sed solum quod in ratione conveniant, sicut forma hominis in statua aurea, quale esse habet forma hominis in carne et ossibus."

4. French text, p. 132 (Theophile, abbreviated "Th.," represents Leibniz in this dialogue): "Th. [Cette division des objets de nos pensées en substances, modes et relations est assés à mon gré. Je crois que les qualités ne sont que des modifications des substances et l'entendement y ajoute les relations. Il s'en suit plus qu'on ne pense.]"

5. French text, p. 607: "1. La Monade, dont nous parlerons icy, n'est autre chose, qu'une substance simple, qui entre dans les composés; simple, c'est à dire, sans parties.
"2. Et il faut qu'il y ait des substances simples, puisqu'il y a des composés; car le composé n'est autre chose, qu'un amas, ou aggregatum des simples.
"3. Or là, où il n'y a point de parties, il n'y a ny étendue, ny figure, ny divisibilité possible. Et ces Monades sont les veritables Atomes de la Nature, et en un mot les Elemens des choses."

6. French text, p. 598: "Et il faut bien qu'il y ait des substances simples par tout, parce que sans les simples il n'y auroit point de composés; et par consequent toute la nature est pleine de vie.
"2. Les Monades, n'ayant point de parties, ne sauroient être formées ny défaites. Elles ne peuvent commencer ny finir naturellement, et durent par consequent autant que l'univers, qui sera changé, mais qui ne sera point détruit. Elles ne sauroient avoir des figures; autrement elles auroient des parties: et par consequent une Monade en elle même, et dans le moment, ne sauroit être discernée d'une autre que par les qualités et actions internes, lesquelles ne peuvent être autre chose que ses perceptions (c'est à dire, les représentations du composé, ou de ce qui est dehors, dans le simple) et ses appetitions (c'est à dire, ses tendences d'une perception à l'autre) qui sont les principes du changement."

7. Latin text, p. 469: "Cujus rei ut aliquem gustum dem, dicam interim, notionem virium seu virtutis (quam Germani vocant Krafft, Galli la force) cui ego explicandae peculiarem Dynamices scientiam destinavi, plurimum lucis afferre ad veram notionem substantiae intelligendam. Differt enim vis activa a potentia nuda vulgo scholis cognita, quod potentia activa Scholasticorum, seu facultas, nihil aliud est quam propinqua agendi possibilitas, quae tamen aliena excitatione et velut stimulo indiget, ut in actum transferatur. Sed vis activa actum quendam sive ἐντελέχειαν continet, atque inter facultatem agendi actionemque ipsam media est, et conatum involvit; atque ita per se ipsam in operationem fertur; nec auxiliis indiget, sed sola sublatione impedimenti. Quod exemplis gravis suspensi funem sustinentem intendentis, aut arcus tensi illustrari potest."

8. French text, p. 8: "[Car si quelque homme estoit capable d'achever toute la demonstration, en vertu de la quelle il pourroit prouver cette connexion du sujet qui est Cesar et du predicat qui est son entreprise heureuse;] il feroit voir

en effect que la Dictature future de Cesar a son fondement dans sa notion ou nature, qu'on y voit une raison, pourquoy il a plustost resolu de passer le Rubicon . . .

"[On sera donc en estat de satisfaire à ces sortes de difficultés, quelques grandes qu'elles paroissent (et en effect elles ne sont pas moins pressantes à l'egard de tous les autres qui ont jamais traité cette matiere), pourveu qu'on considere bien que toutes les propositions contingentes ont des raisons pour estre plustost ainsi qu'autrement, ou bien (ce qui est la même chose) qu'elles ont des preuves a priori de leur verité qui les rendent certaines, et qui monstrent que la connexion du sujet et du predicat de ces propositions a son fondement dans la nature de l'un et de l'autre; mais qu'] elles n'ont pas des demonstrations de necessité, puisque ces raisons ne sont fondées que sur le principe de la contingence ou de l'existence des choses, c'est à dire sur ce qui est ou qui paroist le meilleur parmy plusieurs choses également possibles, [au lieu que les verités necessaires sont fondées sur le principe de contradiction et sur la possibilité ou impossibilité des essences mêmes, sans avoir égard en cela à la volonté libre de Dieu ou des creatures.]"

9. French text, p. 433: "Cela estant, nous pouvons dire que la nature d'une substance individuelle ou d'un estre complet, est d'avoir une notion si accomplie qu'elle soit suffisante à comprendre et à en faire deduire tous les predicats du sujet à qui cette notion est attribuée."

10. French text, pp. 439-440: "Or nous avons dit cy dessus et il s'ensuit de ce que nous venons de dire, que chaque substance est comme un monde à part, independant de tout autre chose hors de Dieu; ainsi tous nos phenomenes, c'est à dire tout ce qui nous peut jamais arriver, ne sont que des suites de nostre estre; et comme ces phenomenes gardent un certain ordre conforme à nostre nature, ou pour ainsi dire au monde qui est en nous, qui fait que nous pouvons faire des observations utiles pour regler nostre conduite qui sont justifiées par le succès des phenomenes futurs, et qu'ainsi nous pouvons souvent juger de l'avenir par le passé sans nous tromper, cela suffiroit pour dire que ces phenomenes sont veritables sans nous mettre en peine, s'ils sont hors de nous, et si d'autres s'en apperçoivent aussi . . .

"Or il n'y a que Dieu (de qui tous les individus emanent continuellement, et qui voit l'univers non seulement comme ils le voyent, mais encor tout autrement qu'eux tous), qui soit cause de cette correspondance de leur phenomenes, et qui fasse que ce qui est particulier à l'un, soit public à tous; autrement il n'y auroit point de liaison."

11. French text, p. 458: "Aussi Dieu seul fait la liaison ou la communication des substances, et c'est par luy que les phenomenes des uns se rencontrent et s'accordent avec ceux d'autres, et par consequent qu'il y a de la realité dans nos perceptions."

12. Common speech names individuals and groups "liberal" and "conservative." Thus it denominates political consciousness from public record on changing the legality of existing real social relations. So liberal or conservative appraisal of the legality of existing social relations makes these individuals' political consciousness a public object: namely people known as liberal or conservative.

Hence, these distinctive ways of distinguishing the unreal legal relation from the real relational component of social relations become public objects indirectly but immediately experienced. Public representatives who are elected as liberal or conservative make into public objects the political consciousness of the groups they represent.

13. Quine refers to Carnap, 1928.

Notes to Chapter IV

1. German text, pp. 50-51: ''Platons Denken folgt dem Wandel des Wesens der Wahrheit, welcher Wandel zur Geschichte der Metaphysik wird, die in Nietzsches Denken ihre unbedingte Vollendung begonnen hat. Platons Lehre von der Wahrheit ist daher nichts Vergangenes . . .

''Die im Höhlengleichnis erzählte Geschichte gibt den Anblick dessen, was jetzt und künftig noch in der Geschichte des abendländisch geprägten Menschentums das eingentlich Geschehende ist: Der Mensch denkt im Sinne des Wesens der Wahrheit als der Richtigkeit des Vorstellens alles Seiende nach 'Ideen' und schätzt alles Wirkliche nach Werten. Nicht welche Ideen und welche Werte gesetzt sind, ist das allein und erstlich Entscheidende, sondern dass überhaupt nach 'Ideen' das Wirkliche ausgelegt, dass überhaupt nach 'Werten' die 'Welt' gewogen wird.''

2. German text, *ibid*.: ''Gesichtskreis des wissenschaftlichen Vorstellens, das nur das Seiende kennt, kann sich dagegen dasjenige, was ganz und gar kein Seiendes ist (nämlich das Sein), nur als Nichts darbieten. Darum frägt die Vorlesung nach '*diesem* Nichts'. Sie frägt nicht beliebig ins Unbestimmte nach 'dem' Nichts. Sie frägt: wie steht es mit diesem ganz Anderen zu jeglichem Seienden, mit dem, was nicht ein Seiendes ist? Dabei zeigt sich: das Dasein des Menschen ist in '*dieses*' Nichts, in das ganz Andere zum Seienden, hineingehalten. Anders gewendet, heisst dies und konnte nur heissen: 'Der Mensch ist der Platzhalter des Nichts.' Der Satz sagt: der Mensch hält dem ganz Anderen zum Seienden den Ort frei, sodass es in dessen Offenheit dergleichen wie Anwesen (Sein) geben kann. Dieses Nichts, das nicht das Seiende ist und das es gleichwohl *gibt*, ist nichts Nichtiges. Es gehört zum An-wesen.''

3. German text, p. 75: ''Gegen den Humanismus wird gedacht, weil er die humanitas des Menschen nicht hoch genug ansetzt. Freilich beruht die Wesenshoheit des Menschen nicht darin, dass er die Substanz des Seienden als dessen 'Subjekt' ist, um als der Machthaber des Seins das Seiendsein des Seienden in der allzulaut gerühmten 'Objectivität' zergehen zu lassen.

''Der Mensch ist vielmehr vom Sein selbst in die Wahrheit des Seins 'geworfen', dass er, dergestalt ek-sistierend, die Wahrheit des Seines hüte, damit im Lichte des Seins das Seiende als das Seiende, dass es ist, erscheine. Ob es und wie es erscheint, ob und wie der Gott und die Götter, die Geschichte und die Natur in die Lichtung des Seins hereinkommen, an- und abwesen, entscheidet nicht der Mensch. Die Ankunft des Seienden beruht im Geschick des Seins.''

4. German text, p. 16: ''Der Mensch 'besitzt' die Freiheit nicht als Eigenschaft, sondern höchstens gilt das Umgekehrte: die Freiheit, das ek-sistente,

entbergende Da-sein besitzt den Menschen und das so ursprünglich, dass einzig sie einem Menschentum den alle Geschichte erst begründenden und auszeichnenden Bezug zu einem Seienden im Ganzen als einem solchen gewährt. Nur der ek-sistente Mensch ist geschichtlich. Die 'Natur' hat keine Geschichte.''

5. German text, *ibid.*, pp. 139-140: ''Was so heisst, verweist unser Denken in den Bereich, den zu sagen die Leitworte der Metaphysik, Sein und Seiendes, Grund—Gegründetes, nicht mehr genügen. Denn was diese Worte nennen, was die von ihnen geleitete Denkweise vorstellt, stammt als das Differente aus der Differenz. Deren Herkunft lässt sich nicht mehr im Gesichtskreis der Metaphysik denken.''

6. ''1° qu'il existe une essence universelle de l'homme;
''2° que cette essence est l'attribut des *'individus pris isolément'* qui en sont les sujets réels.
''[Ces deux postulats sont complémentaires et indissociables. Or, leur existence et leur unité présupposent toute une conception empiriste-idéaliste du monde. Pour que l'essence de l'homme soit attribut universel, il faut en effet que des *sujets concrets* existent, comme des données absolues: ce qui implique un *empirisme du sujet.*] Pour que ces individus empiriques soient hommes, il faut qu'ils portent chacun en eux toute l'essence humaine, sinon en fait, du moins en droit: ce qui implique un *idéalisme de l'essence.* [L'empirisme du sujet implique donc l'idéalisme de l'essence et réciproquement.]''

7. ''L'idéologie est bien un système de représentations: mais ces représentations n'ont la plupart du temps rien à voir avec la 'conscience': elles sont la plupart du temps des images, parfois des concepts, mais c'est avant tout comme *structures* qu'elles s'imposent à l'immense majorité des hommes, sans passer par leur 'conscience'. Elles sont des objets culturels perçus-acceptés-subis, et agissent fonctionnellement sur les hommes par un processus qui leur échappe. [Les hommes 'vivent' leur idéologie comme le cartésien 'voyait' ou ne voyait pas—s'il ne la fixait pas—la lune à deux cents pas: *nullement comme une forme de conscience, mais comme un objet de leur 'monde'*—comme leur *monde* même.] Que veut-on dire, néanmoins, quand on dit que l'idéologie concerne la 'conscience' des hommes? D'abord qu'on distingue l'idéologie des autres instances sociales, mais aussi que les hommes *vivent* leurs actions, communément rapportées par la tradition classique à la liberté et à la 'conscience', dans l'idéologie, *a travers et par l'idéologie*; bref, que le rapport 'vécu' des hommes au monde, y compris à l'Histoire (dans l'action ou l'inaction politique), passe par l'idéologie, bien mieux, est *l'idéologie elle-même.*''

8. ''[Dans l'idéologie, les hommes expriment, en effet, non pas leurs rapports à leurs conditions d'existence, mais *la façon* dont ils vivent leur rapport à leurs conditions d'existence: ce qui] suppose à la fois rapport réel et rapport 'vécu', 'imaginaire'. L'idéologie est, alors, l'expression du rapport des hommes à leur 'monde', c'est-à-dire l'unité (surdéterminée) de leur rapport réel et de leur rapport imaginaire à leurs conditions d'existence réelles.''

9. Green, 1878: 243 par. 286, thus construes Hume's doctrine of causality: ''It is their supposed necessary connection which distinguishes objects related as

cause and effect from those related merely in the way of contiguity and succession, and it is a like supposition that leads us to infer what we do not see or remember from what we do. If then the reduction of thought and the intelligible world to feeling was to be made good, this supposition, not being an impression of sense or a copy of such, must be shown to be an 'impression of reflection,' according to Hume's sense of the term, *i.e.* a tendency of the soul, analogous to desire and aversion, hope and fear, derived from impressions of sense but not copied from them; and the inference which it determines must be shown to be the work of imagination, as affected by such impression of reflection. This in brief is the purport of Hume's doctrine of causation.''

10. Aquinas, 1266-1274g: *Summa*, II-II, q. 49, art. 8: ''RESPONSIO: Dicendum quod ea circa quae est prudentia sunt contingentia operabilia, in quibus, sicut verum potest admisceri falso, ita et malum bono, propter multiformitatem hujusmodi operabilium in quibus bona plerumque impediuntur a malis, et mala habent speciem boni.''

11. Aquinas, 1266-1274c: *Summa*, I, q. 83, art. 3 ad 2: ''[Ad secundum dicendum quod judicium est conclusio et quasi determinatio consilii. Determinatur autem consilium primo quidem per sententiam rationis, et secundo per acceptationem appetitus; unde Philosophus dicit quod *ex consiliari judicantes desideramus secundum consilium*.] Et hoc modo ipsa electio dicitur quoddam judicium, a quo nominatur liberum arbitrium.''

Notes to Chapter V

1. The subtitle of a collection of essays edited by W.D. Hudson (1969). The complete title and subtitle reads: *The Is/Ought Question. A Collection of Papers on the Central Problem in Moral Philosophy*.

2. ''[L'existentialiste, au contraire, pense qu'il est très gênant que Dieu n'existe pas, car avec lui disparaît toute possibilité de trouver des valeurs dans un ciel intelligible; il ne peut plus y avoir de rien a priori, puisqu'il n'y a pas de conscience infinite et parfaite pour le penser;] il n'est écrit nulle part que le bien existe, qu'il faut être honnête, qu'il ne faut pas mentir, puisque précisément nous sommes sur un plan où il y a seulement des hommes.''

REFERENCES

(Historically Layered by Authors)

ADDIS, Laird, and LEWIS, Douglas.
  1965. *Moore and Ryle: Two Ontologists* (Hague: Nijhoff).
ADLER, Mortimer J.
  1958. *The Idea of Freedom* (Garden City, N.Y.: Doubleday), Vol. 1.
  1961. *The Idea of Freedom* (Garden City, N.Y.: Doubleday), Vol. 2.
ALTHUSSER, Louis.
  1965. *Pour Marx* (Paris: François Maspero).
AQUINAS, Thomas. (For the dating of Aquinas' works, I have relied principally
    on Weisheipl, 1974, pp. 355-405).
  c.1252-1256. *Scriptum Super Libros Sententiarum Magistri Petri Lombardi*, in 4
    volumes; Vols. 1 and 2 ed. R.P. Mandonnet (Paris: Lethielleux, 1929);
    Vols. 3 and 4 ed. R.P. Maria Fabianus Moose (Paris: Lethielleux, 1939,
    1947).
  c.1256-1259. *Quaestiones Disputatae de Veritate*. Leonine edition; Vol. 1, qq. 1-7
    (Rome: Santa Sabina, 1975); Vol. 2, qq. 8-20 (Rome: Santa Sabina,
    1970); Vol. 3, qq. 21-29 (Rome: Santa Sabina, 1976). English transla-
    tion, *Truth*, as follows: Vol. 1, qq. 1-9, by Robert W. Mulligan (Chi-
    cago: Regnery, 1952); Vol. 2, qq. 10-20, by James V. McGlynn (Chicago:
    Regnery, 1953); Vol. 3, qq. 21-29, by Robert W. Schmidt (Chicago:
    Regnery, 1954).
  c.1256-1272. *Quaestiones Quodlibetales*, ed. Raymund M. Spiazzi (8th ed.;
    Turin: Marietti, 1949).
  c.1260-1272. *De Memoria et Reminiscentia*, in the *Opera Omnia*, Parma ed. (1852-
    1873), Vol. XX, pp. 197-214.
  c.1266-1267. *De Malo*, in the Parma ed. (1852-1873) of the *Opera Omnia*, Vol.
    VIII, pp. 219-424.
  c.1266-1274. *Summa Theologiae*. From this work, references are made only to
    the critical bi-lingual text of the 60 volume Blackfriars edition, speci-
    fically to the following volumes:
    a. Vol. 2: *Existence and Nature of God* (la. 2-11) by Timothy McDermott
       (New York: McGraw-Hill, 1964).
    b. Vol. 6: *The Trinity* (la. 27-32) by Ceslaus Velecky (New York:
       McGraw-Hill, 1965).
    c. Vol. 11: *Man* (la. 75-83) by Timothy Suttor (New York: McGraw-
       Hill, 1970).
    d. Vol. 12: *Human Intelligence* (la. 84-89) by Paul T. Durbin (New York:
       McGraw-Hill, 1968).
    e. Vol. 13: *Man Made to God's Image* (la. 90-102) by Edmund Hill (New
       York: McGraw-Hill, 1964).
    f. Vol. 28: *Law and Political Theory* (la2ae. 90-97) by Thomas Gilby (New
       York: McGraw-Hill, 1966).
    g. Vol. 36: *Prudence* (2a2ae. 47-56) by Thomas Gilby (New York: McGraw-
       Hill, 1975).
    h. Vol. 49: *The Grace of Christ* (3a. 7-15) by Liam G. Walsh (New York:
       McGraw-Hill, 1974).
    i. Vol. 58: *The Eucharistic Presence* (3a. 73-78) by William Barden (New
       York: McGraw-Hill, 1965).

c.1269-1270. *In Octo Libros Physicorum Aristotelis Expositio*, ed. P.M. Maggiolo (Turin: Marietti, 1954). All English translations are by the present author.

c.1269-1272a. *In Duodecim Libros Metaphysicorum Aristotelis Expositio*, ed. M.R. Cathala and Raymund M. Spiazzi (Turin: Marietti, 1950). The English translation by John P. Rowan, *Commentary on the Metaphysics of Aristotle*, in 2 volumes (Chicago: Regnery, 1961).

c.1269-1272b. *In Aristotelis Libros Posteriorum Analyticorum Expositio*, ed. Raymund Spiazzi from the Leonine edition (Turin: Marietti, 1955), pp. 145-404. The English translation by F.R. Larcher, *Commentary on the Posterior Analytics of Aristotle* (Albany, N.Y.: Magi Books, 1970).

c.1270-1271. *In Aristotelis Libros Peri Hermeneias Expositio*, ed. Raymund Spiazzi from the Leonine edition (Turin: Marietti, 1955), pp. 3-144.

ARISTOTLE.
c.348-330BC. ΑΡΙΣΤΟΤΕΛΟΥΣ ΤΩΝ ΜΕΤΑ ΤΑ ΦΥΣΙΚΑ
Loeb Classical Library bi-lingual edition, *Metaphysics*, with facing English translation by Hugh Tredennick, in 2 vols. (Cambridge: Harvard University Press, 1933). In this work, only Vol. 1, covering books 1-9 of the *Metaphysics*, was used.

c.335-334BC. ΑΡΙΣΤΟΤΕΛΟΥΣ ΗΘΙΚΩΝ ΝΙΚΟΜΑΧΕΙΩΝ
Loeb Classical Library bi-lingual edition, *The Nicomachean Ethics*, with facing English translation by H. Rackham (Cambridge: Harvard University Press, 1962).

c.335-322aBC. ΑΡΙΣΤΟΤΕΛΟΥΣ ΚΑΤΗΓΟΡΙΑΙ
Loeb Classical Library bi-lingual edition, *The Categories*, with facing English translation by Harold P. Cook (Cambridge: Harvard University Press, 1962).

c.335-322bBC. ΑΡΙΣΤΟΤΕΛΟΥΣ ΦΥΣΙΚΗΣ
Loeb Classical Library bi-lingual edition, *The Physics*, with facing English translation by Philip H. Wicksteed and Francis M. Cornford, in 2 vols. (Cambridge: Harvard University Press, Vol. 1, 1957; Vol. 2, 1960).

AYER, Alfred Jules.
1936. *Language, Truth and Logic* (1st edition; London: V. Gollancz).
1946. *Language, Truth and Logic* (2nd edition; London: V. Gollancz).
1963. *Philosophical Essays* (New York: St. Martin's Press).

BALLARD, Edward G.
1960. *The Philosophy of Jules Lachelier*: see LACHELIER entry for full information.

BARTLETT, John.
1882. *Familiar Quotations* (13th ed.; Boston: Little, Brown and Company, 1956).

BENNETT, Jonathan.
1965. "Substance: Reality and Primary Qualities," in *Locke and Berkeley*, ed. C.B. Martin and D.M. Armstrong (Notre Dame: University of Notre Dame Press, 1968), pp. 86-124.

BRAIN, Sir Walter R.
  1959. *The Nature of Experience* (London: Oxford University Press).

BROAD, Charles D.
  1952. *Ethics and the History of Philosophy: Selected Essays* (London: Routledge and K. Paul).

"BURGERSDYK, Francis."
  1878. Unsigned entry in *The Encyclopaedia Brittanica* (9th ed.; New York: Samuel L. Hall), Vol. 4, p. 533.

CAMPBELL, Charles A.
  1967. *In Defense of Free Will* (London: Allen and Unwin).

CARNAP, Rudolf.
  1928. *The Logical Structure of the World*, English trans. by Rolf A. George (Berkeley: University of California Press, 1967) of *Der Logische Aufbau der Welt* (Berlin-Schlachteness: Weltkreis-Verlag).

CASTAÑEDA, Hector-Neri.
  1967. "Private Language Problem," in *The Encyclopedia of Philosophy*, ed. Paul Edwards (New York: Macmillan), Vol. 6, pp. 458-464.

CASSIRER, Ernst.
  1946. *The Myth of the State* (New Haven: Yale University Press).

CHRISTIAN, William A.
  1959. *An Interpretation of Whitehead's Metaphysics* (New Haven: Yale University Press).

CONVERSE, Philip E.
  1964. "The Nature of Belief Systems in Mass Publics," in *Ideology and Discontent*, ed. David E. Apter (London: Free Press of Glencoe), pp. 206-261.
  1975. "Public Opinion and Voting Behavior," in *Nongovernmental Politics*, being Vol. 4 of *Handbook of Political Science*, ed. Fred. I. Greenstein and Nelson W. Polsby (Reading, Mass.: Addison-Wesley Pub. Co.), pp. 75-169.

CRICK, Bernard.
  1964. *In Defense of Politics* (rev. ed.; Baltimore, Maryland: Penguin Books).

CRONIN, Timothy J.
  1966. *Objective Being in Descartes and in Suarez* (Rome: Gregorian University Press).

DALBIEZ, Roland.
  1929. "Les sources scolastiques de la théorie Cartesienne de l'être objectif," in *Revue d'Histoire de la Philosophie*, 3, 464-472.

DEELY, John N.
  1971. "Animal Intelligence and Concept-Formation," *The Thomist*, XXXV (January), 43-93.
  1982. *Introducing Semiotic, Its History and Doctrine* (Bloomington: Indiana University Press).
  1983. Establishment of the text, translation, notes and Editorial Afterword for the bilingual edition of Poinsot, 1632, q.v.

DESCARTES, René.
  1641a. *Meditationes de Prima Philosophia*, in *Oeuvres de Descartes*, ed. Charles E. Adam and Paul Tannery (Paris: J. Vrin, 1957), Vol. 7, pp. 1-90. The English translation by Elizabeth S. Haldane and G.R.T. Ross, "Meditations on First Philosophy," in *The Philosophical Works of Descartes* (New York: Dover Publications, 1955), Vol. 1, pp. 133-199.
  1641b. *Responsio ad Quartas Responsiones*, in *Oeuvres de Descartes*, ed. Charles E. Adam and Paul Tannery (Paris: J. Vrin, 1957), Vol. 7, pp. 218-256. The English translation by Elizabeth S. Haldane and G.R.T. Ross, "Reply to the Fourth Set of Objections," in *The Philosophical Works of Descartes* (New York: Dover Publications, 1955), Vol. 2, pp. 96-122.
  1644. *Principia Philosophiae*, in *Oeuvres de Descartes*, ed. Charles Adam and Paul Tannery (Paris: Vrin, 1905), Vol. VIII, pp. 1-348.

DUNS SCOTUS, Joannes.
  c.1302-1303. *Ordinatio, Liber Primus*, Vol. III of the *Opera Omnia*, ed. P. Carolus Balic (Rome: Typis Polyglottis Vaticanis, 1954).
  c.1303-1304. *Ordinatio, Liber Secundus*, Vol. VII of the *Opera Omnia*, ed. P. Carolus Balic (Rome: Typis Polyglottis Vaticanis, 1973).
  c.1302-1304. *Philosophical Writings: A Selection (from the Ordinatio)*, ed. and trans. Allan Wolter (Edinburgh: Nelson, 1962).

FABRO, Cornelio.
  1961. *God in Exile: Modern Atheism*, being the English translation by Arthur Gibson (Westminster, Md.: Newman Press, 1968) of *Introduzio All'ateismo Moderno* (Rome: Tip. R. Pioda).

FEIGL, Herbert.
  1958a. "The Mental and the Physical," in Vol. 2 of *Minnesota Studies in the Philosophy of Science* (Minneapolis: University of Minnesota Press), pp. 370-497.
  1958b. "Other Minds and the Egocentric Predicament," in *The Journal of Philosophy*, 55, 978-987.

FLEW, Antony.
  1951. "Locke and the Problem of Personal Identity," in *Locke and Berkeley: A Collection of Critical Essays*, ed. Charles B. Martin and D.M. Armstrong (Notre Dame: University of Notre Dame Press, 1968), pp. 155-178.

FLYNN, Thomas V.
  1953. "The Cogitative Power," *The Thomist*, XVI (October), pp. 542-563.

FOOT, Philippa.
  1959. "Moral Beliefs," in *The Is-Ought Question: A Collection of Papers on the Central Problem in Moral Philosophy*, ed. William D. Hudson (New York: St. Martin's Press, 1969), pp. 214-227.

GAUTHIER, René Antoine, and JOLIF, Jean Yves.
  1958. *L'Ethique à Nicomaque*, Vol. I, Introduction et traduction (Louvain: Publications Universitaires de Louvain).
  1959. *L'Ethique à Nicomaque*, Vol. II, Commentaire (Louvain: Publications Universitaires de Louvain).

GEERTZ, Clifford.
  1968. *Islam Observed: Religious Development in Morocco and Indonesia* (New Haven: Yale University Press).

GIBSON, James.
  1960. *Locke's Theory of Knowledge and Its Historical Relations* (Cambridge, 1960).

GILSON, Etienne.
  1937. *The Unity of Philosophical Experience* (New York: Scribner's).
  1952. *Jean Duns Scot: Introduction à Ses Positions Fondamentales* (Paris: J. Vrin).

GOODALL, Kenneth.
  1972. "Shapers at Work," in *Psychology Today*, 6 (November), 53-63, 132-138.

GREDT, Josephus.
  1899-1901. *Elementa Philosophiae Aristotelico-Thomisticae*, ed. Euchario Zenzen (13th rev. ed.; Barcelona, Spain: Herder, 1961), in 2 vols.

GREEN, Thomas H.
  1878. "General Introduction" to Vol. I of *David Hume. Philosophical Works*, ed. Thomas Hill Green and Thomas Hodge Grose (Darmstadt: Scientia Verlag Aalen, 1964 reprint of the new edition London 1886), pp. 1-299.

HARE, Richard M.
  1963. *Freedom and Reason* (Oxford: Clarendon Press).
  1969. "Descriptivism," in *The Is-Ought Question: A Collection of Papers on the Central Problem in Moral Philosophy*, ed. William D. Hudson (New York: St. Martin's Press, 1969), pp. 240-258.

HEGEL, Georg Wilhelm Friedrich.
1830a. *Die Logik*, being the *Erster Teil* of *System der Philosophie*, in *Sämtliche Werke*, Vol. 8 (Stuttgart: Frommann, 1958), i.e., Part I of the 3rd edition of *Encyklopädie der philosophischen Wissenschaften*, first published in 1816. The English translation by William Wallace, *The Logic of Hegel* (2nd rev. ed.; London: Oxford University Press, 1965), was consulted.
1830b. *Die Naturalphilosophie*, being the *Zweiter Teil* of *System der Philosophie*, in *Sämtliche Werke*, Vol. 9 (Stuttgart: Frommann, 1958), i.e., Part II of the 3rd edition of *Encyklopädie der philosophischen Wissenschaften*, first published in 1816. The English translation by Michael J. Petry, *Hegel's Philosophy of Nature*, in 3 vols. (London: George Allen and Unwin, Ltd., 1970), was consulted.

HEIDEGGER, Martin.
1927. *Sein und Zeit*, originally published in the *Jahrbuch für Phänomenologie und phänomenologische Forschung*, ed. E. Husserl (10th edition; Tübingen: Niemeyer, 1963). English translation by John Macquarrie and James T. Robinson, *Being and Time* (New York: Harpers, 1962), based on the 7th German ed., was consulted.
1930. *Was ist Metaphysik?* (9th ed.; Frankfurt A.M.: Klostermann, 1965).
1943. *Vom Wesen der Wahrheit* (4th ed.; Frankfurt: Klostermann, 1961; actual composition, 1930). The English translation by R.F.C. Hull and Alan Crick, "On the Essence of Truth," in *Existence and Being*, ed. Werner Brock (Chicago: Regnery, 1949), pp. 319-351, was consulted in preparing this work.
1947a. *Platons Lehre von der Wahrheit* (2nd ed.; Bern: A. Francke, 1954), pp. 1-52; trans. by John Barlow as "Plato's Doctrine of Truth" in *Philosophy in the Twentieth Century*, ed. William Barrett and Henry D. Aiken (New York: Random House, 1962), Vol. III, pp. 251-270.
1947b. *Einen Brief über den "Humanismus"* in 1947a, pp. 53-119. The English translation by Edgar Lohner, "Letter on Humanism," in *Philosophy in the Twentieth Century*, ed. William Barrett and Henry D. Aiken (New York: Random House, 1962), Vol. 3, pp. 271-302, was consulted.
1949. *Was ist Metaphysik; Einleitung: Der Rückgang in den Grund der Metaphysik* (Frankfurt: Klostermann). English translation by Walter Kaufmann under the title: "The Way Back into the Ground of Metaphysics," in Vol. 3 of *Philosophy in the Twentieth Century*, ed. William Barrett and Henry D. Aiken (New York: Random House, 1962), pp. 206-218.
1950. *Holzwege* (4th ed.; Frankfurt A.M.: Klostermann, 1963).
1954. *Vorträge und Aufsätze*, Teil II (3rd ed.; Pfullingen: Neske, 1967).
1956. *Zur Seinsfrage*. English translation by Jean T. Wilde and William Kluback, published with facing German original under the title *The Question of Being* (New Haven: College and University Press, 1958).
1957. *Identity and Difference*, being the bi-lingual edition of *Identität und Differenz* (Pfullingen: Neske), trans. Joan Stambaugh (New York: Harper & Row, 1969).
1961. *Nietzsche* (Pfullingen: Neske; actual composition 1936-46), in 2 vols. Only Vol. 1 was used in this work.

HIRST, Reginald J.
  1967a. "Perception," in *The Encyclopedia of Philosophy*, ed. Paul Edwards (New York: Macmillan), Vol. 6, pp. 79-87.
  1967b. "Phenomenalism," in *The Encyclopedia of Philosophy*, ed. Paul Edwards (New York: Macmillan), Vol. 6, pp. 130-135.
  1967c. "Realism," in *The Encyclopedia of Philosophy*, ed. Paul Edwards (New York: Macmillan), Vol. 7, pp. 77-83.

HOCKETT, Charles F.
  1958. *A Course in Modern Linguistics* (New York: Macmillan).
  1977. *The View from Language* (Athens, Ga.: University of Georgia Press).

HOSPERS, John.
  1967. *An Introduction to Philosophical Analysis* (2nd ed.; London: Routledge and K. Paul).

HUDSON, W.D., ed.
  1969. *The Is-Ought Question. A Collection of Papers on the Central Problem in Moral Philosophy* (New York: St. Martin's Press).

HUME, David.
  1739. *A Treatise of Human Nature*, in the edition of T.H. Green and T.H. Grose, *David Hume, The Philosophical Works* (London, 1886; 4 vols.), Vol. I, pp. 301-560 (Introduction and Book I), and Vol. II, pp. 73-374 (Books II and III).

INDEX THOMISTICUS.
  1974-1980. *Index Thomisticus: Sancti Thomae Aquinatis Operum Omnium Indices et Concordantiae*, ed. Robertus Busa (Stuttgart-Bad Cannstatt: Friedrich Frommann Verlag & Günther Holybooz K G, 1974-1980), in 41 vols.

JAMMER, Max.
  1957. *Concepts of Force: A Study in the Foundations of Dynamics* (Cambridge: Harvard University Press).

JOLIVET, Regis.
  1929. *La Notion de Substance: essai historique et critique sur le développement des doctrines d'Aristote à nos jours* (Paris: G. Beauchesne).

KANT, Immanuel.
  1787. *Kritik der reinen Vernunft*, in *Kant's gesammelte Schriften*, ed. Royal Prussian Academy of Science (2nd ed.; Berlin: Reimer, 1911), Band III. The English translation by Norman K. Smith, *Critique of Pure Reason* (New York: St. Martin's Press, 1965), was consulted in preparing this work.
  1790. *Kritik der Urteilskraft*, in *Kant's gesammelte Schriften*, ed. Royal Prussian Academy of Science (Berlin: Reimer, 1913), Band V, pp. 165-485. English trans. James Creed Meredith, *The Critique of Judgment* (Oxford: Clarendon Press, 1952), was consulted.

1793. *Die Religion innerhalb der Grenzen der blossen Vernunft,* in *Kant's ge-sammelte Schriften,* ed. Royal Prussian Academy of Science (Berlin: Reimer, 1914), Band 6, pp. 1-202. The English translation by Theodore M. Greene and Hoyt H. Hudson, *Religion within the Limits of Reason Alone* (2nd ed.; LaSalle, Ill.: Open Court Publishing, 1960), was consulted.

KEY, Vladimir Orlando, Jr.
1966. *The Responsible Electorate: Rationality in Presidential Voting, 1936-1960* (Cambridge, Mass.: Harvard University Press).

KIM, Jaegwon.
1967. "Explanation in Science," in *The Encyclopedia of Philosophy,* ed. Paul Edwards (New York: Macmillan), Vol. 3, pp. 159-163.

LACHELIER, Jules.
1905. Comment on the entry "Idéalisme" in Lalande, 1962 (q.v.), pp. 438-440. Extracted by Lalande from the discussion of Société Française de Philosophie on July 4, 1905. All but the last par. of these remarks are translated by Edward G. Ballard on pp. 112-113 of his edition of La-chelier's writings titled *The Philosophy of Jules Lachelier,* including: Du Fondement de l'induction. Psychologie et métaphysique. Notes sur le pari de Pascal. Together with contributions to *Vocabulaire technique et critique de la philosophie* and a selection from his letters (The Hague: Martinus Nijhoff, 1960).

LALANDE, André.
1962. *Vocabulaire Technique et Critique de la Philosophie,* revu par mm. les membres et correspondants de la Société Française de Philosophie et publié, avec leurs corrections et observations par André Lalande (9th ed.; Paris: Presses Universitaires de France). The original editings of this work by Lalande himself took place over the period 1902-1923.

LANGAN, Thomas.
1972. "Formal Insight into Material Natures," in *Phenomenology in America: Studies in the Philosophy of Experience,* ed. James M. Edie (New York: New York Times Books), pp. 109-124.

LEIBNIZ, Gottfried Wilhelm Freiherr von.
1686. "Discours de Métaphysique," being the untitled section II of "Philo-sophische Abhandlungen," in *Die Philosophischen Schriften von Gott-fried Wilhelm Leibniz,* ed. C.I. Gerhardt (Hildesheim: Olms Verlagsbuch-handlung, 1960), Band 4, pp. 427-463. The English translation by Leroy E. Loemker, "Discourse on Metaphysics," in *Philosophical Papers and Letters* (Chicago: University of Chicago Press, 1956), Vol. 1, pp. 464-506, was consulted in this work.

1694. "De primae philosophiae Emendatione, et de Notione Substantiae," in *Die Philosophischen Schriften von Gottfried Wilhelm Leibniz*, ed. C.I. Gerhardt (Hildesheim: Olms Verlagsbuchhandlung, 1960), Band 4, pp. 468-470. The English translation by Leroy E. Loemker, "On the Correction of Metaphysics and the Concept of Substance," in *Philosophical Papers and Letters* (Chicago: University of Chicago Press, 1956), Vol. 2, pp. 707-710, was consulted.

1704. *Nouveaux Essais Sur L'Entendment Par L'Auteur du Système de L'Harmonie Preestablie*, in *Die Philosophischen Schriften von Gottfried Wilhelm Leibniz*, ed. C.I. Gerhardt (Hildesheim: Olms Verlagsbuchhandlung, 1960), Band 5, pp. 41-509. The English translation by Alfred Gideon Langley, *New Essays Concerning Human Understanding* (3rd ed.; LaSalle, Ill.: Open Court Publishing, 1949), was consulted in preparing this book.

1714a. "Monadologie," being the untitled section IX of "Philosophische Abhandlungen," in *Die Philosophischen Schriften von Gottfried Wilhelm Leibniz*, ed. C.I. Gerhardt (Hildesheim: Olms Verlagsbuchhandlung, 1961), Band 6, pp. 607-623. The English translation by Leroy E. Loemker, "The Monadology," in *Philosophical Papers and Letters* (Chicago: University of Chicago Press, 1956), Vol. 2, pp. 1044-1061, was consulted in preparing this book.

1714b. "Principes de la Nature et de la Grace, fondés en raison," in *Die Philosophischen Schriften von Gottfried Wilhelm Leibniz*, ed. C.I. Gerhardt (Hildesheim: Olms Verlagsbuchhandlung, 1961), Band 6, pp. 598-606. The English translation by Leroy E. Loemker, "The Principles of Nature and of Grace, Based on Reason," in *Philosophical Papers and Letters* (Chicago: University of Chicago Press, 1956), Vol. 2, pp. 1033-1043, was consulted.

LOCKE, John.
1690. *An Essay Concerning Human Understanding* (New York: Dover, 1959), in 2 vols. Only Vol. 1 was cited in the present work.

1693. "Remarks upon some of Mr. Norris' Books," in *The Works of John Locke* (Darmstadt: Scientia Verlag Aalen, 1963), Vol. 10, pp. 247-259.

1697-1698. *The Works of John Locke* (Darmstadt: Scientia Verlag Aalen, 1963), Vol. 4, being Locke's correspondence with the Bishop of Worcester.

MACINTYRE, Alasdair C.
1966. *A Short History of Ethics* (New York: Macmillan).

1979. "Why is the Search for the Foundations of Ethics so Frustrating?" in *The Hastings Center Report*, 9 (August), 16-22.

MACKIE, John L.
1977. *Ethics: Inventing Right and Wrong* (Harmondsworth, New York: Penguin).

MAGNUS, Bernd.
1970. *Heidegger's Metahistory of Philosophy: Amor Fati, Being and Truth* (The Hague: Nijhoff).

MALCOLM, Norman.
  1958. "Knowledge of Other Minds," in *Journal of Philosophy*, 55, 969-978.

MARCUSE, Herbert.
  1964. *One-Dimensional Man* (Boston: Beacon Press).

McMULLIN, Ernan.
  1963. "Matter as a Principle," in *The Concept of Matter*, ed. E. McMullin
        (Notre Dame, Ind.: University of Notre Dame Press), pp. 169-208.

MEAD, George Herbert.
  1934. *Mind, Self and Society: From the Standpoint of a Social Behaviorist*, ed.
        Charles W. Morris (Chicago: University of Chicago Press, 1952).

MERLEAU-PONTY, Maurice.
  1960. *Signs*, being the English translation by Richard McCleary (Evanston,
        Ill.: Northwestern University Press, 1964) of *Signes* (Paris: Librairie
        Gallimard).

MONOD, Jacques.
  1970. *Chance and Necessity: An Essay on the Natural Philosophy of Modern
        Biology*, being the English translation by Austryn Wainhouse (New
        York: Knopf, 1971) of *Le Hasard et la Nécessité: Essai Sur la Philosophie
        Naturelle de la Biologie Moderne* (Paris: Editions du Seuil).

MOORE, George E.
  1903. *Principia Ethica* (Cambridge University Press, 1962).

NAGEL, Ernest.
  1961. *The Structure of Science: Problems in the Logic of Scientific Explanation* (New
        York: Harcourt, Brace and World, Inc.).

OCKHAM, William of.
  c.1320-1328. *Summa Logicae*, ed. Philotheus Boehner (St. Bonaventure, N.Y.:
        Franciscan Institute). An English translation (with no critical appara-
        tus) of the *Prima Pars* of this work has been published by Michael J.
        Loux as *Ockham's Theory of Terms* (Notre Dame, Ind.: Notre Dame Uni-
        versity Press, 1974).

POINSOT, John ("Joannes a Sancto Thoma").
  1632. *Tractatus de Signis* (Berkeley: University of California Press, 1983),
        originally published embedded within the larger *Artis Logicae Secun-
        da Pars* (Alcalá, Spain), as explained in Deely, 1983. The Reiser edition
        of the *Artis Logicae Secunda Pars* (*Cursus Philosophicus*, Vol. I; Turin:
        Marietti, 1930, pp. 249-839) was used as the basis for all page, col-
        umn, and line references in the present work.
  1633. *Naturalis Philosophiae Prima Pars: De Ente Mobili in Communi* (Madrid,
        Spain). Reiser Edition (Vol. II; Turin: Marietti, 1933, pp. 1-529).
  1635. *Naturalis Philosophiae Quarta Pars: De Ente Mobili Animato* (Alcalá,
        Spain). Reiser Edition (Vol. III; Turin: Marietti, 1937).

POWELL, Ralph.
  1958. *Truth or Absolute Nothing. A Critique of the Idealist Philosophy of Jules Lachelier* (River Forest, Ill.: The Aquinas Library).
  1970. "The Late Heidegger's Omission of the Ontic-Ontological Structure of Dasein," in *Heidegger and the Path of Thinking*, ed. John Sallis (Pittsburgh: Duquesne University Press), pp. 116-137.

QUINE, W.V.O.
  1953. "Two Dogmas of Empiricism," in *From a Logical Point of View* (2nd ed.; New York: Harper and Row, 1961), pp. 20-46.

RENOIRTE, Fernand.
  1945. *Cosmology: Elements of a Critique of the Sciences and of Cosmology*, being the English translation by James F. Coffey (New York: Joseph F. Wagner, Inc., 1950) of *Eléments de Critique des Sciences et de Cosmologie* (2nd ed.; Louvain: Institut supérieur de philosophie, 1947).

REPASS, David E.
  1971. "Issue Salience and Party Choice," in *The American Political Science Review*, 65 (June), 389-400.

RICHARDSON, William J.
  1963. *Heidegger: Through Phenomenology to Thought* (The Hague: Nijhoff).

van RIET, Georges.
  1946. *Thomistic Epistemology: Studies Concerning the Problem of Cognition in the Contemporary Thomistic School*, English translation by Gabriel Franks of *L'Epistémologie Thomiste: recherches sur le problème de la connaissance dans l'école Thomiste* (3rd ed.; Louvain: Editions de l'Institut supérieur de philosophie; originally published in 1946), published in two volumes by Herder of St. Louis, Vol. I, 1963, Vol. II, 1965.

ROKEACH, Milton.
  1973. *The Nature of Human Values* (New York: The Free Press).

ROSS, William D.
  1923. *Aristotle* (5th ed.; London: Methuen and Co., Ltd., 1953).
  1936. *Aristotle's Physics: An Introduction and Commentary* (Oxford: Clarendon Press).

RUSSELL, Bertrand.
  1914. *Our Knowledge of the External World* (2nd ed.; New York: W.W. Norton and Co., 1929).
  1944. "My Mental Development," in *The Philosophy of Bertrand Russell*, ed. Paul Arthur Schlipp (3rd ed.; New York: Tudor Publishing Co., 1951), pp. 3-20.

RYLE, Gilbert.
  1954. *Dilemmas* (Cambridge University Press).

SANDERS, Thomas G.
  1977. *Secular Consciousness and National Conscience in Southern Europe* (Hanover, N.H.: American Universities Field Staff).

SARTRE, Jean-Paul.
  1946. *Existentialism and Humanism,* being the English translation by Philip Mairet (London: Methuen, 1949) of *L'Existentialisme est un Humanisme* (Paris: Editions Nagel).

SASSEN, F.L.R.
  1967. The article "Dutch Philosophy," trans. R.L. Colie, in *The Encyclopedia of Philosophy,* ed. Paul Edwards (New York: The Free Press), Vol. 2, pp. 440-442.

SCHUMPETER, Joseph A.
  1954. *History of Economic Analysis,* ed. Elizabeth Boody Schumpeter (New York: Oxford University Press).

SCOTUS: see DUNS SCOTUS.

SINGER, Marcus George.
  1961. *Generalization in Ethics: An Essay in the Logic of Ethics, with the Rudiments of a System of Moral Philosophy* (New York: Knopf).

SKINNER, Burrhus F.
  1971. *Beyond Freedom and Dignity* (New York: Knopf).

SMITH, Norman Kemp.
  1941. *The Philosophy of David Hume: A Critical Study of Its Origins and Central Doctrine* (London: Macmillan and Co.).

STEPHEN, Leslie.
  1900. *James Mill,* being Vol. 2 of *The English Utilitarians* (New York: Peter Smith, 1950: three volumes bound as one).

STEVENSON, Charles Leslie.
  1944. *Ethics and Language* (New Haven: Yale University Press).

SUAREZ, Francis.
  1597. *Disputationes Metaphysicae* (Salamanca: Renaut Fratres). The "Opera Omnia editio nova, a Carolo Berton" (Paris: Vivès, 1861), Vols. 25 and 26. All the citations in this book are from Vol. 26.

TOULMIN, Stephen Edelston.
  1950. *An Examination of the Place of Reason in Ethics* (Cambridge University Press).

TURABIAN, Kate L.
  1973. *A Manual for Writers of Term Papers, Theses, and Dissertations* (4th ed.; Chicago: University of Chicago Press).

WALLACE, William A.
1974. *Classical and Contemporary Science*, being Vol. 2 of *Causality and Scientific Explanation* (Ann Arbor: University of Michigan Press).

WEISHEIPL, James A.
1967. The entry, "Scholasticism," in the *New Catholic Encyclopedia* (New York: McGraw-Hill), Vol. 12, pp. 1153-1170.
1974. *Friar Thomas D'Aquino. His Life, Thought, and Work* (New York: Doubleday).

WHITEHEAD, Alfred North.
1925. *Science and the Modern World* (New York: Macmillan Co.).
1929. *Process and Reality: An Essay in Cosmology* (New York: Macmillan Co.).
1948. *Science and Philosophy* (New York: Philosophical Library).

WITTGENSTEIN, Ludwig.
1936-1949. *Philosophical Investigations*, being the English translation with facing German text by G.E.M. Anscombe (2nd ed.; Oxford: Basil Blackwell, 1958) of *Philosophische Untersuchungen*.

INDEX
OF
PROPER NAMES